D0421380

RED'S COLLEGE
...R

WITHDRAWN FROM
THE LIBRARY

UNIVERSITY OF
WINCHESTER

KA 0150108 9

CRY FOR LUCK

CRY FOR LUCK

Sacred Song and Speech Among the Yurok, Hupa, and Karok Indians of Northwestern California

RICHARD KEELING

UNIVERSITY OF CALIFORNIA PRESS
BERKELEY   LOS ANGELES   OXFORD

KING ALFRED'S COLLEGE
WINCHESTER

782.25
KEE   0150108 9

University of California Press
Berkeley and Los Angeles, California

University of California Press
Oxford, England

Copyright © 1992 by
The Regents of the University of California

Library of Congress Cataloging-in-Publication Data

Keeling, Richard.
    Cry for luck: sacred song and speech among the Yurok,
Hupa, and Karok Indians of northwestern California /
Richard Keeling.
        p.   cm.
    Includes bibliographical references (p.   ) and index.
    ISBN 0–520–07560–9 (cloth: alk. paper)
    1. Yurok Indians—Music—History and criticism.
2. Hupa Indians—Music—History and criticism.   3. Karok
Indians—Music—History and criticism.   4. Folk songs,
Yurok—California—History and criticism.   5. Folk songs,
Hupa—California—History and criticism.   6. Folk songs,
Karok—California—History and criticism.   I. Title.
ML3557.K43   1992
782.25'089'970794—dc20   91–39128
                                                CIP
                                                MN

Printed in the United States of America

1   2   3   4   5   6   7   8   9

The paper used in this publication meets the minimum
requirements of American National Standard for Information
Sciences—Permanence of Paper for Printed Library Materials,
ANSI Z39.48–1984 ⊗

Contents

Preface

In aboriginal times, California was the most densely populated region of comparable size in all of North America.[1] There were at least sixty tribes in the area, but even this figure fails to indicate the diversity of cultures that existed, as the word "tribe" has a special meaning in this context. In general, these were not terms used by Indians themselves but designations imposed by linguists and anthropologists who plotted the distribution of Indian cultures for classificatory purposes. In most cases they are overly inclusive from a native perspective, and one scholar has estimated that there were about five hundred ethnic groups or independent communities in California, each with a certain degree of cultural distinctness (Kroeber, in Klimek 1935:10).

Indians of California were also among the last to have their lifestyles greatly altered by contact with whites. To be sure, native civilizations of the coastal areas and southern California were severely devastated by the missionization that took place between 1769 and 1832. However, those of the northernmost and Sierra Nevada regions were relatively untouched before the Gold Rush of 1850, so that even after 1900 it was possible to locate literally scores of elderly persons with knowledge of native culture as it existed before the Indians had ever seen a white person. Much attention has been given to the spectacular phenomenon of Ishi, a "wild" Yahi Indian who wandered into the town of Oroville in 1911 and was studied at Berkeley and San Francisco until his death in 1916, but in fact he was only one of many California Indian persons whose knowledge of aboriginal culture survived the white invasion.

These unique circumstances stimulated one of the most intensive programs of regional ethnographic research in the history of anthropology. The Ethnological Survey of California (1900–1946) to a great extent resulted from the efforts of one man, Alfred L. Kroeber (1876–1960). Kroeber not only produced the monumental *Handbook of the Indians of California* (Kroeber 1925) and scores of other publications on Indians of the region, but he also directed the work of other researchers in the area, often arranging for funds to support their fieldwork and making sure that the results of their research were published. These investigators—many of whom would launch distinguished careers on the basis of their California fieldwork—collected recordings of Indian songs from various parts of the state and produced an extensive literature providing translations and other information concerning the cultural contexts and functions of native music. In many cases, rituals including group performance of songs are described in detail, thus greatly enhancing the value of the recordings as ethnological documents. Other important figures such as John P. Harrington (1884–1961) and Helen H. Roberts (1885–1985) worked independently from Kroeber's University of California–based survey during these years, so that a truly enormous body of evidence concerning California Indian music and related subjects was amassed during the early decades of this century.[2]

Surprising as it might seem, relatively little of this information has been integrated into the general literature on North American Indian music. From the standpoint of ethnomusicology, California has been described as a neglected field of research (Wallace 1978b:648) and one of the least well-known regions of all of North America (Vennum 1979:349). To this extent, the present volume concerning Indian music from the northwestern corner of the state can rightly claim to address an important gap in the literature. But at the same time it relies upon a very large body of published writings, manuscripts, and archival recordings that were the work of earlier writers and researchers in this area. Although I shall occasionally refer to some of the published sources in a critical manner, I hasten to acknowledge what will soon become obvious to any reader: that this study could never have been attempted except on the basis of these previous accomplishments.

A now a word about my own contribution seems in order.

This book describes a living musical tradition largely in relation to earlier beliefs and practices as documented by recordings and narratives that were collected between 1900 and 1942. The conclusions found here are to a great extent my own interpretations rather than based directly on information that was given to me by Indian people I knew while living in northwestern California. Nobody ever told me that singing was supposed to sound like crying, and my speculations about music and culture history are even more foreign to the thinking of Indians in the rural community.

Questions such as "What do they mean when they sing?" or "Why do they seem to cry when they sing?" have great interest to a member of the world community. But the more traditional Yurok and Hupa people whom I knew in Humboldt County did not generally speak about things in this way. Rather, they were more likely to concern themselves with the meaning of a particular song, or with issues such as the order in which singers performed during a dance or who brought regalia or where certain persons were sitting during the meal in between dances. These are subjects—I feel— which have less meaning if a person is not one of the players, while in the close texture of things it seems arrogant and phony to talk about what something represents as a symbol.

If we must engage in cross-cultural hermeneutics, this is perhaps best justified by an honest desire to give these cultures the fairest possible representation in the English language record of man. More than anything this means trying to capture some essence of the local perspective, but the very process of translating these folkways for an outside audience involves a style of discourse which is by nature cosmopolitan rather than local in character. I have come to accept the fact that there is one way of thinking for those who live along the lower Klamath River or in Hoopa Valley, and another for those who live in town and read (or write) about it. And even for the same person, what is worth knowing in one place is not necessarily useful information in the other. I apologize to any local persons who might take offense at my opinions or because I have repeatedly used the names of Indian persons who are no longer living.

Throughout this volume I have been careful to identify all Indian persons who were the source of information presented here, as this was considered necessary for the sake of accuracy and to provide due credit for their knowledge. The names of collectors and other scholarly writers whose work I have relied upon are also given, but there are two others whom I wish to acknowledge separately. Victor Golla (Humboldt State University) was immensely helpful for his knowledge of Hupa language and culture and for generously providing manuscript copies of texts collected by Edward Sapir during the 1920s, even though these were scheduled to appear in a more comprehensive volume that he has edited (Golla, in press). I am also indebted to Arnold Pilling (Wayne State University), a specialist in Yurok studies, who pointed out specific errors and other problems which existed in earlier drafts of the present work. At the same time, I reiterate that the interpretations offered here and any errors of fact that might remain are entirely my own responsibility.

Finally, I am pleased to mention that this formulation of my research on music and culture of the Indians of northwestern California was made possible by a fellowship from the National Endowment for the Humanities.

Richard Keeling

Chapter One

Introduction

*Whoever knows this seat of mine will have good luck.
Let him come at night and cry here. He will not lack
money. . . . Somehow he will get dentalia easily.
Whoever thinks of me will always be lucky, and will
never lack for women, because that is the kind I am.
Whoever thinks of me, and knows this seat, will be
well off. Let him come in the middle of the night, when
no one sees him, and begin to cry while he thinks of
me.*

Portion of a formula from Wohpekemeu as
spoken by Barney of Sregon (Yurok), circa
1901–1907 (Kroeber 1976:378–379)

Wohpekemeu's Legacy

In Yurok mythology, Wohpekemeu was a powerful and impulsive
being who could obtain his desires simply by wishing or hoping
for things. Although he created human beings and resembled the
Christian God in certain other respects, Wohpekemeu (whose
name means "Widower from Across the Ocean") was also an impa-
tient and rapacious character who was obsessed with sexual con-
quest. Everywhere he pursued women and other female creatures,
and nearly always he satisfied his huge appetites, using a form of
willpower to get what he wanted. This was indeed what caused him
to leave the world in which humans came to dwell. He had coupled
with Nospeu (a female skate) down on the beach at a place near
Big Lagoon, but as the surf rolled in and breakers pounded against
them Nospeu suddenly surprised him. She clasped his member
tightly within herself and carried him out to sea and far across the
ocean to the foggy realm of Nepewo (the headman of the salmon)
and other immortal beings.

1

Originally, Wohpekemeu lived underground with Mole.[1] He heard the other spirit-persons moving about on the earth, so he suggested to Mole that the two of them should up and join them. "No, I am afraid," said Mole. "I have heard stones breaking and I heard them say that they would cut my navel off." Irritated by this, Wohpekemeu said, "I hope you die if you ever go out on the earth." Then, after he had sentenced Mole to dwell underground forever, Wohpekemeu tore off his own navel string and emerged into the light. He needed a blanket, and—to the amazement of the other spirit-persons around him—a blanket appeared as soon as he said he wanted one. Needing a place to live, he called for a house, and this came to exist as well. In this way, he not only obtained all that he wished for but also created the very conception of these things, as indicated in the following segment from Kroeber's translation of the myth as originally explained by Jack of Murek (Yurok) in 1907:

Then he thought, "I want a place to live. I want a house." That is why it is called "house," because Wohpekemeu said, "I should like a house." Then he went indoors, into the house. So he had a house. Then suddenly he thought in himself, "I am hungry." That is why it is called "I am hungry," because that is what Wohpekemeu thought in himself. Then, he saw food there and took it, and so customarily it was with him like that: whatever he thought of he got: thus he existed and possessed whatever he wanted. (Kroeber 1976:360)

After this, he made the sweathouse, human beings, and childbirth. And yet the central place of Wohpekemeu in Yurok thought probably owes less to these specific creations than to the general idea that a person could satisfy his needs by visualizing things and hoping for them. This was his real legacy, and the following story illustrates how mythic beliefs concerning Wohpekemeu (or other spirit-persons) became transformed into vehicles through which humans could also obtain power.

All the animals were more like people in Wohpekemeu's time, and the incident described here grew out of Wohpekemeu's obsession for the lovely daughters of Blue Crane, who then occupied a traditional-style Yurok house in the village of Wohkero.[2] Wohpekemeu lusted after those two girls, and he used to sit across the river watching them every day. He cried as he thought about them, so intense was his concentration, and he did so every day, crying constantly until finally the deposit of his tears produced something like a stool or a chair. We can presume that the powerful one succeeded in obtaining his desires, though this is not specifically stated in the mythic text (Kroeber 1976:378–379), and when humans came they recognized the outcropping of rock which his tears produced as a special place where a man could obtain power for money or for women just as Wohpekemeu had done.

This was only one form of medicine that Wohpekemeu had given, and countless other spirit-persons had also revealed such things to human beings. By repeating what had been done across-river from Wohkero, a man could succeed as Wohpekemeu had. In this type of medicine making, the formulist not only described what Wohpekemeu had done but also imitated his actions as much as possible. Seated on that hoary rock of tears, he actually tried to impersonate Wohpekemeu and spoke part of the formula using words that should be translated in first person singular as shown in the quotation at the head of this chapter.

In Yurok medicine making (or that of the Hupa and Karok Indians) nothing was more prominent than tears: humans were usually expected to cry when asking the spirit-persons for help and it was understood that the immortals had also cried when performing miracles through force of will. Such beliefs seem to have had a formative influence on traditional Indian singing among these tribes, and among the early (circa 1900–1910) wax cylinder recordings collected in the region there are a number of "songs" which (to most modern listeners) seem to consist mainly of crying.

Although many types of medicine songs are no longer used in modern times, the overall tradition of vocal music is far from extinct. Rather, group singing forms the major focus of an indigenous ritual life which is thriving today and even gaining in strength among modern Indians living in Hoopa Valley and along the lower reaches of the Klamath River and adjacent coastal areas. While it is poorly documented in published works on North American Indian music, this is one of the most unusual and distinctive musical styles found anywhere on the continent. Some have focused on its multipart texture in describing the special properties of this music, but I have always been more fascinated by the "sobbing" quality

which is so prominent in the voices of Yurok or Hupa singers.
Much like a fossil locking traces of a distant past in the breccia of
a geological deposit, this mannerism bears the imprint of a remote
civilization, one that was vastly different from our own and even
from that of modern Indians living in Hoopa Valley and along the
Klamath River. This "sobbing" has a central place in our study,
which interprets modern Indian singing in relation to the aboriginal
practices that shaped it.

Ethnographic Background

The Indians we now refer to as Yuroks lived before 1850 in permanent villages along the Klamath River from modern Bluff Creek to
the mouth of the river at Rekwoi (forty-five miles downstream) and
north and south along the coast from Crescent City to Trinidad (see
maps on pp. 42–43). Upriver from Bluff Creek, as far as Seiad Valley (where the Klamath turns sharply eastward), Indians pursuing
a similar mode of life were known as Karoks. These were not tribal
names used by the Indians themselves, nor indeed was the concept of a "tribe" as a political unit generally known among Indians
of the California region. The terms "Yurok" and "Karok" were
coined during an early attempt to classify Indian languages of the
region, and they are merely rough approximations of the Karok
words meaning "downriver" and "upriver" respectively (Powers
1877 [1976]:19).

The Trinity River is the Klamath's main tributary and joins the
Klamath at Weitchpec, five miles downriver from Bluff Creek. Following the Trinity back upstream (as it cuts through a steep, rocky
gorge), one arrives at a wide valley six miles long. The Yurok word
for the valley was *hupo:*, and Yuroks called the people *hupo:-la*
just as they called the adjacent group *tsilu-la* (Chilula), the "people"
(*-la*) of the Bald Hills (*tsilu*). These Indians came to be identified
by their Yurok name even though they originally called themselves
na:tinixwe:, a Hupa name that has been translated "Hoopa Valley
People."[3] The disparity of spellings between geographical (Hoopa)
and cultural (Hupa) labels adds yet another twist to the situation.

This study considers aspects of music and culture that are largely
held in common by the Yurok, Hupa, and Karok Indians. Parallels

between the three tribes have led to their being grouped together in this manner ever since Kroeber produced his earliest essay on California Indians (1904), and the present study continues in this tradition, acknowledging that there are distinctions but for the most part regarding the three groups as representing different facets or "moods" of a common civilization.

That they had widely different roots in remote prehistoric times is evident from their differing linguistic affiliations: (1) the Karok are related to many other California tribes in that they speak a language of the Hokan family; (2) the Yurok would seem to be distant relatives of the Algonkian speakers, a small western offshoot of the woodland peoples who occupied nearly all of eastern North America;[4] and (3) the Hupa are Athapaskan speakers, part of a migration from the northwestern part of the continent to Oregon and California, as opposed to the separate and later movement of Athapaskan speakers due south to become what are today known as "Apache" and "Navajo."

Somehow, these three tribes came to share a common civilization and a ceremonial life which stood clearly apart from that of the surrounding Indian peoples in northern California and Oregon. To address the differences between them in a systematic way would not only require a separate study, but also might tend to obscure the variability that exists within each group. Pliny Earle Goddard prefaced his description of Hupa religion with the following disclaimer:

Hupa mythology is very inconsistent when taken as a whole, for not only did each village have its own versions, but each family had myths which, seldom being told outside of the family, came to differ from those in the same village. (Goddard 1903–1904:74–75)

This caveat applies equally to Yurok and Karok mythology and underlines one of the primary characteristics of the religious system described here: that it was and continues to be extremely individualistic, allowing much room for personal vision and creativity. Rather than being uniform or even widely agreed upon, the beliefs and practices described here are dazzling in their variety, and it was partially in order to emphasize this that I sought to employ an approach that presents evidence collected from many Indian persons over the years since 1900, rather than relying more heavily

on information given by knowledgeable individuals I have known
personally.

While readers may note a tendency to view things from a Yurok
perspective, this is mainly because Yurok culture has been documented with such exceptional thoroughness. To a certain extent,
the civilization described here was also shared by neighboring
tribes including the Tolowa, Chilula, and Wiyot. Except for the
Tolowa, however, these bordering cultures are virtually extinct
today, and their descendants have generally become absorbed into
one or another of the three main groups considered here.

In the years before 1850, these Indians enjoyed a fantastic wealth
of natural resources. Salmon and acorns were plentiful. Contra-
dicting the pejorative image of California Indians as "diggers" (a
dehumanizing label originated by journalists of the Gold Rush
period), the Yuroks and their neighbors enjoyed considerable time
for leisure and reflection, living somewhat like displaced Brahmins
along the rugged coast and heavily forested lower reaches of the
Klamath and Trinity rivers. Rather than taking any old shelter as
a refuge against the elements, they occupied permanent semisubterranean houses made of thick redwood boards.

They also placed much importance on symbols of wealth. The
main type of "money" was dentalium shells, but other classes of
objects were also recognized as treasures. These included bright
red woodpecker scalps, large obsidian blades shaped by a flaking
technique, fine deerskins (especially the rare albino pelts), and
other things which were precious for their significance in religious
ceremonies. Men (and even some women) had their forearms tat-
tooed so as to measure the length of strings of dentalium beads,
and these strings of shells served as a standard by which the value
of virtually anything could be measured.

Central authority was minimal among these peoples, and affairs
in any given village were settled in meetings held by a few of the
richest males. A person like this was known by the Yurok word
pergerk, which might be translated as "real man" or "real person,"
and it was generally believed that such wealth accrued largely from
a type of spiritual power. This power and the knowledge of how
to obtain it were controlled by persons of aristocratic birthright,
although one should hasten to note that numerous myths and
medicine formulas refer to "bastards" or to poor persons who be-

come rich. Power was also correlated with certain manners or etiquette, and it was generally believed that dentalium shells would become offended and leave the house of a person who lacked the discipline to live correctly.

Much of the year, aristocratic males slept in the sweathouse apart from their women and children, and indeed there was a clear separation between the male domain and that of food, family, females, and sexuality. For the aristocrats it was important to dwell on mental power and to transcend the appetites of the body. Thus, it is not surprising that the lifestyle called for abstinence, and well-born Indians would refrain from taking food or water when they purified themselves in the sweathouse or made medicine at special places in the high country.[5]

This civilization was greatly altered by 1900, when Alfred Kroeber first visited with Yuroks living along the lower reaches of the Klamath. Prospectors and other settlers had flooded into the region after gold was discovered on the upper Trinity River, and they greatly disrupted the economic basis of Indian life. Kroeber interviewed elderly Indian people and sought mainly to reconstruct an image of Indian culture as it existed more than fifty years before, when these individuals were growing up. Thus the portrait given in Kroeber's *Handbook of the Indians of California* (Kroeber 1925) seeks to depict Yurok culture largely as it existed in the 1830s or 1840s.

In Kroeber's day, it was generally assumed that Indian cultures were rapidly becoming extinct, and this use of a fictional "ethnographic present" was widely adopted because it allowed the writer to concentrate on cultural documentation while freeing him from addressing the broad gamut of legalistic, moral, social, political and other issues which would otherwise complicate his writing greatly. This approach is no longer accepted among modern scholars, and very few would be salved by the modest disclaimer in which Kroeber presents himself basically as a specialist who is simply unqualified to comment on the destruction of Indian societies (1925:vi). Besides trying to be more sensitive about ethical aspects of our work, we no longer accept a static model of culture, and indeed modern research on North American Indian cultures tends to focus on the very transformations that use of an ethnographic present obscures. Most important, we reject the approach to the

extent that it implies Indian culture of the present is somehow less
authentic than that of earlier eras. This interpretation is certainly
not intended in the present study, which employs a historical approach mainly in order to describe the living tradition more
adequately.

While changing times have accentuated the flaws in his work,
Kroeber's research produced dramatic results and it is largely due
to him that a study like this one can be attempted. Elsewhere in
North America, there had been contact between Indians and Euro-
Americans for hundreds of years by the time the Edison phonograph was invented, but the Indians whom Kroeber interviewed
could remember a lifestyle as it existed before upriver Yuroks had
ever seen a white person. Thus, the songs and spoken texts he collected bear traces of great antiquity and reveal an unusually rich
pattern of identifications between spiritual understandings and
practical or scientific aspects of culture.

Toward an Interpretation of Yurok Music

> *One cultural activity of the greatest emotional import*
> *I have regretfully felt compelled to refrain from con-*
> *sidering—music. There can be no question that any*
> *attempt at a well-rounded description of the culture*
> *of a people which omits music from its consideration*
> *is imperfect. But in the present case the difficulties*
> *were enormous.*
>
> From the preface to Kroeber's *Handbook of*
> *the Indians of California* (1925:vii)

Very few people realize the extent of Alfred Kroeber's involve-
ment with ethnomusicology, but it was indeed Kroeber who initi-
ated the study of music among Indians of California. He assembled
a vast collection of wax cylinder recordings from all over the region during the years between 1900 and 1938,[6] and later, evidently
with some guidance from the distinguished scholar George Herzog
and with help from a local musician named William Krestchmer,
Kroeber produced hundreds of pages of musical notations and
analytical notes which are found today in the Manuscripts Division
at Bancroft Library.[7]

Early in his career, Kroeber seems to have felt that music held the key to understanding emotions of profound cultural significance; yet in spite of all his efforts he never felt confident enough to publish an article on the subject. Besides the general apology that appears in the preface of Kroeber's *Handbook*, there is a lengthy passage in which Kroeber expresses his frustration at failing to define the special characteristics of Yurok music in particular: he states that even the most casual listener can distinguish Yurok singing from that of other California tribes such as the Yana or the Yokuts, but that it is impossible for him to say why (1925:95–96).

Kroeber briefly discusses California Indian music in an essay on culture area theory, stating that a relatively uniform style is found through most of California and Nevada while Yurok music stands clearly apart from it. Of Yurok music he writes,

The effect certainly is that of a deliberate endeavor to express a mood or feeling tone; and there can be little doubt that analysis will show a different structure than that of the music of most of California. (Kroeber 1936:114)

Though his publications on the Yurok span a period of more than fifty years, Kroeber never does attempt to interpret Yurok music in print, nor does he speak of music generally in his later and more theoretical works on culture. In retrospect, this failure is not difficult to explain: the approach that Kroeber employed was not well suited to the musical style considered here, nor was it the type of analysis that was likely to yield insights into musical meaning or symbolism in any case.

Kroeber's methodology relied mainly upon quantitative analysis of melodic patterns and formal structures as derived from standard musical notations. This sort of approach was capable of producing elegant results when applied to simpler vocal styles, and Herzog's study tracing the spread of the Ghost Dance and transformations in the musical style connected with it is one of the finest essays in the entire literature on American Indian music (Herzog 1935a). But an examination of the manuscripts at the Bancroft Library reveals that Kroeber was examining melodic characteristics much more closely than Herzog did, and his efforts to graph scalar structures or analyze intervallic frequencies suggest a closer affinity to the work of Herzog's own mentor, Erich von Hornbostel, as for exam-

ple in von Hornbostel's essay on Thompson River Indian songs
(Abraham and von Hornbostel 1906).

From various clues in the notebooks, it is clear that Kroeber relied upon William Kretschmer to transcribe the recordings, and
then Kroeber himself produced graphs and other analyses that
were based mainly on Kretschmer's notations. The songs do not
appear to have been differentiated by genre but only by tribe, and
the same basic approach was used for songs that Kroeber had collected among various tribes of the California region. This methodology failed miserably when applied to Yurok music, and this was
largely due to the character of the music itself.

For one thing, the style relies heavily upon shouts, percussive vocal techniques, and other unusual mannerisms that are not
clearly focused in pitch and can only be notated in an arbitrary manner. In Keeling (1982a) the presence of these "special effects" and
the manner in which they are combined with more clearly sung
tones was examined through use of sound registrations produced
by a melograph. The study also showed that intonation was very
inconsistent even when focused (clearly sung) pitches were involved, and that in some examples it was necessary to describe
tonal structures in terms of "scale tone areas" rather than scale
tones per se (1982a:220–228).

Rhythmic and formal aspects of the music were found to be
equally imprecise (1982a:129–130), and my interviews revealed
that singers placed little premium on exactitude in musical performance while focusing much more upon "feeling" and concepts
of what a song represented to the singer. This pointed up another reason why Kroeber's methods failed to produce the sort
of interpretive results that he was evidently hoping for: while
analysis of formal structures and even melodic characteristics might
be effective for comparative research, the significance or semiology of Yurok music becomes much more accessible through a
look at vocal quality and an exploration of what it seems to dramatize or represent.

Singing tends to reveal emotion through the very phonology of
vocal production, and facial gestures reveal even more about what
a singer is trying to express. However, while voice and gesture may
be useful indicators of "meaning" in music, these clues are quite
nonspecific and even equivocal in character. Because of this am-

biguity, such expressions can only be interpreted in relation to the particular culture or symbolic system to which they belong. Even then, there may be a tendency to confuse our interpretations with observations of a more objective nature, and thus it seems useful to describe the stages through which I became aware of the connection between singing and crying in Yurok culture.

I first became acquainted with the music in 1976 while editing a series of videotaped interviews with American Indian musicians produced by Professor Charlotte Heth at the University of California, Los Angeles. Two of the programs focused on Indian music of northwestern California, and these featured three very entertaining and knowledgeable individuals who performed songs and described Indian cultures of the region in a general way. Besides Dr. Heth (a Cherokee), the sessions included Loren Bommelyn, a young man of Tolowa and Karok descent, and two Yurok women, Joy Sundberg and Aileen Figueroa (Bommelyn et al. 1976, 1977).

From these two sessions I learned that Yurok songs were often considered to be magical in function rather than sung merely for entertainment. The singers explained how people obtained songs, and from this it became clear that the songs were often viewed as representations of something such as a personal experience or an image inspired by an animal. They also said that Indian men sometimes went off alone to pray for power, but crying was not specifically mentioned, nor did traces of "sobbing" seem evident in the singing.

I decided to focus on Yurok music as a topic for my dissertation, and over the next year I prepared myself for fieldwork by studying some of the more basic ethnographic sources. Almost at once I became confused because Kroeber (1925) and other sources described various elements of the spiritual life somewhat differently than the Indian persons in our interview. For example, Loren Bommelyn had spoken of "the Creator" a number of times in describing his beliefs concerning the nature of things, but Kroeber never mentioned the concept of a monotheistic deity among these tribes, and I had the distinct impression that Loren was not referring to Wohpekemeu but rather to some larger teleological agent not unlike the Christian God.

This confusion persisted and grew even worse during much of the time that I lived in Humboldt County (1978–1980), and it took nearly the entire two years of my residence there before I felt that I was beginning to understand some of the transformations that had affected Indian religious thought over the previous hundred years. I attended numerous dances in Hoopa Valley during that period, and it was then that I began to notice that the participants (nearly always men) often seemed to be crying as they sang. In retrospect, I feel a little foolish for not having addressed the subject in my interviews, but the importance of it simply was not clear to me then. Besides, toward the end of my stay at Weitchpec I was beginning to think of myself as a local person and I had begun to shy away from asking questions that I thought would be perceived as stupid by my friends.

On leaving the reservation I regained a bit of distance on the subject and again began to view Yurok culture from a broader and more scholarly viewpoint. I took a job in Washington, D.C. that year (1981) and there became acquainted with Alan Lomax, who had a great influence on the subsequent course of my work. While Lomax's cantometrics methodology has received a good deal of criticism, some of which strikes me as valid, it certainly helped me discover a key to the symbology of Yurok music and also provided a tool for understanding what the vocal style seems to represent from an ethnohistorical perspective, a question that is addressed toward the end of this book.[8]

While some of the cantometrics parameters did not seem particularly relevant for Yurok music in particular, the coding process itself revealed a cluster of phonological traits (vocal tension, much slurring, much nasality, much glottalization, much glissando) that could be directly equated with the actual act of crying. This made me place greater significance on the "sobbing" in the music, as opposed to melodic characteristics or other musical properties, and I soon noticed that the mannerism proved to be a reliable way of distinguishing Yurok (or Hupa or Karok) singing from that of neighboring tribal groups in northern California and Oregon. During the same period, I began to discover ethnographic writings that mentioned crying in early spiritual life, but the connection between singing and crying was still unclear in a paper I wrote at the time (Keeling 1982b).

During the next few years (1982–1985) I worked among the archival recordings at the Lowie Museum of Anthropology and discovered a number of early wax cylinder recordings in which the "sobbing" mannerism was even more marked than in the modern singing I had heard previously. Even then, however, it seemed impossible to express what was meant by the gesture, beyond the fact that it clearly seemed to indicate a state of heightened emotions in the singer.

Later yet I began to look more closely at spoken medicine formulas, and this brought a descriptive strategy into focus. I found numerous references to crying in the early narratives and discovered much about its significance in precontact religion. The texts not only revealed crying as a symbol of spiritual contact but also showed its relationship to a larger matrix of mythological beliefs which shaped the character of practical knowledge, subsistence methods, doctoring, etiquette, child rearing, and other domains of native culture. From that point I became committed to the idea of trying to explain modern ritual singing by relating it to the kaleidoscopic world of medicine making from which it emerged.

Overview of the Chapters to Follow

Part I (Aboriginal Religion) provides an introduction to beliefs and institutions of the precontact period. In relating contemporary music to earlier spiritual practices, our first problem is that of accounting for major differences between these eras. Therefore, the section begins with a chapter ("Secularization in the Period Since 1850") which describes some of the transformations that have affected Indian culture during the historical period. The depiction of modern Indian culture is based mainly on experiences I had while living at Weitchpec on the Klamath River between 1978 and 1980.

Chapter 3 ("The Sacred Landscape") discusses aboriginal ideas about the physical environment and the relationship between human beings and the spiritual entities that governed their fate. The quest for wealth and for acquisition of shamanistic power were particularly important domains for medicine making, and these are discussed separately in chapter 4 ("The Sweathouse and the High Country").

Part II (Ceremonial Singing) considers the major group rituals performed among these tribes and describes the musical styles associated with each of them. Chapter 5 ("Rituals to Repair the World") describes rituals that have been regarded as comprising a unified "cult system" (Kroeber and Gifford 1949), while chapter 6 ("Rituals to Help Human Beings") looks at three ceremonies that have little in common with one another. The chapter titles are my own rather than based on verbalizations given by Indians.

Musical notations illustrate nearly every musical genre that has been performed in recent years (since 1950), and in some cases modern examples are discussed in relation to recordings collected shortly after 1900. These vocal styles are virtually undocumented in the literature of ethnomusicology; therefore I have felt obliged to describe them in a general way rather than in an overly analytical or detailed fashion. While lay readers may find the discussion highly technical at times, I sincerely hope that the notations and commentary will make the songs more accessible to anyone who can read music or obtain assistance from a musician.

Part III (Individual Use of Songs and Formulas) examines personal medicine rituals in a wide range of different contexts. As an introduction to the topic, chapter 7 ("Making Medicine") summarizes basic characteristics of a private ritual and discusses certain elements, such as offerings of tobacco or the burning of angelica root, which seem to have had a general significance in these activities. After outlining the typical structure of a spoken text, the chapter looks closely at some specific narratives and describes how they would be used in actual context.

Chapters 8 and 9 ("Medicine Songs and Formulas") provide an overview of spoken formulas and songs that were used for various practical applications. The corpus includes 216 items, most of which were collected between 1900 and 1942, and represents a fairly comprehensive survey of the available evidence. These two chapters seek mainly to identify some of the more salient themes in various types of spoken formulas, and the style of medicine songs is also discussed in a general way. For those wishing to examine these materials in greater depth, an inventory is provided in Appendix 2, including complete references and brief summaries of the spoken formulas which are not discussed in the text.

In the context of medicine making, song and speech operated at a comparable symbolic level, for both functioned mainly as vehicles through which humans re-created the utterance of spirit-persons, and it is largely to emphasize this affinity that they are described together in the chapters on personal medicine making. Readers will also note that there is no clear demarcation between song and spoken formula from a descriptive perspective, as many of the recorded examples are rendered in a form of "heightened speech" which falls somewhere between the two categories.[9]

Part IV (Interpretations) explores the significance of the musical tradition on two different levels. Chapter 10 ("Music and Culture History") takes a comparative approach, describing general characteristics of the music and discussing its place in the overall picture of North American Indian music. While previous chapters examine individual songs in relation to a particular performance context, this one looks at the music from a more abstract perspective. That more than one style is present here becomes evident; therefore the chapter describes each of the elements which comprise the tradition as a whole and then offers speculations about what each seems to represent in relation to local culture history and in the broader sphere of North American prehistory.

Chapter 11 ("Crying and Singing") returns to the question of what the music expresses within its own cultural context. The essay begins by reviewing what others have written about crying in relation to Yurok music and then uses evidence given in previous chapters to explain this instance of musical symbology more adequately.

This is, then, a book that examines its subject from many different points of view, and some chapters will be more interesting to certain types of readers than others. For some anthropologists, particularly those with a comparative orientation, the most important findings will be those in chapter 10, while local Indian persons who read the book may have strong objections to that chapter, insofar as it tends to contradict basic tenets of indigenous religious thought and assigns historical priorities in a manner that some may find insulting. While some may regard this lack of coherence as a flaw, these disparities truly reflect the state of my own thoughts on these subjects: the mixed understandings of an outsider who is fascinated by a world he can never really call his own.

Part One

Aboriginal Religion

Chapter Two

Secularization in the
Period since 1850

*One half of him was lost in the dim past of concep-
tions that are almost unintelligible to the White man.
The other half of him seemed utterly at home in the
modern world of scientific application and religious
scepticism. At one moment Sam would speak of some
mysterious rock, which one is forbidden to touch,
with obvious faith and awe. At another he would
turn around and declare that the old beliefs were
"all imagination."*

> From Edward Sapir's description of Sam
> Brown (Hupa) in 1927 as a man caught be-
> tween two worlds (Golla, in press)

The End of Indian Time

In explaining their culture to an outsider, elderly Indian persons
most often begin with a statement about the past: the first thing
they want understood is that in ancient times, everything used to
be religious. Even the act of walking along a trail, they might say,
was made religious because of certain places where a person was
supposed to rest, speak a certain prayer, or simply drop a piece of
twig onto a pile of other twigs—just as some *wo'gey* had done.

Wo'gey is the Yurok word for the prehuman beings who occupied
the landscape before Indians came, while in Hupa they are called
kixunai and the Karok word is *ikhareyev*. In aboriginal thought
there was no conception of a human history, but rather all culture
was believed to have been inherited from these miraculous beings,
who had occupied the territory just a few generations before. The
early Indians believed that they lived where the *wo'gey* had lived,

fished where they had fished, and spoke prayers and sang just as the *wo'gey* had done. Indeed, the prayers and songs Indians used were gifts from the *wo'gey*, who felt sorry for humans and wanted them to have medicine. Aristocratic Indians sought to emulate the *wo'gey* in all things, as this was the key to power, while departures from the *wo'gey* lifestyle caused bad luck for a person and ruined the world in general.

But curiously, the word *wo'gey* also means "white person," and a Yurok might even use the expression very derisively today, so that it has the connotation of "white boy" or "honkie." This was something I discovered quite soon after moving to Weitchpec, and the experience was all the more shocking because I was honestly confused about what he meant. Here was a word that I had heard mentioned only in reverence, but now I was being called *wo'gey* in a clearly insulting voice. I had a Yurok friend named Dick Myers, who lived downriver at Sregon, and I asked him about it the next day.

"Oh Rich," he said, answering me as if I were a child even though we were both in our thirties, "when they brought Indians to live in the world, they never said it would last forever. They said they'd be back, and then that'd be the end of Indian time. So when Indians seen the first white people, they figured it was them come back."[1]

For me, that always explained the sardonic fatalism that set Yuroks apart from the Hupas and the upriver Karoks. During the late 1970s, when I was staying in Humboldt County, the main spokesman for this brand of thinking was Calvin Rube, who had a small ranch on the hillside at Wahsek, not far from the Martin's Ferry bridge, a few miles downriver from Weitchpec.

Mr. Rube said it was wrong to put on dances like the Hupas did, now that Indians didn't live the way they were supposed to. If a dance were done wrong or conducted by an improper person (and some objection always seemed to apply), then the Creator's power would work in a "vice-versa" manner, according to him. Moreover, he said that people violated "the Creator's Program" so openly nowadays that the world was going to end pretty soon anyway. The San Francisco earthquake of 1906 and other, more recent disasters such as floods or tidal waves were cited as evidence.[2]

While Calvin Rube's reactionary teachings were far from typical, feelings of antagonism between past and present seem to have been shared among other, more moderate persons I met. Indians of the 1970s were no longer so divided between two worlds as Sam Brown had been during the 1920s, but the disparity between an idealized past and an imperfect present was still troublesome for many in the rural community. The character of the dissonance and the specific nature of the disparities between past and present can be illustrated by describing a Brush Dance I attended in 1979.

A Brush Dance in Hoopa Valley

To begin with, I noticed that people found things to criticize about nearly any dance that came up during the year. The main complaint against the Brush Dance at Matilton Ranch was that the pit was built on a cemetery. That was considered reason enough not to go, and some people made it pretty clear to me that they didn't intend to. One Yurok woman (Ella Norris) said,

They put [that pit] right on a cemetery. Something's going to happen. They found bones when they was digging it, and you're not supposed to disturb the dead. You're supposed to show respect. And something's going to happen. You just watch.

I talked to one Hupa man (Elmer Jarnaghan) who had even more to say about the pit at Matilton Ranch. He said that he had known the two men who first got the idea of building a pit up on that flat above the riverbank, a long time back.

They're both dead now. They was gonna fix a pit there, and some older people told them, "No. Don't bother. That's a cemetery." So they covered it up and never bothered no more. Two or three years ago, some boys got to fixing it up. My grandson was one who helped work on it. And believe it or not, when they got through working, he couldn't walk. . . . Damn near a year. He could walk, but he had a hell of a time.

I wanted company for my first Brush Dance, but it seemed as if none of the Yuroks I knew intended on going. That afternoon, I mentioned it to some younger guys outside of Pearson's Store in Weitchpec and asked them if they were going. They just laughed off my question, and one guy just shook his head and said, "We weren't invited." They said they were going to spend the night hooking eels down by Tuley Creek, so I dropped the subject.

Others who considered themselves more respectable than the bunch outside Pearson's told me that the Brush Dance was not important anyway. They would attend the Deerskin Dance or the Jump Dance, but in their opinion the Brush Dance wasn't even religious anymore. "Nowadays," one Christian woman said, "I call it the Devil's Playground," presumably because the dance had occasionally been marred by drinking and other roughhouse behavior during recent decades. Another person said that I would probably enjoy the dance quite a bit, as long as I didn't go walking around by myself in the parking lot. If I stayed around the area of the pit, I would be fine.

On the night of the dance, I found myself standing on a gravel turnout off Highway 96, considering this advice and wondering if anybody I knew would be at the dance, which I could see in the distance out across the river. From this high embankment, I could make out several camps in a small grove of fruit trees. Several separate groups of people seemed to be having a nighttime picnic, each little bunch illuminated by the cooking fire in the middle, and I gathered that they were taking a break between dances.

This was Matilton Ranch, the family name being derived from a Hupa word meaning "boat place." The Trinity River makes a huge hairpin turn around the Matilton plain, and below where the yellowish grass starts growing, the beach is wide and sandy. Even though the moon was new, I could see water eddying in great slow spirals, and two sleek Indian boats, carved from redwood logs, slanting into the water. For a city person like myself, the scene looked much like a museum display, except that some young Hupas had placed stones on the sand so as to spell out the words FISH ON. This was a protest against federal restrictions on Indians taking salmon with their gill nets, and the words were written in letters as tall as a man and designed to be read by someone standing on the turnout, as I was.

But here on the opposite bank, I realized that I had driven too far, and that I should have turned off the highway about five miles back, before even crossing to this side. I had to drive back to Hoopa Valley, cross a cement bridge, and head back upstream along Tish Tang Road. Turning off where the sign said "Hospital," I soon passed the small but modern Hupa Tribal Clinic. The road went on for a quarter mile to where there was a small airport, and then the blacktop ended. For about three hundred yards I avoided potholes that pocked a dusty construction road, and then my Volkswagen climbed a steep bank to bring the area of the Brush Dance pit into view.

There were about thirty or forty pickup trucks, vans, and cars parked helter-skelter around the fireplaces, and when I killed my engine, I felt at once how pleasant it was to be there. I could hear gently syncopated singing emanating from the pit, and saw silhouettes of the dancers lit by firelight. Out under the stars there was a pervading silence which framed the music, and the songs had a sobering and spiritual character that more consciously artful music could never have achieved.

The earth was built up around the pit, and split logs made four rows of seats, as if the pit was a miniature amphitheater. There were a couple of families who stayed well after midnight, but only a handful of people had committed themselves to watching the dances until dawn. Tomorrow, Sunday morning, the seats would all be taken as sleepers awoke and others arrived to watch the climactic final dances, but now there was plenty of room, and some of us even stretched out on the logs between dances to stare up at the stars.

There were two middle-aged women, probably the wives of singers, who left the pit between dances to govern the cooking and other family affairs, then returned for each set of songs. They watched very carefully, in a critical yet approving way. They were very nice and, seeing that I was alone, they decided to chat. Before long, one began explaining that the dance had been different in earlier times.

She pointed out that the dance was originally held in the family house and not in one of these permanent Brush Dance "pits." She explained that the modern pit was a stylized replica of the (semisubterranean) houses in which precontact Indians actually lived.[3] She also noted that the dancers only came from two "sides" tonight, whereas before (when there were more dancers), groups came from several different villages, each competing to outshine the others with their songs.

Most important, she wanted me to know that the original Brush

Dance was not just an annual affair, but rather something that could happen any time during the warm season that began with the spring salmon run. Originally, the ceremony was held in order to cure a child who was weak or sickly. The parents hired a specialist to make medicine for the baby in the family house, and this curing was the core event around which the rest of the singing and dancing took place. The roof planks were removed from the house during the dance so that people could watch from outside, and gradually the Brush Dance developed into an occasion for community entertainment and courtship, as well as serving its central purpose.

Since it was now an annual community event, I concluded that the dance had become largely symbolic in function, but I found out later that this impression was incorrect. I became acquainted with Alice Pratt (Hupa), a medicine woman for the Brush Dance, and then I learned that concessions to modernization in the modern Brush Dance were remarkably slight. The culture around it had become much more secularized, but the ritual itself had remained very much the same, despite (or perhaps because of) the criticism it received.

For Alice Pratt, the ritual begins well before the dance itself, as she gathers the plant substances that will be needed, going without food or water and speaking prayers as she collects the medicine.[4] On the first night of the public ritual, she builds a fire in a particular way,[5] and then she makes medicine over the baby for three days in much the same way as it has been done for at least one hundred years.

One important element is the waving of burning sticks of pitch-wood over the baby. The wood must be sugar pine, and a certain song is sung while this is done. Mrs. Pratt described the fire waving in these words:

First we take that salal brush and we throw it on our fire, and it just burns. It goes click, click, click. My father used to call it firecrackers because it crackles like that. Then you stick your pitch on the end and get it started, and it's got to be rotten. Used to be some nice ones but they've logged everything out and it's getting hard to find. You stick it in the fire and it blazes. So that's what we go this way with [she sings, swinging the sticks at waist level as if waving them over the baby]. If the baby is sick or not doing well, that is why we wave that fire. It scares away things. It helps the baby to grow stronger.

She also uses the bark of the sugar pine, pounding it up and mix-ing it in water that the child will drink. Other medicines are used to steam the child at various points in the three-day ritual.

This is my medicine basket. We put herbs in it, and we steam it with hot rocks. You put it underneath the blanket and steam the baby. It cleans them out, and it works on them so they grow up healthy. Some of the same stuff goes into these [other] two baskets, only it's not steamed. It's Colt's Foot, and you put that in there, and you put a pine, a *new* growth of pine bough, on top. I pick them about three o'clock in the morning. Both of them. And I dance. (August 24, 1979)

On the last night of the dance, Mrs. Pratt speaks a medicine for-mula which is perhaps the single most important element in the ritual.

About three in the morning I pick up both of the medicines and I dance. Towards Mount Shasta. That's where we call for our medicine. There's a sharp rock, and you pound on the rock and you talk. Then you hit it again twice. No answer. Talking in Indian all the time. You pound three times, and the third time he's giving it to you. (August 24, 1979)

Alice Pratt told me that she had learned the entire Brush Dance ritual from her mother, who in turn was instructed by a woman named Queen McCann (Hupa). An explanation of the ceremony was obtained from Queen McCann by Goddard in 1901, and it is interesting to compare the information given by Mrs. Pratt with that found in Goddard (1904:241–251) and in another account given by Sam Brown (Hupa) during the 1920s (Golla, in press). Each of the three versions gives only a partial view of this complex event, besides having been affected by the interviewer's methodology and other factors, but nonetheless it seems clear that the medicine has remained remarkably intact.

Some slight changes seem to have occurred, though it is hard to be sure, and these seem significant. The spoken formula given by Alice Pratt seems to be less detailed than that collected by God-dard, and she made it very clear that her prayers were largely im-provised rather than fixed in form. The significance of this is not perfectly clear, as Goddard may have failed to note the improvisa-tory element in Queen McCann's prayers, and I may have failed to obtain a complete account from Alice Pratt. She may have had her own reasons for not giving me more complete information, for knowledge of spoken formulas is traditionally quite valuable.

Asked if she always spoke the same prayers, Alice said,

No, just whatever you think. Whatever comes into your heart that's beautiful. You begin [thinking], "Oh what am I going to say?" And before you know it you'll be just talking, on and on.

She also made it clear that she prayed for the dancers and not only for the child being doctored. This was not indicated in the earlier accounts, and it struck me that this fits perfectly with the modern status of the dance as an event that serves the entire community (rather than only the family of a single child). She said the following words in Hupa, then translated,[6]

I wish my people would be good. I wish they wouldn't go up against anything bad. *Hey in sah* [spoken like an amen].

Then (only in English) she said,

And the little fellers they get in there. I say a special prayer for them. It's supposed to be in the spring of the year when they have this Brush Dance, so I pray that the child will grow with the leaves and everything else that's growing. That he or she will grow up *in* that, the blossoms and the grass, everything. And he'll *be* just like that.

It was also highly interesting to me that even Alice Pratt had complaints to make about the modern Brush Dance. I mentioned another dance I had attended and Alice criticized the medicine woman for not being active enough.

She just sat there. Every time the dancers [leave the pit], well you're there, and you pick up the *miewluh* and make your flame go again, and brush off the baby again. When the singers go out, you're supposed to raise up that pitch again. So we sat there and sat there, and she never did.

More important, she complained at several points during our talk that logging activities were making it hard to obtain sugar pine for the medicine.

I went to Pekwan, and they told me, "Oh there's a lot of pitch out there." Then I said I'd go [to perform a Brush Dance], and we walked and walked. I don't know how many miles. We just found a few. I told him it wasn't going to be enough. Then one guy says there's lots that way. We traveled all around, and only found a few. It's terrible.

Because of that, she had to allow about two weeks for gathering the medicine substances, and even then it was not possible to wave the fire as many times on the first night as one really should.

Generally speaking, however, it was clear that the Brush Dance had changed relatively little over the past one hundred years or so, and indeed I learned that the ceremonial life as a whole was among the most conservative to be found anywhere in North America. Nonetheless, other aspects of society had changed considerably during the historical period, and it seems important at this point to speak about the genocide that prompted these transformations.

The Devastation of Indian Cultures in Northwestern California

The earliest definite contacts between coastal Yurok Indians and whites was in 1775, when the Spanish explorer Juan Francisco de Bodega y Quadra landed at the Yurok village of Tsurai, which is now called Trinidad.[7] However, accounts of that visit indicate that the Yuroks who met Bodega's boats were already using iron implements and that they were prepared to trade pelts for more of them. Spanish ships had presumably been passing relatively close to these beaches since the start of the regular Manila galleon run in 1565.

The first known contacts between inland Yuroks and whites occurred much later, in 1827. In that year, fur traders from the Hudson's Bay Company reported having seen various trading articles from American ships. In May, 1828, Jedediah Smith crossed through the area from the southeast. Beginning from the Sacramento Valley, the Smith party first reached the upper Trinity River, then descended along the Trinity and the Klamath rivers downstream to the Pacific Ocean. Reports of this expedition stated that the Yuroks possessed what must have been glass trade beads and iron knives and arrowheads. Again it was noted that the Indians wanted to trade beaver pelts for more knives.

Except for these incidental contacts, the indigenous civilization was not seriously disrupted until 1850, when prospectors began flooding into the local Indian territories. During the course of the next fifty years, mainly on account of the Gold Rush, the aspects of Yurok, Hupa, and Karok culture which derived from aboriginal patterns were much diminished. Several adjacent tribes were driven virtually to extinction during the 1850s and early 1860s, including the Indians now known as Konomihu, Chilula, Wiyot, Chimariko, and Whilkuts.[8]

Since Karok land on the Klamath offered the best prospects for mining, the Karoks suffered most, initially. In 1852, most of the Karok towns between present-day Bluff Creek and the mouth of the Salmon River were burned to the ground, the Indians having been driven out. On returning to their villages, the Indians found houses and farms of white settlers on their land (Bright 1978:188). The Karoks fought back, and their persistence was noted in newspaper accounts, but these reports of the Indians' resistance only fed the temper of indignation and incited vigilante groups to greater violence against them.

There was also a climate of outright violence downriver at Weitchpec, but as might be expected the Yuroks responded as individuals rather than by fighting collectively.[9] This anarchic temperament played right into the hands of white journalists: they portrayed Yuroks who resisted as outlaws, observing that many other Indians took decent jobs working for whites. Pilling notes that Yuroks of the period (circa 1850) were indeed working for whites at Trinidad, Gold Bluffs, Klamath City, Kepel, and Weitchpec, while other Yuroks were openly hostile (Pilling 1978:140).

Meanwhile, greater populations of whites flowed into the cities that were developing on the coast. Adequate seaports were necessary to transport goods and supplies for the inland mining industry, and soon there was also a booming trade in lumber and commercial fishing. Warnersville, now called Trinidad, and Klamath City (near the mouth of the river) were both founded in 1850, and the town of Union, now called Arcata, was founded shortly thereafter. Rather than bringing a civilizing influence to the region, however, the growth of urban populations only intensified the violence against Indians, who were hounded and killed on the least excuse.

Government officials spoke out against these crimes, but were unable to stop them. George M. Hanson, a federal Indian agent assigned to northern California, makes the following charges concerning the treatment of Indians in Humboldt and Mendocino counties in a report for the year 1861.

Indian children are seized and carried into the lower counties and sold into virtual slavery. These crimes against humanity so excited the Indians that they began to retaliate by killing the cattle of Whites. At once an order was given to chastise the guilty. Under this indefinite order, a company of United States troops, attended by a considerable volunteer force, has been pursuing the poor creatures from one retreat to another. Ten kidnappers follow at the heels of the soldiers to seize the children when their parents are murdered and sell them to the best advantage. (Coy 1929:167)

In Hoopa Valley, things went somewhat differently than along the Klamath, as the valley became a center for government administration of Indians quite early. By the year 1858, the Hupa had not been involved in direct conflict with the white settlers, but they were suspected of assisting some Bald Hills Indians who were known as "outlaws." Settlers in the valley wanted to defuse Indian resistance before it could develop, and one fellow came up with the idea of taking a respected elder down to San Francisco, to show him how futile it would be to resist against the newcomers who were moving into the valley.

A Hupa leader named John Matilton was taken south by steamboat, and a witness describes his response as follows:

[He] could not control his wonder when our city burst into view . . . as the steamer rounded the point, and he very anxiously inquired, "How long it took to build it?", expressing strong doubt of the statement that it had all been done in ten years. He said that his people had never seen so many Whites, and they believed our numbers to be few, and thought that by killing five or six at one time, and as many at another, in a short while they would have killed them all off, but now he felt how greatly they had deceived themselves. (Anderson 1956:97; quoted in Nelson 1978:68)

When he returned to the valley and stood before his people, Captain John scooped up dry sand from the riverbank and let it trickle through his fingers to show how numerous the whites really were (Nelson 1978:68).

The reservation at Hoopa Valley was established soon after-

wards. This provided a place where Indians from all over northwestern California could be moved, to keep them safe from mur-
derous whites, and at the same time it provided a base for dealing
with Indian "lawlessness." Goddard, whose "Life and Culture of
the Hupa" (1903–1904) would be published some forty years later,
assesses the impact of martial law on the Indian populations in
Hoopa Valley in these words:

One company of soldiers, and sometimes two, had been kept here twenty-
five years after all need of their presence had passed. This was done in
the face of oft-repeated protests of the Agents in charge, civilian and mili-
tary alike. Nothing could have been worse for these Indians than the
maintenance of these men in their midst. It may be said in truth that if
the government, in 1864, had resolved to do all that lay in its power to
demoralize this people, it could hardly have taken a course more sure to
reach that end than the one followed. (Goddard 1903–1904:11)

He also includes the following comment from H. S. Knight, a
lawyer from Eureka who spent several months on the Hoopa Reservation in 1871.

If the reservation was a plantation, the Indians were the most degraded
slaves. I found them poor, miserable, vicious, dirty, diseased, and ill-fed.
The oldest men, or stout middle-aged fathers of families, were spoken to
just as children or slaves. They know no law but the will of the Agent.
(Goddard 1903–1904:11)

As time went on, reservation officials systematically began trying
to educate the Indians in modern Western culture and to dissuade
them from traditional customs and beliefs, which were viewed as
immoral by those in charge. There was compulsory attendance at
a reservation school, but this seems to have been little more than
a farm which supported itself through the labor of Indians who were
supposed to be its students. Nelson provides this account of the
reservation school (circa 1895) based on information in a letter sent
by William E. Dougherty, Acting Indian Agent, to another official.

At Hoopa, as at many reservation schools, "manual labor" made up fifty
percent of the curriculum. Boys worked on a small farm, and girls did
the cooking, sewing, and housekeeping. Since the students did this as
"part of their training," the school did not have to hire many employees.
(Nelson 1978:122–123)

By 1900, this forced acculturation had largely succeeded, and Goddard would summarize the accomplishments of the reservation in these words:

Allotments of land have now been made, and the Hupas are now self-supporting and capable of becoming useful citizens. They are good farmers and stock-raisers. A few adults have enough education to do smith and carpenter work. They are fairly honest, a few perfectly so, and nearly as temperate as White men under similar temptation. (Goddard 1903–1904:11)

William Wallace has stated that the concentration of Indian populations at the Hoopa Valley Indian Reservation tended to assist the survival of indigenous traditions and slowed down the disruption of native culture (1978a:176). This seems valid enough, especially since the Indians here shared a similar culture, unlike those at other California reservations (or at the Missions), where Indians of many tribes were often mixed together. But the reservation experience also left these people severely demoralized by 1900. From that date onward, they would tend to view their customs as whites saw them, and even the most elderly Indians who are alive today tend to describe their customs in terms that have been very much influenced by Euro-American values.

Carl Meyer, who traveled among the Yurok at Trinidad in 1851, left notes describing them as a proud people who considered themselves morally superior to whites and little interested in them except to acquire iron tools and other trade goods. The Yuroks that Meyer met were secretive and aloof, as the following comment reveals.

[The] beliefs of the Indians are very involved, and it is very difficult, in the absence of an exact knowledge of their language, to investigate their significance . . . for they strive to conceal them even from their most trusted alien friends. (Meyer 1855, in Heizer and Mills 1952:131)

The Yurok of 1900 were also secretive, but sometimes for different reasons. By that time, some had become ashamed of their own customs, which were viewed as "old-fashioned" and stigmatizing. One writer of the period notes that this was especially true of the younger generation.

Of the Indian ceremonial and tradition it is very hard to gain satisfactory information. The things one learns must be learned a little here and a little there. . . . [The] younger generation of Indians . . . does not wish to talk about the old ways because [they] feel [themselves] above them. (Fry 1904:8)

Even after 1900, however, there were pockets of real resistance, especially in those places farthest from the sphere of white authority. This was something that T. T. Waterman notes in describing his fieldwork among the Yuroks near Sregon.

This place was not large; but its people were all related and all excessively rich. Even yet, the Sregon people assume a rather overbearing attitude toward other Indians. The people here were unwilling to tell me anything about house-names or geography, and I think they passed the word around that I was not to be told by anybody else. (Waterman 1920:244)

No matter how proud or defiant they were, all would have their lives greatly altered through influence from the economically dominant culture, and the delicate relationship between Indians and *wo'gey* became more tenuous with the passing of each decade.

Transformations

Today, some families take considerable amounts of salmon through gill-netting; other traditional foods such as deer, eel, sturgeon, and acorn soup are also still consumed, but nowadays the Indians of this region rely mainly on markets for their supplies. Those living in Hoopa Valley have a modern tribal facility (with indoor basketball court), two schools, a shopping center, an airport, a medical clinic, and a tribal museum. By comparison, Yuroks living along the lower Klamath have much less in the way of modern American conveniences. The only public buildings in Weitchpec are Pearson's Store and an elementary school; twenty-five miles downstream from there, the road ends at a place called Johnson's, which is smaller yet, and the only telephone in the whole area today is a radio phone setup at Pearson's Store. But even in these remote "downriver" locations, Indian life has been dramatically transformed.

Economic Dimensions of Secularization

The influence of American economy and values connected with it naturally had a central importance in this process. Stephen Powers notes that Yuroks of the 1870s did not consider American gold and silver pieces to be as valuable as Indian shell money (1877 [1976]: 56),[10] but he also reveals that the Yuroks and Karoks had already become very much involved in the white economy by that time.

Though they have not the American's all day industry, both these Klamath tribes are job thrifty, and contrive to have a considerable amount of money by them. . . . I often peeped into their cabins, and seldom failed to see there wheaten bread, coffee, matches, bacon, and a very considerable wardrobe hanging in the smoky attic. They are more generally dressed in complete civilized suits, and more generally ride on horseback, than any others, except the mission Indians. . . . How do they get these things? They mine a little, drive pack trains a good deal, transport goods and passengers on the river, make and sell canoes, whipsaw lumber for the miners, fetch and carry about the mining camps, go over to Scott Valley and hire themselves out on the farms, etc. These Indians are enterprising. When we remember that they learned all these things by imitation, never having been on a reservation, it is no little to their credit. (Powers 1877 [1976]:46)

Comments such as these tend to obscure the fact that the Yurok was always enterprising in his own way. In aboriginal times, the aristocrat was energetic in the quest for wealth and influence, but the ecstatic practices connected with Indian medicine were viewed with disdain by the early white settlers, as indicated in the following comment from Powers's description of a Karok person gathering sweathouse wood.

While crying and sobbing thus, as he goes along bending under his back load of limbs, no amount of flouting or jeering from a white man will elicit from him anything more than a glance of sorrowful reproach. (Powers 1877 [1976]:25)

Early medicine making seems to have been repressed because it was both offensive to whites and also alien to the American work ethic, and the decline of Indian gambling might be interpreted as part of the same trend. Today, the local Indian gambling game is demonstrated on special occasions, and many young singers can perform the distinctive songs which are used in playing. But social and economic transformations have greatly diminished the primary status it once had as an indicator of spiritual power. Its place in aboriginal culture is revealed in Powers's description of gambling among the South Fork Hupa (Kelta) Indians.

Like all savages, the Kelta are inveterate gamblers, either with the game of "guessing the sticks" or with cards; and they have a curious way of mortifying themselves for failure therein. When one has been unsuccessful in gaming, he frequently scarifies himself with flints or glass on the outside of the leg from the knee down to the ankle, scratching the limb all up criss-cross until it bleeds freely. He does this "for luck," believing that it will appease some bad spirit who is against him. (Powers 1877 [1976]:91)

The Influence of Christianity

The aboriginal belief system was also influenced by Judeo-Christian thought at a very early period. Powers (1877 [1976]) notes that Indians of the 1870s were fascinated by biblical imagery and had little problem viewing Christian themes in familiar terms. According to him, Karoks of the period already believed in God but rated him slightly lower than Coyote as "a useful and practical deity" (1877 [1976]:24). He also mentions a Yurok legend in which the aboriginal superhero Wohpekemeu was banished from the world because he disobeyed one of God's commandments (Powers 1877 [1976]:62).

The early blending of Indian thought and Christian monotheism is poignantly illustrated in the following remark, though these are of course the words of Powers himself rather than being those of an Indian person.

The Supreme Being of Yurok mythology is called Gard; he created all things, and gave them their language, and now lives in the mountains. Anyone who will for the space of ten or fifteen days eat only acorn soup and think only of him will have good fortune and get rich, and when he goes out hunting will find a white deer—the highest earthly object of desire to a Yurok. (Powers 1877 [1976]:64)

Besides introducing the concept of monotheism, Christian thinking has also produced a greater emphasis on religiosity and on moralistic aspects of the local belief system. This was evident in the modern teachings of Calvin Rube (Yurok), who often referred to "the Creator's Program" and spoke of sickness or bad luck as a "penalty" for violating one of the Creator's Laws. Far from being unique to Calvin Rube, the same basic ideas were shared by many of the Indian people I knew. They reflect a distinctly Indian view of sickness but also have been influenced by Christian thought and contemporary social circumstances.

The accommodation to modern conditions could be illustrated by any number of examples. In one case, a Yurok man's child started having mild seizures, and they were talking about having him doctored down at the Shaker Church. Later, when the man was gone, I heard an elderly Indian woman say, "Of course he [the child] got sick, poor thing. He [the father] was on drugs when he made the baby."

Drinking was another new problem that Indian religion had to address. During the 1970s, young male Indians often spoke of "training" and of being "clean." This no longer means using the sweathouse, but the men do train in the high country, and they also have to avoid using alcohol. Calvin Rube (Yurok) often said that he did not want any visitors at his ranch unless they were "clean," and when I asked Dick Meyers (Yurok) what he meant by this, specifically, Meyers said no sex or alcohol for at least three days.

The blending of Indian belief and Christian thought is nowhere more evident than in the Indian Shaker Church.[11] In a Shaker service, songs and prayers are addressed to God or to Jesus Christ, and in return the worshiper sometimes receives a curative power which is manifest in the spasmodic trembling that gives the church its name. Once blessed with "the shake," a church member will try to cure another by rubbing the person and scraping the "sickness" off onto candles standing at the altar of the church. Confessions and hymns, sung amidst the ringing of large handbells, comprise the remainder of a Shaker service.

Here again, despite the obvious accretion of Christian elements, the curing is based on distinctly Indian notions of sickness or misfortune as a penalty for some spiritual offense, whether committed by a troubled person himself or by a relative. Accordingly, personal confessions have a central importance in Shaker services, and at one meeting I attended in 1979 a woman blamed a certain problem on the fact that her father was always gambling Indian style. Thus, ironically, her "testimonial" seemed to imply that the sickness derived from following what she called "old Indian ways" instead of modern Christian ones.

The growth of Shakerism may even have contributed to the extinction of shamanism among these tribes, according to Barnett (1957). He argues that the social function of the Indian sucking doctor was replaced by the Indian Shaker Church, which also allows for ritual curing in a communal setting, and in his opinion this is confirmed by conflicts that occurred during the 1930s and 1940s between Shakers and those who supported shamanism (1957:172–173). While Barnett's explanation may be partially true, the ascendance of Shakerism and the decline of shamanism are perhaps better understood by viewing them in relation to the general process of secularization that occurred as white influence disturbed the delicate balance between Indian culture and the natural environment.

Secularization of the Natural Landscape

Many of the rituals relating to assuring subsistence needs gradually fell into disuse during the historical period as Indian life was increasingly shaped by patterns of the dominant American economy. Like the Brush Dance, surviving dances of the so-called World Renewal complex have assumed a slightly different significance than they once had, but in most respects they have remained remarkably intact. Similarly, songs and formulas used by individuals for practical reasons have also become less common, but many have survived. I recorded some myself during the late 1970s, and others were mentioned to me by persons who declined to sing them except when they were actually needed.

The most severe transformations are in those areas where modern technology has alienated the Indians from mythological understandings they once relied upon for survival, and changing methods and attitudes toward deer hunting provide a dramatic example of this. In earlier times, as the next chapter reveals, a hunter relied upon pleasing the spirit-animal, and one tried to live correctly in order to avoid insulting him. A violation of the flesh was always necessary, but the early hunter seems to have been highly sensitive to this and sought to excuse himself through rituals which placated deer and other game animals.

By contrast, modern deer hunting is not much different whether done by Indians or whites in this area. In my experience, both generally use a pickup truck or a car and usually hunt at night. Places where a walking Indian might have been obliged to stop and pray in passing are ignored as the hunter speeds by, perhaps tuned in to the radio or maybe even using a CB to keep tabs on the Forest Service. When he does spot a deer, he hypnotizes the animal with his spotlight for as long as it takes to blow him down with a rifle. A headshot is about the only consideration that the animal can hope for nowadays.

Adaptability and Survival

In the introduction to his book on the Yurok language (1958), R. H. Robins paints a grim picture of cultural extinction in describing the character of modern Indian life.

The fabric of Yurok culture . . . has completely disintegrated under the impact of American contacts. . . . The ceremonies and rituals described by Kroeber have been extinct for some years. Debased derivatives of one or two Yurok dances have occasionally been incorporated, much to the annoyance of "old time Indians," into commercial festivities organized by members of the white community in Klamath. (Robins 1958:xiii-xiv)

It should be emphasized from the outset that this view resulted at least partially from inadequate fieldwork. A visiting researcher from the University of London, Robins obtained his linguistic data from six Yurok speakers who lived near the mouth of the Klamath and only stayed in the area from March until June of 1951. As noted previously, the coastal Indian communities were influenced by white settlement at a very early period, and it is not clear that Robins ever visited the more rural Indian communities in Hoopa Valley or along the Klamath River between Pekwan and Happy Camp. Moreover, the dates of his visit would seem to preclude his attendance at any traditional ceremony, as the earliest in the year (the Brush Dance) is held no sooner than the last part of June.

What I found during the 1970s was that Indian culture was not only still alive but was growing in so many directions that it was hard to get a grip on it. There was cranky old Calvin Rube (Yurok), spreading a sort of neoconservative message that helped produce a generation of Yuroks who were probably more intense about "training" and being "clean" than their parents. There was gentle Alice Pratt (Hupa), quietly performing the Brush Dance medicine much as it had always been done. There were literally scores of Yurok, Hupa, and Karok people I knew personally for whom traditional culture had a slightly different meaning.

None lived as Indians had lived before 1850, but all seemed to regard Indian heritage as the central fact of their personal identity. If there was anything that most of them had in common it was that tendency to criticize whatever transformations did occur: first they want you to know that everything used to be religious, and next they want to tell you that it is not that way anymore. It is not difficult for me to visualize the elderly people whom Robins interviewed complaining to the visitor from England that some people were doing religious dances for demonstration purposes, for this type of finger pointing is a traditional mode of Yurok discourse. This is one thing that the Indians always like to talk about, either to an outsider or among themselves. Far from being a symptom of cultural extinction, this could be viewed as the muscle that holds everything together so tightly as Indian life is grudgingly adapted to modern conditions. And rather than being a modern characteristic, this complaining is probably rather ancient, as earlier Indians also seem to have been obsessed with the disparities between their own lives and that of the *wo'gey* whose existence they sought in vain to duplicate. Viewed from this perspective, Indian culture has changed very little in the years since 1850.

Chapter Three

The Sacred Landscape

Ii, you are very ill. You are about to die. If you eat
me, you will recover, because it is from this, from
your eating everything, eating dead humans, eating
everything reptilian, and rattlesnakes, it is from this
that you are sick. You will eat me. Prepare well, with
a keyom-*dipper, pound me up, put me into it. Then,*
talk to me. You will get well from that, even though
you are weak now and have no flesh. Look at yourself!

A plant spoke thus to Buzzard as he was
walking along the ridge of the Bald Hills.
From a Yurok formula for stomach sickness
as spoken by Domingo of Weitchpec in 1907
(Kroeber 1976:313)

It would be virtually impossible to list every feature of the natural
environment which was regarded as a spiritual entity according to
aboriginal belief. All of nature was thought to have been shaped
through incidents that occurred in the period before humans
existed, and in their modern form not only the plants and animals
but even the trails were believed to have "feelings" and power to
influence human life.

This chapter describes some of these early Indian beliefs concerning nature and the human condition, and readers should note
from the outset how sharply these ideas differ from Judeo-Christian
thought. In Western civilization, the idea that man is created in
the image of God seems to have been associated historically with
a drive to control and regulate the physical environment through
science and technology. By contrast, the Yurok viewed humans as
the main contaminating element in a world that was otherwise perfect. Far from seeking to control nature he tried to purify himself,
hoping that he could share in the miracles of the *wo'gey* if he were
"clean" enough.

Sacred Places

As noted in chapter 1, these were among the last North American
Indians to have their aboriginal civilization altered by contact with
outsiders, and it was probably due to this that spoken narratives
and other information collected shortly after the turn of the century
reveals such a close correspondence between mythology and practical knowledge. The degree of congruence is most strikingly demonstrated in Waterman's "Yurok Geography" (1920), which contains thirty-four annotated maps of Yurok territory and is certainly
one of the most detailed studies of its kind ever made.

Waterman begins by telling us that aboriginal Yuroks conceived
the world as a flat body of land, roughly circular, and surrounded
by ocean, with the Klamath River running down the center.[1] Thus,
it was believed that if a person left the mouth of the river and went
far enough upstream, he would reach the water again. The land,
with all its forests and mountains, was thought to float upon the
ocean, constantly rising and falling as it heaved and settled in a
rhythm too vast to be perceived by human beings (see diagram 1,
p. 44).

Roughly in the center of the world lies the village of Kenek.
Here, a being called "World-Maker"[2] made the sky, which was
woven like a fish net. Upon finishing this, he heaved it aloft where
it became solid, stretching over the world as the great blue sky.
Above this ceiling, there was another region called "sky country,"
which could be reached by climbing an invisible ladder located just
downstream from Kenek. In this conception the solid sky formed
a sort of canopy that came down to meet the ocean on all sides. If
one paddled far enough out to sea, it was theoretically possible by
timing the rise and fall of the waves to slip through underneath,
and thus one could leave the world. It was thought that Geese left
the world regularly through their own special "sky hole."

Far across the ocean, well beyond the edge where the sky came
down to touch it, was the home of Nepewo (the headman of the
salmon) and of Dentalium Shell Money, both of whom lived there
in wooden houses much like those the Indians occupied. Wohpekemeu also made his home there, and it was believed that these
and other godlike beings visited the human world on a regular basis
despite the terrific distances involved.

Within that part of the physical environment which was actually inhabited by humans were many places where mythic beings had left evidence of their presence. There was, for instance, a certain cliff by the seashore where Wohpekemeu had lain on his back, singing and slapping himself on the chest. When the tide was out, one could still see the marks that Wohpekemeu's feet had made as he kicked them about against the vertical face of the cliff (Waterman 1920:231). Not far from there, the Indians also showed Waterman an offshore rock that was known by a Yurok word meaning "refuse," as this was the place where Chickenhawk had thrown the guts of an enemy he had killed (1920:233). The number of similar examples in Waterman (1920) suggests that any natural configuration might come to have mythic relevance in Yurok thought.

These connections with the prehuman world were especially close at the village of Kenek, near the mouth of Tuley Creek on the Klamath River. Besides being the place where "World-Maker" made the sky, this was where Wohpekemeu first emerged from the earth, and the Indians who lived there during Waterman's visits (circa 1902–1909) could actually point to the pits where there had been houses occupied by deities such as Thunder, Porpoise, and Earthquake only a few generations before. Waterman also mentions that Kenek was regarded with special reverence by Indians of other villages.

Ordinary people do not dare step around in Kenek. Visitors used to come as far as the place where the trail crosses Tuley Creek and call. Then the people who belonged there would come down and get them, and show them around, so that they might not inadvertently step on some supernatural being's "place" and get into trouble. (Waterman 1920:252)

Not just at Kenek, but all over the region, walking trails were regarded as conscious beings, and in traveling the Indian had to observe certain rules in order to avoid insulting them. It was considered wrong, for example, to step out of a trail and in again without making some gesture of respect, and indeed the traveler had to observe many such customs. There were certain places where it was expected that a person would stop and rest while using a trail, whether he was tired or not, and there the Indian was often supposed to speak a prayer. The following example was recited by Sam Brown (Hupa) in 1927 and translated by Edward Sapir.

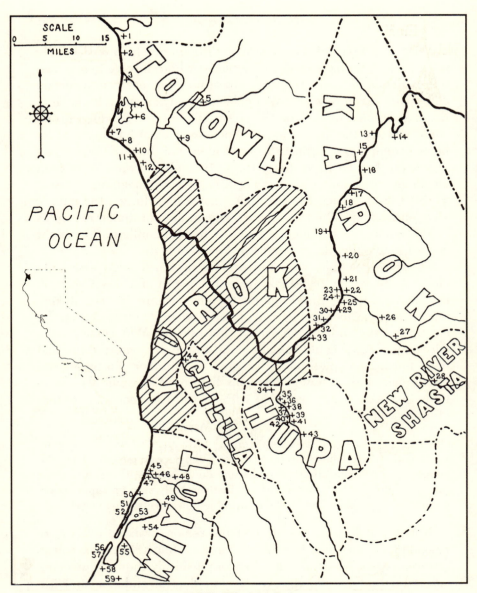

KEY TO MAP 1

1. rkr'
2. noro'rpeg
3. hinē'i
4. logeno'ʟ
5. hine'g
6. tolo'qʷ
7. pĕkʷtsū
8. ko'hpi
9. mistsi'ks
10. rʟ
11. ne'keʟ
12. osme'tsken
13. äko'nileʟ
14. äyo'omok
15. rä'yoik
16. häʟkutso'r
17. posī'r
18. äpye'ʷ
19. tsäno'ʟ
20. me'legoʟ
21. tū'noiyoʟ
22. higwoni'k
23. segwe'ʷ
24. e'nek
25. ma''a
26. sepola'
27. keski'ʟ
28. ke'per
29. nä'ästok
30. we'tsets
31. ko''omen
32. olege'ʟ
33. oprgr'
34. plo'kseʷ
35. oknü'ʟ
36. rgr'its
37. qrrwr'
38. o'plego
39. qä'xteʟ
40. rlr'n
41. pyä'ägeʟ
42. petso'ʷ
43. wo'xtoi
44. otle'p
45. ko'hso
46. sepora'
47. tegwo'ʟ
48. pegwe'
49. we'skwenet-o-tnä'ʷ
50. enikole'ʟ
51. rtr'qr
52. tepa'axk
53. olo'g
54. hike'ts
55. oknü'ʟ
56. weyo'
57. pi'min
58. le'plen
59. äyo'

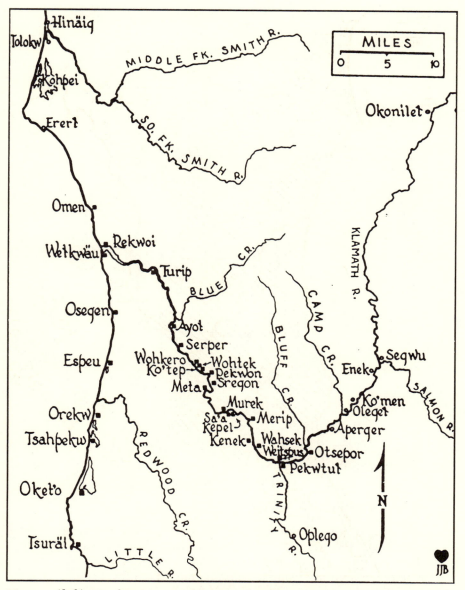

Map 1. (*left*) Northwestern California, showing distribution of Yurok place names outside Yurok territory. Inset map: California, showing the location of Yurok territory (shaded). (From Waterman 1920)

Map 2. (*above*) Principal Yurok towns, indicated by black squares, along the Klamath River and the northern California coast. Towns of the Tolowa, Hupa, and Karok are indicated by circles. The names shown for these are the Yurok ones. (From Spott and Kroeber 1942)

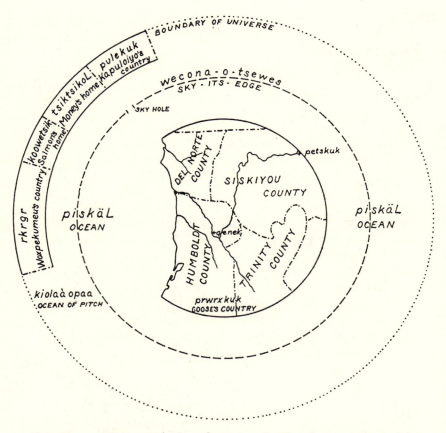

Diagram 1. Waterman's map depicting the Yurok conception of the
world (1920:192).

[You] lie here still. Let me go about without criticism. Let me grow old
doing things this way. Let me keep coming back along this trail only with
something good. Let me live happily. You have plenty of power, they
say, oh [resting place]. May you look on me. May I live happily. May I
grow old in the way I'm telling you. May you preserve my body. (Golla,
in press)

There were other places where the traveler was expected to
make a certain offering. In some instances, this meant dropping a

twig or branch where trails crossed one another, while in others the Indian was supposed to shoot an arrow into certain sacred trees so as to assure good luck.

The twig dropping is best described by Powers, who writes,

They have a curious custom of dropping twigs and boughs at the junction of trails, which sometimes accumulate in heaps several feet high, like the nests of woodrats. Every Indian who passes deposits a twig on the pile, but without observing any method that a white man can discover. No one will explain the custom, though it is probably observed, like so many other things, merely "for luck." (Powers, 1877 [1976]:58)

The custom of offering arrows to a sacred tree is described by Waterman, who explains that the arrow was a valuable piece of property in precontact times, since much time and effort were required to produce one. He also notes that the custom became distorted after the introduction of firearms, as the trees were then sometimes shot with bullets, leaving them scarred and stripped of bark (Waterman 1920:230–231).

The annotated maps in Waterman (1920) identify a number of special locations that were known as places where a Yurok person could pray or ask for help, and the following examples give an indication of their character:

1. A certain place on Bald Hills where there is an echo. One goes there to shout for help and the response tells whether or not the spirit will help (1920:197).
2. A rock offshore from Wilson Creek (False Klamath Rock). One of the *wo'gey* came to live in this rock, and he invites people to cry and ask for money while looking at the place (1920:230).
3. A place on the coast near the village of Omen. People would look around in the saltwater here for rocks to make arrowheads. After shaping them, they would "cook" the points by speaking a formula over them, after which they would be strong enough to shoot right through an elk (1920:233).
4. A submerged rock in the Klamath River (Posir Rock), just upstream from Ah Pah Creek. This rock was a "charm" for snaring deer. The hunter would dive underwater to touch it, and then

he rubbed his hands upon the snares, which guaranteed a catch (1920:238).

5. A large rock in the Klamath River below Pekwan. Pelintsiek ("Great Dentalium") used to live in the water here. In passing the rock by canoe, one stops alongside it in midstream, there clapping the hands and speaking a short prayer for luck (1920: 243).

6. A certain rock formation near the village of Merip. Arrowheads were placed in a cleft in the rock, and there they became "rusted" or covered with a poison that made them certain to kill (1920:250).

7. A point of rocks on Trinidad Head. The Yurok name for this rock formation is translated "He Sits Forever." A man went there to cry for luck and ask for money. Then he saw dentalium shells in the water, numerous as sardines. He sat there looking and refusing to leave until he gradually turned to stone (1920:270).

8. A cave at Trinidad Head. Its Yurok name has been translated "Where it Drops (or Trickles)." People went inside this damp cave to pray for money. If one drop fell on a person, then he would soon become wealthy. But if two fell upon him, then the rock would close up and he would never escape (1920:270).

Waterman felt that the Yurok had an unusually large number of named places within their territory, by comparison with other North American Indians, and he said that his monograph contained only about one half the places that might have been indicated if there were adequate time or space to include them clearly on the maps (1920:195). This very intensive view of the surrounding landscape was something which also impressed Powers, who commented on the care with which this information was transmitted from one generation to the next.

The boundaries of all tribes . . . are marked with the greatest precision, being defined by certain creeks, canyons, boulders, conspicuous trees, springs, etc., each of which has its own individual name. Accordingly, the squaws teach these things to their children in a kind of sing-song. . . . Over and over, time and again, they rehearse all these boulders, etc., describing each minutely and by name, with its surroundings. Then, when the children are old enough, they take them around . . . and so faithful has been their instruction, that [the children] generally recognize the objects from the descriptions given them previously by their mothers. (Powers 1877 [1976]:109–110)

These teachings relating to geography were expressed in mythic terms, and mythic tales were also loaded with useful knowledge about the landscape. We learn, for example, from one Yurok narrative that Wohpekemeu used to fish at a place near the village of Kenek, just below the mouth of Tuley Creek (Kroeber 1976:110), but any fisherman could see why this is a good spot. Just above there is a very strong rapid, and this is the first real barrier that salmon and other species encounter on moving upstream from the mouth of the river. In this fashion, mythic belief and practical or scientific knowledge were woven into a single fabric.

Heroic Beings

In this and the sections that follow, the multitude of spiritual beings which animated the environment are divided into categories for descriptive purposes. This is only a convenience and does not reflect a classification that Indians themselves would be likely to express. The discussion focuses mainly on characters of Yurok mythology, but similar beings were also known by the Hupa and Karok. For example, Wohpekemeu figures in several Hupa myths, where he is identified as Yumantuwinyai. In Karok mythology Wohpekemeu is sometimes equated with Coyote, as shown by a text in which Coyote invents childbirth (Harrington 1932:25–27), and other times equated with a character called Yeruxbihii (Kroeber and Gifford 1980:288–289).

While Wohpekemeu is generally portrayed as having the physical appearance of a human being, another heroic figure called Pulekukwerek ("At the North End of Creation Sharp One") was a monstrous creature, covered with horns or spines, who smoked tobacco but never ate food. Like Wohpekemeu, he lived across the ocean, but Pulekukwerek avoided females altogether and spent all of his time in the sweathouse. Thus, as character models, these two superheroes seem to represent opposing tendencies toward virility on the one hand and asceticism on the other. In Yurok mythology, Pulekukwerek is mainly known for having killed off the sea serpents who inhabited the estuary at the mouth of the Klamath (Waterman 1920:228). The physical characteristics of these beings often seem fantastic and contradictory from a modern American perspective. Thus, for example, Pelintsiek ("Great Dentalium") was conceived as a dentalium shell as large as a sturgeon, but in narrative texts he is also able to speak and walk like a man (Kroeber 1976:200–204).

Other Yurok deities included Megwomits, the bearded dwarf known mainly as a provider of acorns and other vegetable products, and imposing natural entities such as Sun, Moon, Earthquake, and The Thunders. Like Pelintsiek, each of these awesome beings had human qualities despite the apparent contradictions this sometimes implied, and each was responsive to the thoughts and deeds of human beings. The Thunders, for example, were known as patrons of men who wanted to become stronger and more fearsome. To obtain their help, one would go to a mountain lake in the dead of night; he would dive to the bottom, holding his breath until he nearly lost consciousness, and then the man would not only obtain power for fighting but would also get luck for obtaining wealth (Spott and Kroeber 1942:163).

While the heroes described here are identified in narratives collected early in this century, not all were mentioned by Yuroks I knew during the 1970s. Wohpekemeu is by far the most important heroic figure in mythic tales or anecdotes told by modern Yuroks.

Monsters and Creek Devils

The most awesome beings in this category were the sea monsters who raised havoc in the estuary at the mouth of the Klamath River. There were twelve monsters there, each different in type, and they not only seized canoes but also caused a terrific turbulence so that people often drowned. The estuary was an important ferrying point in aboriginal times, as it was part of a major trail that Indians had to use in moving north or south along the coast. Fortunately, Pulekukwerek managed to kill the monsters so that the water became quite calm (Waterman 1920:228). In another account Pulekukwerek used a song to make the water still, and this became a form of medicine that travelers could use whenever they were using a boat in rough water (Kroeber 1976:423–424).

Smaller monsters were sometimes adopted as "pets" by the *wo'gey*, and narratives collected from Wets'owa of Pekwon (Yurok) around 1900 mention two of these creatures: a giant bird known as an *erl'erm* and a type of water serpent called *knewollek* ("long one") in Yurok. In the first of these texts, a spirit-person brought the *erl'erm* into his house, where it began to dance around and then vomited up some bulbs. Later the man got married, and the *erl'erm* did not like this and left. The family began eating the bulbs, but they proved to be poisonous and made the baby sick, because the man should not have used the bulbs after he had taken a wife. This mythic incident became the basis of a formula for curing, and the text is also significant for illustrating the concept of sickness as a penalty for a spiritual offense (Kroeber 1976:409).

The text involving the *knewollek* ("long one") has a similar theme: A hunter found one of these water serpents, and he decided to take it home, though he didn't know what it was. He kept it hidden from his wife and always gave it a share of the deer he took. This became his "pet" and gave him tremendous luck in hunting deer. However, one day the man's wife noticed the serpent as it reached out to snatch a piece of meat. She struck it with a stick and it ran away. The hunter never did find out why his "pet" had left. This story also serves as the basis of a spoken medicine formula, in this case one used for a baby with cramps. The cramps were said to be caused by the *knewollek*, who was causing pain by holding the child in a tight grip (Kroeber 1976:410).

Both of these texts depict a male whose "pet" comes into conflict with his domestic life, and in the latter the *knewollek* is explicitly a creature that gave the hunter good luck. This theme that a man's luck or spiritual interactions are corrupted by contact with females or sexuality is pervasive in the texts of spoken medicine formulas to be described later, especially in those collected from men.

Aside from beasts such as these, the Yuroks interviewed by Kroeber shortly after 1900 also believed that ghosts of dead could haunt the living and corpses sometimes came back to life (1925:47). This was not discussed in conversations I had during the 1970s, but Indians I knew often mentioned a creature known by the Yurok word *uma'a* and called "devil" or "Indian devil" in English. The *uma'a* were thought to live in dark, bushy thickets, and they had magical arrows of burning flint with which they could kill someone who passed nearby. The arrows (which come in sets of twelve or more) sometimes fell into the hands of humans, and then they could be used for sorcery.[3] A person who does this is also called an "Indian devil" and some are accused or suspected of practicing this form of black magic even today. Waterman cites at least one location that was known to have been frequented by *uma'a* around the turn of the century (1920:238).

Animals

All of the animals were thought to have been more like people in the prehuman period, and the transformation of animals is described in one Yurok narrative in which several animals join forces to kill a giant bird in order to obtain the feathers and fur that they would need when humans arrived. This happened somewhere near Shelton Butte (Kroeber 1976:329).

Mythic narratives involving animals are particularly important as vehicles for expressing cultural values, and Erik Erikson mentions several animal stories which were used in the education of Yurok children. In one example, Buzzard is described as a greedy character who got his ugly pinkish head by scalding himself when he plunged into a bowl of soup before it had time to cool. Then he became afraid to eat anything warm, and that is why he flies around waiting until his food gets so old that it stinks (Erikson 1943:287). Another story involved Negenich the Mouse. She was pretty, but boys did not want to marry her because she stole things all the time. Her sister Frog did not steal, so she got married and raised a nice family despite being rather plain (Erikson 1943:288).

Some of these animal tales are sung or dramatized. While used mainly for entertainment today, these animals songs were previously also used for medicine making. All of them involve an element of impersonation or mimicry, and they are not "sung" but delivered in a form of heightened speech which is supposed to represent the thoughts or speech of an animal spirit-person. The songs are all rather brief and each contains much hidden meaning or relies upon knowledge of things not mentioned in the song itself.

One excellent example is an Elk Song that was performed by Frank Douglas (Yurok) during an interview on March 8, 1979. Using a tense and nasalized voice which is supposed to represent that of the female elk, Frank intoned Yurok words which could be translated,

> It hurts me. It hurts me.
> I hope it gets daylight soon. I hope it gets daylight soon.

Then he switched to a lower pitch level and imitated the masculine voice of her mate, who said (in a modern translation quite characteristic of Frank),

> I hope it don't get daylight too damn quick.

In this example, the sexual connotations of the song are not explicit, and this is precisely what makes it clever or amusing from a Yurok perspective. Most important, Frank emphasized that the song was not only for entertainment, but could also be used as a hunting song.

In a Dog Song performed during the same interview, the practical function was much more evident. In this case, Frank prefaced the song with an explanation, and instead of being humorous and slightly vulgar, this song had the darker character of a curse.

A dog was a person at one time, according to the Indian. One fellow's dog was barking all the time. He got tired of that, and he put him outside rough-like. And the dog sang this song. If you're mean to your dog, that's the worse thing you can do, and the dog will say:

> Osh-a-la-moy . . . Key-ku-wen
> Osh-a-la-moy . . . Key-ku-wen
> Osh-a-la-moy . . . Key-ku-wen

And that means, "I hope that person dies, because he's mean to me."

Here was a song that a person could use to wish harm on someone who had treated him unfairly. In later chapters we shall examine more songs of the same general type, most of which were collected between 1900 and 1927, but many of these ancient songs were still known by Frank Douglas and other Indian persons whom I interviewed during the 1970s.

Animals upon which the Indians depended for sustenance, especially deer and salmon, were regarded with special reverence. In aboriginal times, it was believed that the most effective means of attracting salmon was to imagine their presence, visualizing the fish as they moved into the net underwater. Then, if you lived correctly they would indeed come and fill your net. But no matter how many were taken, their number was never diminished, and the species was viewed (collectively) as a single immortal being. Nepewo, the "headman" of the salmon, lived across the ocean with Wohpeke-meu and other deities, and Nepewo spoke for all salmon when he declared the following:

I shall travel as far as the river extends. I shall leave my scales on nets and they will turn into salmon, but I myself shall go by and not be killed. (Kroeber 1925:68)

One might say that the Indians excused their violating the salmon's flesh by viewing the species in this manner, and a description of the First Salmon Ceremony reveals the extent to which indigenous attitudes toward the salmon were basically conciliatory or apologetic.[4] The ceremony was performed at the beginning of the spring salmon run, and it was forbidden for anyone to take salmon before it was done. A formulist prepared for the ritual by praying and gathering sweathouse wood for ten days. During this period he was not allowed to drink water, nor indeed could he drink water until the fall. There was also a taboo against his having sex, and this extended for an entire year after he conducted the ceremony.

In the ritual itself, the fish was prepared and eaten according to strict guidelines. The medicine man was not supposed to use his hands to lift the salmon from his net, but rather he fashioned a twine of green hazel bark and threaded it through the gills for handling. Next, he lay the fish on its belly and held his breath while drawing a stone blade along the backbone from head to tail. It was believed that the spirits on either side of the river watched very closely while this was done, in order to make sure that the proper etiquette was observed. If a modern hafted knife were used, for example, or if the salmon were lifted carelessly by its tail, then this would make for poor fishing all year long and would also "ruin the world."

Before eating the salmon, the medicine man spoke a formula in which he consulted with the leader of the salmon and obtained his permission to be eaten. Like many prayers of this kind, this text had the form of a dialogue but was spoken by one person. In asking and answering the questions, the medicine man also outlined the proper guidelines for consumption of salmon. He asks if it would be all right for a person to eat salmon and then eat bear meat afterwards, and then he describes how the fish just lay still in the water, signifying assent. Then he asks if it were all right to eat trout afterwards, and the fish also allowed this. Finally, he asks what the salmon would do if eaten by a woman who had a miscarriage, and he describes how the fish floated belly up as if dead. After this dialogue was enacted, the medicine man cooked and ate the first salmon, and it was considered good luck to eat the whole thing. He would not be permitted to eat salmon again until the fall, but through his actions the community received permission to do so.

Hunters were also careful to obtain the good will of deer, which were also regarded as immortal beings. It was believed that the deer only gave their flesh to those who observed proper manners in eating, and it was even thought that they compared notes in this regard.

"How do you like that house?" the elder [deer] would ask. "I do not like it," [the younger one] says. "He does not wash his hands, and his women shift their feet while they sit at the meal." Or it answers: "He is good. He acts rightly. Smell my hand." They sniff it, like [the smell of] the pepperwood, and frequently go into that man's snares. (Kroeber 1925:68)[5]

While eating the deer, the hunter saved the bones and other offal, and he returned these to the spot where the deer was taken so that the deer would rise again. This practice was described by Aileen Figueroa (Yurok) in a relatively recent interview conducted by Charlotte Heth.

Every time we'd eat a deer we'd have a basket or a can or something. We'd throw all our bones in there, all our bones, until we got the whole deer used up, and then we'd either go up in the mountains or out in the brush and [we] take the whole bunch of bones and [we] dump it. And then, as you dump it, the deer takes off. If you just throw your bones here and there, well the deer doesn't have all the bones together [laughs]. This way you put all your bones together and there goes your deer, ready for another catch. (Bommelyn et al. 1976)

The propitiatory attitude toward deer is evident in other beliefs and customs relating to deer hunting and consumption of venison.

For example, deer hunting was thought to be incompatible with sex, and the successful hunter had to abstain or use a medicine formula to counteract the effects of intercourse, otherwise the deer would not allow themselves to be found. Besides being a prominent theme in hunting narratives to be described later, this belief is documented in Powers (1877 [1976]).

Before going out on a chase the Karok hunter must abstain three days from touching any woman, else he will miss the quarry. Mr. A. Somes related an incident which happened to himself when hunting in company with a venerable Indian. They set out betimes and scoured the mountain-tops with diligence all day, and were like to return empty-handed, when the old savage declared roundly that the white man was trifling with him, and that he must have touched some woman. No ridicule could shake his belief, so he withdrew a few paces, fell on his knees, turned his face devoutly toward heaven, and prayed fluently and fervently for the space of full twenty minutes. Somes was so much impressed with the old savage's earnestness that he did not disturb him. Although able to speak the language well, he understood nothing the white-haired petitioner uttered. When he made an end of praying he rose solemnly, saying they would now have success. They started on, and it so fell out that they started upon a fine pricket in a few minutes and Somes picked him off. (Powers 1877 [1976]:31–32)

It was also believed that having sex after eating venison (or sea lion flesh) could cause a person or one of his children to get sick (Kroeber 1925:69). And finally, Valory notes that it was considered repulsive to eat the portion of the game that had been struck by the arrow (1970:83).

Plants and Herbs

Plants were also thought to have been more like human beings in the period before humans arrived. Acorns were the most important vegetable food in aboriginal times, and a story about acorns told by Phoebe Maddox (Karok) in 1926 and recorded by Harrington (1932:5–6) provides another example of the manner in which practical knowledge was cast in the form of a mythic narrative.

The acorns are depicted as a group of young ladies. They are told to weave nice hats, because human beings are about to arrive, and the girls will soon be transformed into acorns. Thus, the story is based on a resemblance between the woman's traditional woven hat and the woody cup which holds the hard acorn seed. The girls begin to weave, but their work is abruptly interrupted when humans appear sooner than expected. As a result, one of them does not finish her hat, and she wears a woven bowl instead. Another one (Tan Oak Acorn) finishes her hat, but without completely trimming away the straws that projected toward the inside. She just turned it wrong side out and wore it that way. Finally, the last one finished her hat perfectly.

After being transformed, Tan Oak Acorn got so angry about this that she cursed the others.

Tan Oak Acorn wished bad luck toward Post Oak Acorn and Maul Oak Acorn, just because they had nice hats. She was jealous of them. . . . [That is why] nobody likes to eat Post Oak Acorn. And Maul Oak Acorn does not taste good either, and is hard. [Their] soups are black. And Maul Oak Acorn is hard to pound. They were all painted when they first spilled down. Black Oak Acorn was striped. When one picks it up on the ground it is still striped nowadays. But Tan Oak Acorn did not paint herself much, because she was mad. (Harrington 1932:6)

Plants and herbs were especially prominent in doctoring, and the effectiveness of a given plant substance was expressed mainly in terms of its mythological significance. Wallace described the work of Hupa herb doctors as follows:

Lesser disorders like an upset stomach or headache were treated with spoken formulas, almost always accompanied by herbal medicines. The medications were administered in such minute quantity or in such a way as to have little or no effect. Relief was supposed to stem from the words uttered rather than the plant substances. Medicine formulas, handed down in family lines, represented a valuable form of property, since a stiff charge was made for their recital. (Wallace 1978a:175)

In many cases, the formula was to be spoken as the plant substance was being collected. For example, a formulist would actually speak to a cluster of madrone leaves while plucking them from the tree. The leaves themselves were not medicine, but rather it is believed that they become medicine after they were "talked to" in this fashion. The spoken formulas describe a previous cure that was successful in the period before humans. In some cases the mythic cure was effected by a *wo'gey* who used a certain plant substance, but often the plant itself was regarded as a conscious being, as shown in the narrative quoted at the head of this chapter.

The *Wo'gey* and Human Beings

Of all the spiritual beings recognized by the Yuroks, none was more important than the *wo'gey*, for it was they who had originated nearly every form of medicine making and whose continued help the Indians needed if public and private rituals were to be effective. While heroic beings, monsters, animals, and plants all have a certain importance in mythic narratives that were collected from Yurok speakers, the *wo'gey* are the primary characters in this literature and figure in virtually every text. Because of this, we shall be learning more about the *wo'gey* and their lives in chapters to follow, but it seems useful to make some preliminary comments here.

Erikson states that the Yurok conceived the *wo'gey* as being rather small, and he emphasizes the belief that they were always "clean" because they did not know sexual intercourse (1943:260–261). While Erikson may indeed have been told this by one of the individuals he interviewed, this is a rather specialized view and does not reflect Yurok religious conception in general. Indian persons whom I interviewed said that they were not necessarily small but "just different." In mythic narratives the *wo'gey* are generally portrayed as being very much like human beings, and in many cases the literature in translation is likely to be confusing because it is not always explicit as to whether the characters involved are supposed to be *wo'gey* or human beings. In these texts they often have sex and do other polluting things, and this is one reason why they needed to invent medicine in the first place.

Kroeber and Waterman both note that the time frame of Yurok mythology is compressed into a very brief span. Rather than depicting the prehuman world as something ancient, the narratives that Kroeber and others collected generally relate something that happened in the last few days before human beings were to arrive. A sense of immediacy is repeatedly expressed in passages such as the following, which describes two *wo'gey* discussing how to build a sweathouse to be used in the Jump Dance ritual. And one says,

I wanted to know, before making my sweathouse, what sort I should have, and I waited for you. Now I shall make it quickly because I know that there are [human] people all along that [Trinity] river and that [Klamath] river. I want everything to be made when they arrive. I know now that we shall not remain here. There will be another kind of people in this world. We must hurry. (Kroeber 1976:29)

Rather than believing that they had a human history, Indians of the precontact period thought they had inherited their world from the *wo'gey* relatively recently. Thus the nearness of humans and *wo'gey* in time was emphasized even further, and the speaker of the text quoted here actually showed Kroeber a pit where the sweathouse in question had existed, only a few generations before.

The use of medicine formulas and other rituals was also supported by a belief that the *wo'gey* had invented these things mainly in order to help human beings, and this is mentioned in several texts describing medicine formulas. One reason they wanted to help, according to Yurok thought, is because they felt sorry for humans, particularly because humans had to grow old and die while the *wo'gey* themselves were immortal. These sentiments are illustrated in the following comment, which was made by Johnny Shortman (Yurok) of Rekwoi in 1901.

Now the *woge* are always glad when one calls on them in a formula. In all formulas a name has to be called upon, then they are glad that they are talked to. They always pity the people because they are so few. If they had let old people become young, as they wanted to, if [Jerusalem Cricket] had not done wrong and brought death, there would be many people. That is why the *woge* are sorry. (Kroeber 1976:443)

When Indians came, the *wo'gey* took refuge in trees, rocks, springs, and other places. Because humans built homes along the river, many of the spirit-persons went into the upper ridges to live, and this is why Indians traditionally go to the high country to make medicine. The sweathouse was another special place for communicating with the *wo'gey*, and early customs involving these two sacred locations are discussed in the next chapter.

Chapter Four

The Sweathouse and the High Country

As she danced with her eyes closed and her hands stretched out, she heard a song for gambling, then for the Jumping Dance, the Brush Dance, for luck, for money, for the Deerskin Dance, for basketmaking. But to each one she said, "I did not come for that." Then all at once she heard the Doctor Dance song. "That's what I came for," she said, clapped her hands, and held them out. Thereupon, she heard the song again. She danced harder and harder, still sucking in her breath, until she felt something with wings come against her, got something into her hand, and lost consciousness.

> Shamanistic power coming to an Indian Doctor as she danced in one of seven stone chairs on Oka Mountain (Spott and Kroeber 1942: 220)

This chapter examines two important avenues through which Yurok Indians sought to establish contact with the *wo'gey*. Before discussing these institutions, however, it seems necessary to consider certain aspects of culture and society which formed a context for them. Indian concepts relating to wealth and sexuality are fundamental in medicine making, and they differ so greatly from modern Western attitudes that failing to view them in their own terms would almost certainly lead to misinterpretation.

Aristocracy and Wealth

Before our federal government imposed itself upon them, the tribes of the region did not recognize forms of social regulation or government as we understand them. As a matter of fact, the word "tribe" is not strictly appropriate in speaking of California Indians generally, for rather than being political units the so-called tribelets of this region typically consisted of groups of villages that were linked by linguistic or cultural affinities and were otherwise quite independent.

This anarchic tendency was particularly evident among the tribes of northwestern California.[1] From a legal perspective, the male head of a Yurok household was answerable to no one, and indeed there was no authority beyond that which an individual could impose through force of wealth, personality, or physical strength. When the federal Indian agent Redick McKee made the Treaty of 1851 at Weitchpec, the document was signed by "Big Indians" from each village, and four signed from Weitchpec alone (Nelson 1978:appendix 1).

Precontact law was based upon a specialized "blood money" system in which a person who felt that he had been wronged might seek compensation. Matters as serious as a murder or as trivial as a breach of manners would be settled only when the offended party managed to collect what he felt he was owed. In practice, this often implied much haggling and negotiation, and a rich and important person could naturally press his claims more forcefully than one of lesser stature.

In point of fact, his *or her* claims would be more accurate, as Kroeber emphasizes that women had equal rights in law and wealth, and that the only reason men dominated in legal affairs was that they were more able to press their claims by threat of force (1925:22). Readers interested in a case study should consult the detailed description of a dispute over rights to a sea lion harpooned near the mouth of the Klamath River in Spott and Kroeber (1942: 182–199).

Society was based upon a dual caste system which basically dictated whether an individual was an aristocrat or a commoner. Known in recent times as a "headman" or a "big Indian," the precontact aristocrat generally had several other males attached to his household; these might include sons, sons-in-law, and others who simply relied upon him for protection. Kroeber describes Yurok words for status as follows:

The rich man is called *si'atleu*, or simply *pergerk*, "man." Similarly, a wealthy or "real" woman is *wentsauks* or "woman." A poor person is *wa'asoi.* A slave is called *uka'atl.* A bastard is called either *kamuks* or *negenits,* "mouse," because of his parasitic habits. . . . Even a small village group was known as *pegharkes,* "manly," if its members were determined, resentful, and wealthy enough to take revenge. (Kroeber 1925:40)

It was mainly the aristocratic Indians who trained in the sweathouse and made medicine in the high country. These were often intellectuals who traveled widely to gain knowledge of other Indian peoples and took pride in speaking languages other than their own. Moreover, they were expected to observe a special code of manners, described in these words by Kroeber:

A well-brought-up man asked to step into a house its with folded arms, they say, and talks little, chiefly in answers. If he is given food, he becomes conversational, to show that he is not famished, and eats very slowly. Should he gobble his meal and arise to go, his host would laugh and say to his children: "That is how I constantly tell you not to behave." (Kroeber 1925:39)

Among lesser families, such etiquette was not expected, and Indians seem to have felt that aristocratic manners were not only acquired through learning but passed through the very blood in a good family. Even in recent times, modern Yuroks have been noted to say that a particular family "had a history" of poverty or shiftlessness, so that they could never be expected to amount to much (Valory 1970:18).

In assessing these beliefs, it becomes clear that wealth signified something very different for the Yurok of 1850 than it does for us today. Various writers have focused upon the Indians' preoccupation with wealth without placing enough emphasis on its spiritual connotations. Thus, Erikson (1950:142) and Kroeber (1904:88) both describe Yuroks as having been completely obsessed with wealth and determined to lie or argue for the least advantage. Walter Goldschmidt errs yet further in this direction, characterizing Indian society as a "capitalist social structure" (1951).

William Wallace recently described tangible forms of wealth among the Hupa as follows:

Wealth meant, in addition to shell currency, skins of albino or unusually-colored deerskins, large chipped blades of imported black or red obsidian, scarlet-feathered woodpecker scalps glued to white buckskin bands, and a number of lesser valuable items. These rare and precious things, proudly displayed at group festivals, formed the basis of a person's fortune and subsequent social position. (Wallace 1978*a*:170)

While from an extrinsic viewpoint dentalium shell money was used much like modern currency, it is important for us to bear in mind that the Indians viewed all of these treasures as conscious entities. Thus, it was believed that these objects had "feelings" and were capable of leaving a person who was careless enough to insult them or to hurt their feelings.

Yurok aristocrats sought to identify themselves with the *wo'gey* in various ways and even spoke embellished dialects which were sometimes called "*wo'gey* language" (Valory 1970:21). In seeking to become more like the *wo'gey*, the aristocrat sought first of all to control his human appetites, which were regarded as degrading, and well-brought-up children were obliged to observe very strict discipline at meal times. Erik Erikson, whose study of Yurok culture focused primarily on child rearing, described the regimen as follows:

During meals a strict order of placement is maintained. Between the parents a space is always left for a potential guest. The girls sit near the mother, the boys near the father. The father teaches the boys and the mother the girls how to eat. They are told to take a little food with their spoon, to put it in their mouth slowly, to put the spoon back in the eating basket, and to chew slowly and thoroughly, meanwhile thinking of ways of becoming rich. Then, the food is to be swallowed and the child may reach again, without haste, for the spoon. . . . If a child eats too fast, the father or the mother silently takes his basket away from him and the child is supposed to rise silently and leave the house. (Erikson 1943:286)

Sex and Contamination

Institutionalized avoidance between the sexes was also an important element in Yurok society, and in the entire literature on North American Indians there is perhaps no other culture in which females, sex, and menstruation have been pictured in such a negative light. Initially, my own research on modern singing seemed to support this image of male dominance in Yurok spiritual life, for it seemed clear that women had very little role in religious rituals. Viewed more closely, however, in conjunction with archival recordings and narratives collected around the turn of the century, it becomes evident that native views regarding sexuality were not so one-sided. This evidence suggests that Yurok women once had a separate spiritual life, parallel to that of the men, that has never been fully documented.

Most of the anthropological literature describes Yurok spiritual life from a male viewpoint and gives the impression that women were largely excluded from sacred contacts. From this perspective, any contact with females or sex was viewed with ambivalence. Thus, from Kroeber we learn that men and women slept apart through much of the year, the men and boys staying in the sweathouse while women and smaller children lived in the family house (Kroeber 1925:44). The psychoanalyst Erikson states that these two structures tended to symbolize Yurok attitudes equating females with spiritual pollution, as indicated in the following passage:

[The] two house forms not only serve woman and man, respectively, but also symbolize what the man's and woman's insides mean in Yurok culture: The family house, dark, unclean, full of food and utensils, and crowded with babies, the place from which a man emerges contaminated; the sweathouse, lighter, cleaner, more orderly, with selectivity over who and what may enter, a place from which one emerges purified. (Erikson 1943:268)

Writing about Yurok child rearing, Erikson informs us that little girls were forbidden to touch boys' playthings such as toy dugout canoes or small bow and arrow sets (1943:289). Boys, on the other hand, were advised when quite young that thinking of women would spoil their chances of becoming rich. Even if a person fasted and prayed in the high country, the boys were told, one who thought of women too much would always be a poor man and a worthless one (Kroeber 1976:292).

Kroeber also informs us that girls became subject to rather severe restrictions at the onset of puberty. Although Yuroks did not conduct a public ritual for the occasion, there was formalized isolation for the girl, as her first menses was viewed as a powerful and potentially dangerous spiritual process. The custom is described as follows:

When a girl becomes mature she is called *ukerhtsperek*, and sits silent in her home with her back turned to the central fire pit. She moves as little as possible, and scratches her head only with a bone whittled and incised for the occasion. Once each day she goes to bring in firewood; on her way she looks neither to the left nor right, and looks up at no one. The longer she fasts, the more food she will have in her life, it is believed. After four days she may eat, but only at a spot where the roar of the river confounds every other sound. Should she hear even a bird sing, she ceases at once. Each evening she bathes, once the first night, twice the second, and so increasingly until on the eighth she pours the water over herself eight times. The ninth night she bathes ten times, and on the tenth day, with declining day, once, squatting by the river, while the small children of the village, one at a time, wash her back. (Kroeber 1925:45)

Her subsequent menses were surrounded by similar restrictions, and the Yurok woman was virtually isolated for at least ten days each month. During this period, it was considered especially important that she take food separately from others. According to Aileen Figueroa (Yurok), the woman had to stay in a menstrual hut, consuming only a small portion of smoked salmon each day; she also had to wear a flickertail feather in her septum so that others could be alert to avoid her (Bommelyn et al. 1977).

These customs have not been adequately described by researchers, who have mainly described patterns of sexual avoidance from a male perspective. An essay by Thomas Buckley (1982) does attempt to correct this image by discussing Yurok spiritual life from a feminist perspective; much of the information presented there is admittedly speculative, but the basic argument has much validity.

As a result of male bias on the part of earlier scholars, we know little about what women did during their menstrual isolation but have relatively complete information about the male side of things: there is, for example, ample data concerning spoken formulas that men used to counteract the contaminating effects of having had sex or contact with a menstruating woman. For example, spoken formulas to purify the deer hunter after sex are documented among the Chilula by Goddard (1914b:307, 314) and among the Karok by Kroeber and Gifford (1980:293–294, 301–302) and by Bright (1957:259).

The existing anthropological literature leaves us with an impression that women were largely excluded from sacred contacts among the Yuroks and neighboring tribes. The body of evidence supporting this view is not necessarily invalid, but it is only par-

tially true, having been derived mainly from data that male anthropologists collected from Indian men. Erikson's lengthy interview
with Fanny Flounder (Yurok) is a noteworthy exception (1943:260–
269), and other important evidence concerning female spiritual life
is summarized in chapter 9 (see Medicine for Use by Women).

Sweathouse Customs

*When you make a fire in the sweathouse, you will talk
to that fire. You will talk to it continually. You will
tell it what you want, what you want to become, that
you want to be a rich man or whatever else you want
to be. If you want play and good times, tell it that.*

> Instructions of a sweathouse spirit, from a
> myth told by Lame Billy of Weitchpec (Yurok)
> in 1901 (Kroeber 1976:20)

Religious activities connected with purification were centered in
the sweathouse, and before the 1880s men of these tribes generally
slept in the sweathouse throughout much of the year, separated
from their women and small babies. According to one Karok myth,
the sweathouse structure, its restriction to men, and special customs of gathering firewood were given to mankind specifically so
that human beings could acquire dentalium shell money (Kroeber
1925:41).

Besides sleeping in the sweathouse, men lingered there
throughout much of the day, talking business, working on ceremonial regalia, and sharing songs and stories. On certain special
occasions the sweathouse might be used for rituals such as the
"doctor-making" dance (to be described later in this chapter), but
this was primarily a place for personal purification. Not only the
wealth quest, but other practical pursuits such as hunting or fishing
required that a man be "clean," so besides using spoken medicine
formulas to counteract specific infractions, the aristocratic Indian
person ideally purified himself in the sweathouse every day.

Having had intercourse with a woman, or having slept in the same house
with a woman, the fisherman must pass the "test" of the sweathouse. He
enters through a normal-sized door; normal meaning an oval hole through
which even a fat person could enter. However, the man can leave the

sweathouse only through a small opening which will permit only a man moderate in his eating habits and supple with the perspiration caused by the sacred fire to slip through. He is required to conclude this purification by swimming in the river. The conscientious fisherman passes this test every morning. (Erikson 1950:150)

Erikson places much significance on purification in Yurok life, making the Indians seem rather compulsive about it. But being "clean" did not simply mean avoiding impure contacts and seeking to eradicate them; rather it meant lifting oneself above the normal human condition and making contact with mythic forces which animated the physical landscape. This identification with the sacred landscape is revealed in a remark made by Florence Schaughnessy (Yurok) in describing the beauty of the high country.

You come across a place you've never seen before, and it has awesome beauty. Everything above you, below you, and around you is so pure— that is the beauty we call *merwerksergerh,* and the pure person is also *merwerksergerh*. (Matthiessen 1979:62)

This word is translated as "clean person" in Robins (1958:225), and thus it becomes evident how the Yurok conception of purity became depleted of its spiritual connotations as the native word *merwerkergerh* was replaced in common usage by its English equivalent.

The practice of gathering wood for the sweathouse fire was considered a very direct method of obtaining wealth, and boys were advised to start doing this as soon as they were old enough to understand such things (Kroeber 1976:292). This did not mean simply bringing back firewood; the process itself was highly ritualized. Powers described this process as practiced by Karok Indians in the 1870s.

Fuel for the assembly chamber is sacred, and no squaw may touch it. It must be cut from a standing tree, and that tree must be on top of the highest hill overlooking the Klamath, and the branches must be trimmed in a certain particular manner. The Karok selects a tall and sightly fir or pine, climbs up within about twenty feet of the top, then commences and trims off all the limbs until he reaches the top where he leaves two limbs and a top knot, resembling a man's head and arms outstretched. All this time he is weeping and sobbing piteously, shedding real tears, and so he continues to do while he descends, binds the wood in a fagot, takes it upon his back, and goes down to the assembly chamber. (Powers 1877 [1976]:25)

A tree that has been trimmed in this manner is shown in the photo insert.

The ritualized gathering of sweathouse wood is also described in connection with the First Salmon Ceremony at Welkwau, and here again crying is mentioned. In this lengthy narrative, Robert Spott is telling the story of how his father learned the ritual from an older man and writes,

Now it was toward evening. The old man went outside and my father followed. Then the old man sent him to bring down sweathouse wood. On the way he cried at nearly every step because now he was seeing with his own eyes how it was done, when before he had never thought much about it. Also he cried because this was the way the people of old had done from the beginning, and now they had chosen him for that part. (Spott and Kroeber 1942:177)

From passages such as these, we learn that crying tended to symbolize the spiritual purpose of the sweathouse and also served as a traditional vehicle for expressing overwhelming religious feelings. It was also expected of those who sought wealth or power in the high country.

The Sources of
Sregon Jim's Family Wealth

If a person wants to tell me something, let him come up into the hills in the evening and stay all night. Let him take tobacco with him, and angelica root, only those two. And he must be careful of himself before he does that: he must get sweathouse wood, and drink no water, and go with no women. Then, I shall answer him if he calls my name.

Instructions from a *wo'gey* on how to pray in
the high country (Kroeber 1976:291)

As noted previously, it was believed that the *wo'gey* went to live in the hills when Indians arrived, for the humans built their villages at lower elevations close to the rivers. A person had to make special preparations for praying in the high country. He or she must drink no water for ten days, and for this period eat alone, taking only a small portion of acorn soup each day. It was necessary to avoid sex, and some have said that a full year's abstinence was required. When a person finally made this lonely journey and built a campfire up on the ridge, he or she would have to stay up all night, because it was considered dangerous to sleep up there. There was a wind, some said, which could suck away the body of a person who fell asleep, leaving only the skeleton (Matthiessen 1979:61).

Beliefs concerning the high country are splendidly illustrated in a story told by Robert Spott, who was Kroeber's main source for information about Yurok spiritual practices (Spott and Kroeber 1942:167–169). The narrative begins with a lengthy description of Sregon Jim, a man who seems to have personified Yurok ideals of wealth and fierce manliness in the eyes of Spott.

He was rich by inheritance and had augmented this wealth in his own time. Besides having two white deerskins, purchased from Karoks with American gold money, he owned an abundance of dentalium shell money and various other treasures which he loaned for use in communal rituals. His wife was also industrious, as expected of an aristocratic Yurok woman, and always awoke at daybreak to pound acorns. She provided more food than the family could eat, and Jim frequently gave acorn soup, dried fish, and other foods to those who passed by the house. Above all, Spott emphasizes that Sregon Jim was a brave man. He was unafraid of any lake or bad place in the river, and he used to dive deep into the water in such places in order to acquire power for fighting. He was a man, Spott says, who would never attack his enemies without warning, but always sent word of his intentions in advance.

These were the things that made Sregon Jim a man of substance, by Yurok standards. However, this account really concerns an ancestor of his, probably his great-grandfather.[2] He was reputed to have had ten wives, and through praying in the high country he not only received wealth for himself but also a miraculous power through which his descendants could obtain money for generations to come.

This patriarch used to train on a sacred mountain about one and a half day's hike northward from Sregon. On the peak of this mountain there was a stone enclosure[3] with this highly unusual property: if a person sat inside the enclosure he would hear water dripping, as if he were inside a cave. The water would drip and strike the ground with a ringing sound, and yet it was hard to tell exactly where the ringing came from as drops struck the ground. The man had been coming here for many summers until finally the following incident occurred:

Then, the last time, as he was sitting there, he heard the water drip and ring twice, seemingly in front of himself. He wiped his tears away—because they mostly cry on such an occasion, cleared off the grass, and saw a shiny gray rock. He began to rub this, and it slid to the side like a cover. Underneath it was a hole about the size of a can, with blue or green water in it. He felt around in the water with two fingers and there was something very slippery, like a lamprey eel but smaller. . . . Finally, he got hold of it, took it out, and laid it in some manzanita-limb shavings . . . which he had in a *keyem* basket. Then he saw that the thing was of stone and shaped like a deer, with horns. (Spott and Kroeber 1942:168)

The thing described here seems to have been an object similar to the so-called pains which Indian doctors used to hope for in their own quests for power. Whatever it actually was, it had fantastic significance to one who had brought himself to a peak of spiritual expectation by going for days without food, water, or sleep. Using pine needles and dirt to hide the secret compartment, he took the magical object and wrapped it in some herbs. Then he headed back down to Sregon, crying all the way. Before reaching the village, however, he stopped to place his package in the cleft of the trunk of a white oak. He covered the opening with a broken branch and went to gather sweathouse wood before returning to the village.

The first person he saw was his grandfather, but there were others present and all knew that something special had happened.

They thought there that he had found something, because he was crying. . . . Then, the old man said to him, "Go to the creek and wash your face and come on indoors." Then he wiped his eyes with the heel of his hands and told his grandfather he had found what he had gone for. Now the grandfather also began to weep, as if there were a death in the family, and crawled back to the sweat house to get his pipe and tobacco bag. (Spott and Kroeber 1942:168)

Later, when they were by themselves, the young man and his grandfather went together up to the oak tree. After examining the thing carefully, they then took it to a certain rock formation, about three-fourths of a mile back from the river. They placed it in a crevice along with angelica root, shredded manzanita, and other herbs. Sealing the crevice, they also covered the rock with dead leaves, and spread leaves around to hide their footprints as well.

They cried all the while, and did not tell the other men what had happened for many days afterward. According to Spott, this was how Sregon Jim's ancestor had assured the family wealth. The thing that he had found was called a *tsemmin*,[4] and it had many lucky properties. Not only would it tend to attract valuable property ("as if it came of itself"), but it also brought deer close by where they lived, and because of this *tsemmin* the doctors in the family were summoned often and handsomely paid for their services.

Actual use of the *tsemmin* was described as follows:

> Sometimes he would go to where it was and smoke. He would strike his tobacco pouch, wish for luck, fill his pipe, and blow the crumbs of tobacco out of his palm toward the *tsemmin*. . . . All this he did before he was married. After he was married he did not go near it anymore, except sometimes when he lost his luck in hunting; then he would stand in front of the rock where the *tsemmin* was hidden and would clap his hands. This hand-clapping is called *we-terkterpterwerk*. This was something a woman may not do, except a doctor who is seeking power.[5] When he had done this his hunting luck always returned. It was this same young man who later had ten wives. (Spott and Kroeber 1942:169)

This account reveals much about the relationship between crying and spiritual contact in Yurok thought. Even before he discovered the *tsemmin*, we are told, Sregon Jim's ancestor was praying so intensely that he had begun to cry, and later, after discovering the object he kept sobbing continuously, as if to sustain the ecstasy he felt. On returning to Sregon, it was this crying that signified to others in the village that the young man had experienced something miraculous. Finally, upon hearing what had been found, even his grandfather started crying, and the two of them cried constantly while moving the sacred object from the oak tree to its place in the rock called *Kwerap Otek*.

Indian Sucking Doctors and the Acquisition of Shamanistic Power

The Indian shaman should not be confused with the medicine woman of the Brush Dance, nor with the type of practitioner who cured wounds, boils, upset stomach, and other maladies through use of herbal concoctions and spoken formulas.[6] While each of these also worked for a fee, the true Indian doctor was a highly specialized professional. In status and wealth she more closely approximated the modern psychiatrist, and the parallel is especially strong because her doctoring relied much on obtaining confessions through which she could diagnose the spiritual cause of her patient's sickness.[7]

The practice of shamanism among the Yurok was based upon the belief that possession of "pains" within her body made it possible for the Indian doctor to extract similar ones from the bodies of her patients, thus relieving their illness. These "pains" are described as bloody-looking things, about the size of a polliwog (Erikson 1943:262), and it was generally believed that they were somehow shot into the sick person's body through sorcery. In curing, the shaman actually sucks these "pains" from the body of her patient and displays them for all to see. Through releasing the "pain" from the body and by singing her doctoring song, the shaman can tell where it came from. One instance of this was described by Robert Spott (Yurok).

When a doctor sucks out an *uma'a* pain she holds it between her hands, closes her eyes, chants "ᵃhokᵃhokᵃhok" and then begins to sing. Then the pain flies upward, spirals in the air, and suddenly flies in a beeline to where it came from, leaving a trail of fire, by which the doctor can tell from whom it was sent. Usually she does not tell, for fear that the *uma'a* will be sent back into herself. (Spott and Kroeber 1942:166–167)[8]

In other cases, the Indian doctor makes an "interpretation." She fills her pipe and smokes, then has a vision through which she diagnoses the problem. Generally, this involves obtaining a confession from one or more of the family members who are present. In an example provided by Erikson, the Indian doctor said, "I see an old woman sitting in the Bald Hills and wishing something bad to another woman. That is why the child is sick" (1943:261). Upon hearing this, the child's grandmother confessed that it was she who had done this, and this was considered cure enough.[9]

There is no recorded evidence of the type of chanting referred to in the previous quotation, but it is interesting to note that Powers characterized it as "barking" when he witnessed such doctoring during the 1870s.[10] This type of singing should not be confused with songs sung by the shaman in the "doctor dance" (Yurok: *re-mohpoh*), two of which will be mentioned later. Rather, the comments by Spott and by Powers make it appear likely that this "barking" was similar to the type of accompaniment one hears from "helpers" in the Brush Dance.

The process of acquiring shamanistic power might be described in four stages:[11]

1. In a dream, the young woman meets a spirit who somehow implants a "pain" into her body.
2. A *remohpoh* or "doctor dance" is held in the sweathouse in order to help her learn to control her "pain."
3. She dances every summer in the high country, in order to receive a matching "pain" and possibly to receive a song signifying enhanced shamanistic power.
4. Finally, she is taken to the sweathouse again. This time, she dances around a large, hot fire to "cook" the "pains" and to demonstrate that she can swallow the "pains" and vomit them up at will.

This process can be illustrated by reference to Fanny Flounder, a famous Yurok Indian doctor whose experiences are described in several sources.[12] While each offers valuable insights, the account in Spott and Kroeber (1942) seems most useful for present purposes.

Fanny's first experience occurred while she was praying in the high country. She had been dancing at *Wogel-otek*, a mountain peak about three miles north from her home village of Espeu. This place looked out over the ocean, and when she stopped to sleep she had a dream which Spott described as follows:

She dreamed she saw the sky rising and blood dripping off its edge. She heard the drops go "ts, ts" as they struck the ocean. She thought it must be [the place] where the sky moves up and down, and the blood was hanging from [the edge of the sky] like icicles. Then she saw a woman standing in a doctor's maple-bark dress with her hair tied like a doctor. Fanny did not know whether she was dead or alive, but thought she must be a doctor. The woman reached up as the edge of the sky went higher and picked off one of the icicles of blood, said "Here, take it," and put it into Fanny's mouth. It was icy cold. (Spott and Kroeber 1942:158–159)

After this, Fanny could remember nothing. When she came to her senses she was down by the coast again, casting about in the surf as several men tried to revive her. They took her to the sweathouse, but she was unable to dance for five days. Finally, she felt a craving for food, and someone brought her a morsel of crab meat. Upon eating it she became sick, and when she threw up, a "pain" could be seen in her vomit. Then she danced with vigor, and swallowed the "pain" again. At this *remohpoh* she also sang a doctoring song that she would later use in curing, and the words of the song have been translated "Where the sky moves up and down you are traveling in the air" (Spott and Kroeber 1942:159).

Next summer, she went back to the same mountain peak, dancing and trying to obtain the (second) "pain" through which her power would be completed. Valory's version emphasizes that Fanny was going without food or water and "crying nearly all the time" (1970:35–36). She stretched her hands up to the sky and saw a chicken hawk soaring overhead. Soon after this she became drowsy and went to sleep, whereupon she dreamt.

She saw the chicken hawk alight and turn into a person about as tall as a ten-year-old boy, with a martenskin slung on his back. He said, "I saw you coming and came to help you. Take this." And he reached over his shoulder, took something out of his martenskin, and gave her something which she could not see; but she swallowed it. At once she became unconscious. (Spott and Kroeber 1942:160)

Down at the coast, the Indians at Espeu heard her come running down the hill into the village, singing wildly. While ordinary singing is called *rurawok* in Yurok, this kind of singing is called *u-kel-peyok*, according to Spott and Kroeber (1942:160), and Robins informs us that the verb root *kelpey-* should be translated "to lose control of oneself at the doctor dance" (1958:205). As she ran past the sweathouse, the men seized her and took her inside so that she could dance until she came to her senses again. This "pain" was easier for her to control, and when she took it out and swallowed it she saw that it looked like a dentalium.

At her "pain cooking" dance, Fanny had a hard time at first. The first few nights, as she tried to dance with the men, she only grew weaker and weaker until she could hardly stand up. But then she noticed something in between the planks on the south corner of the sweathouse. Upon inspection, this turned out to be a piece of dry salmon. It was the food of a menstruant woman, evidently placed there on purpose in order to spoil Fanny's power. Later, a woman confessed to having put it there, but she said that she did so in order to test Fanny's power, not ruin it. Fanny's mother then told the woman's husband not to beat her, but they did make her promise not to do such a thing again.

After this, Fanny's strength returned. Each night she swallowed and vomited up her "pains" several times, for ten nights in all. Now, her power was established in the eyes of the community, and Spott concludes this account with the following words:

After this and after her experience with the chicken hawk, Fanny had her roadway to *helkau* established. From now on she could get her dreams and her pains in her own house. (Spott and Kroeber 1942:162)

The Yurok word used here refers to the High Country, and Robins translates the adverbial form *helkew* to mean "in the mountains" (1958:198).

From this account, it seems clear that the acquisition of shamanistic power had many parallels with the successful pursuit of power for wealth. In both cases, the Indian went up to the mountains in order to shout and cry for help, and the goal in both instances was to establish a permanent connection with the *wo'gey* world. For the Sregon man, this meant bringing back the *tsemmin* and placing it in a rock close to his village, while in Fanny Flounder's case it meant obtaining "pains" and a song that functioned to validate her power. The crying of Sregon Jim's ancestor and the shaman's "singing out of control" seem to have had similar significance from a spiritual perspective: they served as vehicles for intensifying the person's own ecstatic experience and also proved to society in general that authentic contacts with the *wo'gey* were involved.

Part Two

Ceremonial Singing

Chapter Five

Rituals to Repair the World

*The creation myth tells of a large cloud appearing to
the east over TakimiLdiñ. This was known to be pes-
tilence. Yimantuwiñyai advised that a dance be held.
After each dance and song they saw that the cloud had
gone back a little. After two periods of five days it had
completely disappeared. They then went to Miskut
and danced the Jumping Dance at a place selected by
Yimantuwiñyai. The formula describes this first dance
and says after each dance, "That sickness is afraid,
it goes back."*

Origin of the Jumping Dance as described
in Goddard's "Life and Culture of the Hupa"
(1903–1904:82)

This chapter and the next describe group rituals and the musical
styles which occur in each of them. Several examples have been
transcribed, despite the inherent limitations of Western notation
for this purpose, and the general approach is descriptive and con-
textual.[1] A more abstract analysis is provided in chapter 10, which
examines various elements of the musical tradition from a comparative and historical perspective.

I regret to say that it did not seem appropriate at this time to
produce a recording as a companion to this book. Generally speaking, it is prohibited to make recordings or to take photographs at
any of these sacred events, though I have often seen local Indian
persons doing so at the Brush Dance. The songs transcribed here
were collected in recording sessions or interview situations and
were not recorded in actual context. Nevertheless, I feel sure that
some members of the community would be offended were the recordings made public, and I wish to honor their feelings on the
subject.

World Renewal

Kroeber and Gifford coined the expression "World Renewal" (1949) to encompass a number of separate rituals through which the Indians seek to maintain or regenerate the surrounding environment and its resources. In precontact times, the rituals not only served to assure continuing abundance of salmon, acorns, and other natural foodstuffs but were also intended to drive away sickness and to prevent natural disasters such as earthquakes, landslides, or floods.

As practiced between 1900 and 1942, this religious system included the rituals listed below by tribe. Each included an esoteric component conducted privately by a formulist and assistants and a public component that involved either the Deerskin Dance or the Jumping Dance. These dances are identified by the same terms in native languages: both are called *opyuweg* in Yurok, *wuwuhina* in Karok, and *chitdilya* in Hupa (Kroeber and Gifford 1949:3).

Ritual Components of the World Renewal Complex[2]

Karok

> *Isivsanen Pikiavish* ("World Repairing") Ceremony at Inam
> *Isivsanen Pikiavish* ("World Repairing") Ceremony at Katimin
> *Isivsanen Pikiavish* ("World Repairing") Ceremony at
> 　　Panaminik[3]
> First Salmon Ceremony at Amaikiaram[4]

Hupa[5]

> Acorn Feast
> First Salmon Ceremony
> Fish Dam Ceremony
> First Eel Ceremony
> Jump Dance
> Deerskin Dance

Yurok

> Deerskin Dance at Weitchpec[6]
> Jump Dance at Weitchpec

Fish Dam Dance at Kepel[7]
Rebuilding of Sacred Sweathouse at Pekwan[8]
Rebuilding of Sacred Sweathouse at Rekwoi
First Salmon Ceremony at Welkwau[9]

All these ceremonies are believed to have been originated by
the prehuman beings, and in the esoteric portion a medicine man
usually speaks a formula that describes how the ritual was first
created and assures that the same procedure is being followed now
as before. The formulist also performs actions that replicate those
of the spirit-persons. This can be illustrated through the Karok
ritual *isivsanen pikiavish,* the name of which should be translated
as "world repairing." In this ceremony the *fatavenan* or "priest"
makes a trek to various sacred spots, and at each place he performs
actions symbolizing what the prehuman beings did in order to
renew the world. He is also sometimes called *ixkareya ara,* a term
that means "spirit-person" and thus emphasizes the mimetic
character of the ritual.

The *ixkareya ara* was required to prepare for his role by abstain-
ing from water, sex, and other profane activities for more than a
month. Nor did he take food during this period except for a thin
acorn soup. Instead, he would stay around the sweathouse, continually crying and gathering wood while expressing his gratitude
to the spirit-persons through offerings of tobacco and angelica root.
All of these things were done much as if the priest were an ordinary
person praying for wealth, but in his role as *ixkareya ara* he was
further sanctified. Observers were forbidden to look at him as he
performed the ritual, nor could they make loud noises within ear-
shot for fear of spoiling their own lives. This was because his actions
during these rituals were believed to affect the condition of the
world as a whole. It was assumed, for example, that if he did not
fast on acorn soup, the animals would become ravenous and eat all
the food that Indians needed to gather, thus causing a famine
(Kroeber and Gifford 1949:6).

Various forms of the First Salmon Ceremony focused on prepa-
ration and consumption of the first salmon taken in the spring run.
As in the Hupa version described in chapter 3, the medicine formula spoken is typically conciliatory in nature, as the priest seeks
to obtain permission for Indians to consume the flesh of the salmon

during the coming year. The First Eel Ceremony and the Acorn
Feast had a similar character, and indeed these rituals have numerous parallels in so-called first fruits ceremonies found among other
tribal groups of northern California.

The Acorn Feast of the Hupa merits particular attention as being
the only World Renewal component conducted mainly by women.
Here the formulist asks for abundance of acorns and prays that the
people should be spared from sickness. The following translation
is a segment of a prayer spoken while a formulist and her assistants
grind acorn meal in their mortars. There is the scent of angelica
burning in a ceremonial fire, and her prayer includes words which
can be translated as follows:

Acorns will be plentiful in our district on these mountains. There will be
no sickness. People will gather acorns happily. If one eats little he will
fill as though he had eaten much. Birds and other animals' stomachs will
be upset. They will not eat much. Similarly with insects of all kinds. (Gifford 1940b)[10]

Finally, there are rituals that centered upon the construction of
sacred structures. Fish weirs were ceremonially constructed by the
Yuroks at Kepel and by the Hupas near Takimilding. At Pekwan
and Rekwoi, the Yuroks conducted rituals in which a sweathouse
was rebuilt. Restoration of the sweathouse structure was intended
to symbolize the renewal of the world as a whole.

All these esoteric rituals were conducted in connection with public events known in English as the Deerskin Dance and the Jump
Dance. These dances are sometimes said to serve special functions
within the overall context of world renewal, especially in more
modern times as other elements of the religious complex have declined. Thus, for example, Hupa Indians attributed the following
functions to various public rituals when interviewed around 1940.

The purpose of the [Deerskin] Dance is to wipe out the evil brought into
the world by members of society who have broken taboos. In this way it
is a purification or world-renewal ritual as no other Hupa Dance is. There
are other rites to renew specific foods, salmon, acorns or eels; the Jump
Dance to ward off illness, and the Brush Dance to cure the sick, but only
the White Deerskin Dance wipes away the evil brought on by those who
have spoiled the world. (Goldschmidt and Driver 1940:121)

This explanation corresponds to those given during the late 1970s, but some of the most knowledgeable Indians I knew declined to verbalize on the subject at all. When asked why the dances were performed, Frank Douglas (Yurok) simply said, "That's our religion." Others did make it clear that the dances were intended for the pleasure of the *wo'gey* rather than for the human audiences in attendance. Thus it is not surprising that songs of the Deerskin Dance and Jump Dance have a "sobbing" quality that seems to symbolize the crying expected in spiritual interactions.

The Deerskin Dance[11]

Songs of the Deerskin Dance have a solemn and dignified quality so striking that even the first-time listener can hardly fail to recognize their sacred purpose. Speaking of Yurok mythology, Kroeber repeatedly noted that stories of the *wo'gey* were filled with grief and longing,[12] and the character of this music seems to reflect these emotions. While very apparent in recorded examples, the impression is even stronger when one hears this singing in actual context.

Yurok, Hupa, and Karok versions of the Deerskin Dance are each slightly different, and in earlier times the dance was conducted according to slightly different rules at every village that had a dance. The ceremony always lasts several days, however, and includes several sets of dances each day. Different groups alternate in performing the dances, and there is a spirit of competition between these "teams."[13] Goldschmidt and Driver observed that the Hupa Deerskin dance of 1935 lasted eight days and included six dances each day (1940:110). By contrast, a Yurok Deerskin Dance held at Weitchpec in 1901 lasted eighteen days, with several dances each day (Kroeber and Gifford 1949:68).

A Typical Deerskin Dance

As the men walk from the dressing area to the clearing where they dance, each intones long notes using vocables such as "whoa." These foghornlike sounds are sustained for four or five seconds and are set in the lowest register of the male vocal range. Besides being independent with respect to tonality, these parts are also rhythmically incongruent, yet there is a sense of order because all the tones have a similar timbre and seem to blend into a single body of sound. The effect is very striking when several voices are heard together in this manner.

Between nine and fifteen males generally perform in a single dance, and their procession moves gradually to the dance area where they stand in a line as indicated in the diagram below.

Once the dancers are in position, the main singer begins. Holding his deerskin pole like the others in the row, he starts patting time with his foot. Once all the others are also stamping in time with him, he starts to sing, the assistants singing faintly in unison or trailing the main part heterophonically. These songs are wordless, which is to say the singer uses vocables or syllables without lexical meaning.

After a few phrases, the main singer is accompanied by the dancers who chant an ostinato figure that outlines the 6/8 rhythm as indicated in example 1 below. This "hey-hey" figure is not sung in focused tones; rather, the delivery is percussive in character and indistinct in pitch.[15] The dancers stamp their feet to the beat and hold out their deerskin poles, which bob up and down gently in time to the music. Soon the red flint carriers arise from either side and begin to move across the main line of dancers, holding the flints well out in front of them at arm's length.[16] As they display the blades in this manner, they each blow a constant note on their whistles, adding yet another level to the musical texture. The whistles were traditionally made from a bone of the leg of the blue crane, but toy whistles are often used as substitutes today. The whistles are blown softly and produce a breathy tone that is independent of the ensemble with respect to pitch.[17]

As the flint carriers pass before them, some of the dancers on one side emit a volley of whoops, sounding a high note loudly and letting their voices fade away as they descend in pitch. After a full measure, this whoop is answered by dancers from the other side of the line, so that an echo effect is produced. These whoops are also not related to the main song with respect to tonality, nor are they definitely coordinated with its phrasing.

The songs are brief in duration, lasting between two to three minutes, and the ending is signified by a whoop or "flourish" from the main singer. Usually, the song is ended after the flint carriers o o o

d D D D A S A D D D d

F   F

M

Diagram 2. Position of performers in the Deerskin Dance.[14]

o   Stone seats used by singer and assistants between songs

S   Principal singer

A   Assistant singers

D   Adult male dancers holding deerskins hung on poles

d   Boys holding deerskins in same manner as the men

F   Flint carriers holding obsidian blades

M   Medicine man seated by fire burning angelica root and speaking prayers

have passed in front of the line three times and returned to their original positions. The main singer then signifies conclusion at the end of the next phrase, even though his solo part might be incomplete from a formal standpoint. Between songs, there is a break of about thirty seconds, and during this period any of the dancers may sound one of the long foghornlike sounds described above. The song is sung three times, then a new one is sung and the red flint carriers are replaced by men carrying black ones.

A complete set of songs lasts about thirty minutes, after which the dancers proceed back to the dressing area to remove their ritual clothing and store the deerskin poles until it is time for them to dance again. In the meantime, another set of dancers prepares to appear, and the day passes with alternate periods of dancing and feasting.

The Musical Texture

The various elements in Deerskin Dance singing combine to produce a rich texture which is coordinated rather loosely. The main melodic part is augmented by sound layers of indefinite pitch, and the whole ensemble is unified mainly by rhythm. The musical texture of a typical phrase is illustrated in example 1.

Key to Musical Example 1

A	Main part sung by soloist and assistants[18]
B	Rhythmic accompaniment chanted by dancers
C	Whistles blown by flint carriers
D	Volley of whoops from dancers on one side of the line
E	An answering volley of whoops from the other side

Example 1. Elements of musical organization in the Deerskin Dance.

The Solo Part

The late Abraham Jack (Hupa) was one of the most highly regarded singers in recent decades, and one of his well-known Deerskin Dance songs provides an excellent model for describing the genre in general. A rough transcription is provided in example 2. In keeping with its sacred nature, the song is sung entirely in vocables, as the use of lexically meaningful texts in ritual music is generally more frequent in secular songs such as the "light songs" heard in the Brush Dance.

One important characteristic in this music is the general tendency for the soloist to chant the tonic pitch at the beginning of a song and at the end of each major section. This chanting is called "rhythm" by the Indians themselves. In the song above, for example, the soloist begins by chanting a bit of "rhythm" to get his pitch

Example 2. Deerskin Dance song sung by Abraham Jack (Hupa) and recorded by Mary Woodward in 1953.

and to establish a rhythmic framework for the song to follow. After he has completed at least one major phrase-group, the soloist is joined by others who chant "rhythm" for an accompaniment as indicated in example 1 (part B).

In each major phrase group, the solo part begins at or near the upper limit of its range and gradually descends to merge with the chanting of the accompanists. This downward progression creates a sense of drama and climax in the music. It tends to integrate the solo part with the accompaniment, and at the same time it serves a cadential function by indicating the close of each phrase-group. As a compositional device, it is perhaps the single most important concept in group singing among the tribes considered here, for it occurs in various types of ensemble singing and is even present as an organizing principle in many of the medicine songs used by individuals.

The overall form of the song in example 2 may be described as a simple strophe[19] of the following shape: (Rhythm) A A A$_1$ (Rhythm) B B A$_1$ (Rhythm). The B sections generally feature long sustained notes sung somewhat higher in pitch than the A sections, and this basically binary form may represent a version of "the rise" as noted among the Yumans by George Herzog (1928:193) and among other California tribes by Bruno Nettl (1954:18–19).[20] In actual performance, the ending of the song is determined by the movements of the dancers (see above), and thus the form is not necessarily completed on the last repetition. Whenever the flint carriers complete their circuit, the soloist will signify conclusion by using the ending "flourish" notated in the last line of this example.

The 6/8 or 12/8 meter is a general characteristic of Deerskin Dance songs, and this is intrinsically related to movements of the dance. A strong sense of meter forms the basis for an interlocking relation between the solo part and other elements of the musical texture (see example 1), and there is not much syncopation in these songs. Also in keeping with the dignified character of the music, the tempo is always rather slow.

The melodic range spans an octave and a fifth, and this wide ambitus is a consistent trait which seems to go hand in hand with the use of rather long phrases and descending or terraced-descending melodies. Use of an anhemitonic pentatonic scale is also a general characteristic, and this type of scale is the one most frequently heard in all styles of vocal music. As noted previously, the singer chants "rhythm" on the tonic note at the beginning of the song and again at the end of each major phrase-group. Therefore there is a strong sense of tonal center throughout the song.

Although this style is generally rather consistent, it is interesting to broaden our analysis by looking at another modern Deerskin Dance that diverges from this one in certain respects. This one is sung by the late Ewing Davis (Hupa), another artist of legendary stature in Hoopa Valley, known locally by the nickname "Fido."

The song in example 3 is very similar to the previous one, but there are important differences. The basic form (AAA BBA) is the same, but Ewing Davis chants "rhythm" at more points during the song. The resultant formal structure may be described as follows:

A (Rhythm) A (Rhythm) A (Rhythm) B (Rhythm) B (Rhythm) A_1 (Rhythm)

It is significant that there are extra beats of "rhythm" chanted in example 3 (indicated in the transcription by brackets). These tend to preclude a feeling of symmetry in the melody, and this occurs in so many recordings of various types of songs that it seems to be aesthetically significant. There appears to be a general distaste for overly symmetrical melodies, and this is also reflected in the occasional use of irregular metric groupings and other subtle variations that apparently serve to avoid an impression of perfectly balanced phrasing.

While the first example was clearly in 6/8 meter, this one is best notated in 12/8, mainly because of the melodic phrasing in the B section. Either meter fits nicely with movements of the dance and other elements of the musical texture.

The scalar material in example 3 provides a more significant point of contrast. While the earlier example used a standard pentatonic scale without half-steps, this one uses an irregular scale in which notes of the upper octave do not exactly correspond to those in the lower one. Regular scales such as the one in example 2 are far more common, but the repertory as a whole contains many examples that are unusual or idiosyncratic with respect to scale and tonality.[21]

The transcription provided in example 4 allows us to compare these modern Hupa songs with a Yurok Deerskin Dance song collected by Kroeber in 1906.

In most respects, the style of example 4 parallels that of the

Example 3. Deerskin Dance song sung by Ewing Davis (Hupa) and recorded by Mary Woodward in 1953.

Example 4. Deerskin Dance song sung by Hawley (Yurok) of Meta and recorded by Kroeber in 1906.

Example 4. Deerskin Dance song sung by Hawley (Yurok) of Meta
and recorded by Kroeber in 1906. (continued)

previous ones very closely. This song is built on an anhemitonic
pentatonic scale, and the rhythm is basically similar to that of the
previous examples, even though the tempo is a bit quicker. As in
the previous example, there are instances in which the singer has
added "extra" beats of "rhythm" (indicated with brackets) which
tend to reduce the feeling of symmetry in the phrasing.

The most important point of contrast involves the formal structure. Omitting consideration of the "rhythm" sung between sections, the more modern songs are most often based upon strophic
repetition of an AAA BBA pattern. In example 4 there are traces
of this general outline, but there is more repetition of the A section
and phrase-groups are varied more on repetition. The song is not
strophic but rather of a form that would be best coded as a complex

litany with moderate variation in terms of cantometrics terminology (Lomax 1968:58–59). The overall structure could be analyzed as follows:

$$A\ A_1\ A_2\ B\ A_2\ B\ A_2\ A_2\ B\ A_2\ A_3\ \text{(Ending)}$$

This comparatively loose formal structure seems to be typical in early recordings and it seems likely that the genre has become somewhat more regular in form over the past one hundred years. A similar pattern of apparent stylistic change will also be noted in the next chapter through comparison of recent and early Brush Dance songs.

The War Dance and the Boat Dance

At certain places, an imitation War Dance and a ceremony called the Boat Dance are performed in conjunction with the Deerskin Dance. An early version of the War Dance was described by Pete Henry (Karok), and the following excerpt is quoted from the unpublished fieldnotes of Helen Roberts (1926*a*).

In the War Dance about ten men stand side to side in a row. Two stand, one at each end, a little in advance of the row, facing one another as in the Deerskin Dance. Sometimes the end men squat. The men in the row stand holding out their bows in front of them, using both hands and holding the string nearest to the body, vertically, with the left hand above, the right below, and the arrow at the back of the bow and parallel to it. These ten men lift the right foot and stamp to the beat and sing. They act as a chorus. The two end men have whistles which they also blow on the beat. They carry a fisher skin and some brush which sticks out behind the arm under the shoulder and is thrown away when the dance is over. The two warriors advance toward one another stepping with bent knees and feet lifted high, blowing their whistles and brandishing their bows and arrows. The bow is held in the left hand with the string toward the arm, the bow being vertical. The arrow is held vertically in the right hand. As they advance toward one another down the line they cry ’i, ’i, ’i, on the beat, but when they reach the opposite end from where they started and turn around, they cease crying and blow their bone whistles on the beat as they advance back to their original places, with their bodies upright, not bent forward as before. They may pass on either side of one another as they march. (Roberts 1926*a*)

As described above, this seems quite similar to the Deerskin Dance itself, and the resemblances even led Goldschmidt and Driver to speculate that elements of the Deerskin Dance may have originally derived from some version of the real War Dance, various forms of which were once widespread among Indians of northern California (1940:126–128). From a diffusionist perspective, the idea that the local and highly specialized Deerskin Dance might have evolved from the widespread and presumably more ancient War Dance has much appeal; however, we should bear in mind that this hypothesis is largely speculative and that it also neglects the possibility that local versions of the War Dance may have been influenced by the Deerskin Dance in relatively recent times.

I recently heard that a demonstration War Dance was performed at Rekwa during the early 1980s with Dewey George (Yurok) presiding. However, the dance is mainly performed by Karoks in modern times and is probably more closely associated historically with the Karoks than with other tribes of the area. The dance occurs in the late afternoon at the very end of the Deerskin Dance at various locations in Karok territory and is said to have been invented by Coyote (Kroeber and Gifford 1949:33). There are relatively few recordings of the songs used in the War Dance, but Helen Roberts recorded a few examples as performed by Pete Henry (Karok) and by Bernard Jerry (Karok) in 1926.

The Boat Dance occurs only in connection with the Hupa Deerskin Dance today, though previously it was conducted at various places in Yurok territory. I have seen the Boat Dance twice but I would still quote from the detailed account given in Goldschmidt and Driver (1940), who describe the entire Deerskin Dance as performed in Hoopa Valley in 1935 and 1937. The whole event lasted eight days, and this takes place during the afternoon of the third day:

> There are four boats, two from each camp. Crouched in the bow of each are two flint carriers, wearing all their lesser regalia but without the deerskins, otterskins, and flints. Their faces are painted solid black, and as they sit they hold paddles across the boat prows to keep them abreast and together. The dancers move their heads around slowly, perhaps in imitation of the sea lion, and they blow on their whistles. One paddler propels each boat from the seat carved in the stern, and the medicine man rides in one of the boats.

Behind the flint carriers stand the singers, the first leaning on a stick planted against the bottom of the boat, the others leaning on the shoulder of the man in front. In 1935 there were four dancers in each boat; in 1937, only two. This may have been due to an increased lack of interest, or it may have been simply a precaution against overloading of the aging boats, which had capsized on the previous occasion. The dance consists of a rhythmic bending of both knees to the beat of the song. None of the more valuable objects are worn in the boats, probably because of the danger of losing them. (Goldschmidt and Driver 1940:110–111)

The solid redwood canoes take off from a large rock on the river-bank, but several times they return to shore after paddling about ten yards. Finally they proceed downstream, the singers chanting a special song accompanied by the whistles of the flint carriers.[22] Meanwhile, the audience moves downstream to meet the boats at the landing point. When they seem ready to touch land, however, the boats are pushed back from the bank. The singing continues as several false landings are made, until finally the boats are pulled up onto the beach.

Shortly thereafter the dancers hold a mock Deerskin Dance farther up on the beach. This is an intentionally comic parody in which rags are held upon poles instead of the beautifully decorated deerskins that are used in a real dance.

The Jump Dance

A curious part of this dance is the peculiar expression of countenance assumed by the men who sing the solos. They evidently work themselves up into a hysterical condition, for their faces assume a far-away, ecstatic look, and they seem for the time being to inhabit another world.

Woodruff 1892:54

While the Deerskin Dance has an austere and dignified character, the Jump Dance more clearly displays the extreme pitch of emotion which characterizes the spiritual tradition, and those who have seen the dance will probably recognize the ecstatic facial expression that was noted by Woodruff in 1892.[23] This emotion pervades the singing as well; the "sobbing" mentioned previously is very pronounced in these songs, and the use of slow, irregular rhythms also gives the music a strange and hypnotic quality.

In many respects, the Jump Dance parallels the Deerskin Dance just described. The ritual lasts several days, ten being the norm among the Hupa (Goddard 1903–1904:82) and the Karoks (Kroeber and Gifford 1949:45). Each day there are a number of separate dances performed by alternating groups of performers. One significant difference is that the Deerskin Dance is held in different locations each day of the ritual, while the Hupa Jump Dance is performed in the same location each day.

A Typical Dance

Like the Deerskin Dance, this one is performed by men standing in a line, but in this case they align themselves in front of a fence that was ritually constructed for the purpose of the dance.[24] Not quite six feet tall, the fence is about thirty feet long. While the dance is in progress, no one may stand behind the fence or at either end of the dance area, because these places are reserved for the *kixunai* ("spirit-persons") and their view of the ceremony must not be obstructed.

Each man wears a scarlet-colored headband decorated with scalps of the piliated woodpecker. A single eagle feather projects upward from the back of his head, and each has necklaces of beads and shells around his neck. A hundred years ago, these men would have worn buckskin breechcloths, but today they wear trousers, over which is a deerskin skirt that hangs down almost to the ankles. This skirt is not fastened, but rather the ends of it are clutched in the dancer's left hand so that it can be removed easily at the appropriate time. Each man is barefoot. Most important, each dancer holds a woven Jump Dance basket in his right hand. This is shaped like one of the elk-horn purses in which the Indians traditionally kept dentalium shell money.[25] During the dance, these baskets will be held up high, evidently as an offering to the *kixunai*.

Dressed like this, several dancers (usually between seven and eleven) march single file and align themselves in front of the fence as indicated in diagram 3. At first they are seated. The centerman and the singers sit on three stone blocks, while the other dancers sit on the ground. Throughout the dance, the centerman will take

D D D S C S D D D

M

Key

C   The centerman who leads the dance movements
S   Singers who alternate as soloists
D   Adult male dancers who also chant bass part
M   Medicine man seated by fire burning angelica root and
     speaking prayers

Diagram 3. Position of performers in the Jump Dance.

a leading role, though remaining silent the whole time; he initiates all the dance movements and is more animated than the other dancers. He has fasted specially for the occasion, and throughout the dance he twists and turns his head in movements said to imitate the woodpecker.

Following the centerman's lead, the dancers stand and begin the first phase of the dance. Holding the Jump Dance baskets by the middle of the upper edge, they lift them high over their head in the right hand, and at the same time they lift a foot from the ground. Then, as the basket is lowered, they stamp the foot from a height of six to twelve inches. As Barrett notes, the motion is as if the dancer were taking a long step forward, but actually he does not move out of his place (1963:79). While doing this, the dancers repeatedly chant a figure which might be notated as in example 5.

Then two soloists take turns singing over this accompaniment. After each has sung his song twice and the dancers have repeated their movement thirty or more times, the centerman stops the dance and all sit down to rest. After a minute or two they rise and the group repeats what they have done. Following another break, it is done once more to make three times in all. After the third time, the dancers remove their deerskin skirts and place them on the ground in front of them. The Jump Dance baskets are placed on top of this, and then, after standing in place and intoning the bass pattern once again, they sit down again to rest. This ends the first phase of the dance.

Example 5. Bass figure sung by dancers in the Jump Dance.[26]

After a short time, following a signal from the centerman, they rise again and sound the bass figure once more while standing still. Then each takes the hand of the man on either side, and the dancers all raise their hands in unison, with the fingers interlaced. At the same time, they bend at the knees and jump or hop in place. They sound the bass pattern as they do this.[27] After perhaps thirty jumps, they sit down and rest for a minute. This phase of the dance is repeated twice for a total of three performances, and after picking up their baskets and hide skirts the dancers file out and return to the dressing area.

One complete dance takes between thirty and forty minutes, and two or more dances are generally performed during each of the ten days of the Jump Dance ritual. As in the Deerskin Dance, there are always at least two "sides" that compete in the singing, and in earlier times there were more groups in competition.

The Musical Texture

In this music, two soloists take turns singing over a bass part which is chanted by the rest of the dancers in a low register. Curiously, the bass figure is generally sung at a slightly slower tempo than solo part; thus the two parts are metrically out of phase. For me, this and the slow tempo of both parts produce an "other-worldly" quality that perfectly matches the spiritual purpose of the songs.

In a recording made by Margaret Woodward in 1953, the bass figure illustrated in example 5 was sung together with the solo part notated in example 6. In this instance, the bass part was sung on a scale tone of the solo part. In most actual performances, there is little sense of pitch focus or tonal blend in the collective intonations of the dancers, and tonality is not a major factor in the musical organization. Rhythm seems more important in this respect, as solo and bass parts are similar in tempo and meter, though not perfectly congruent. Since the two parts differ slightly in tempo, they grow out of phase with each other, and this seems to be another instance in which there is an avoidance of musical relationships that are overly symmetrical or congruent and a preference for those which are more complex and "natural" in character.

The Solo Part

Like those of the Deerskin Dance, all of the Jump Dance songs are wordless. While simpler in formal structure, they are sung with a "sobbing" delivery that is often more pronounced than that heard in the Deerskin Dance. Thus the music is rather complex on a microtonal level; the song in example 6 provides a good model for analysis, but readers should bear in mind that the transcription has been simplified somewhat for purposes of clarity. The pitches are not so clearly focused as the notations indicate, nor do the notations adequately indicate the pervasive tremolo and slurred articulations that are used throughout the song.

A song such as this would be sung in alternation with that of another soloist, and this exchange defines the larger formal structure in Jump Dance music. Each man completes his entire song, then repeats it after his partner has sung. In each repeat the song is varied slightly. Since the songs are sung in pairs, it is not surprising that they are each shorter and somewhat less complex than the Deerskin Dance songs considered previously. The form of example 6 might be analyzed as A A B B_1 (Coda), and each motive is briefer in durations than those of the Deerskin Dance.

The tempo is very slow and use of compound meters such as 6/8 or 9/8 is typical. In example 6, the meter is rather consistent throughout, but changing meters also occur often in these songs.

In general, the melodic and tonal characteristics of Jump Dance songs parallel those of the Deerskin Dance songs considered previously. The range is typically rather wide, and the melodies are usually descending in contour. Here again the anhemitonic pentatonic scale is the most common type heard, and the only unusual thing about the tonal structure of example 6 is the occurrence of the nontonic tone c as a finalis.

The same basic style is evident in the Yurok Jump Dance song performed by Frank Douglas (Yurok). In example 7, the solo part

Example 6. Jump Dance song sung by Abraham Jack (Hupa) and
recorded by Mary Woodward in 1953.

also gives the impression of crying, but the effect is achieved somewhat differently than in the previous example, which simply employs a nasal delivery and tremolo throughout. Here the song includes two descending motives (B and B_1) which seem to imitate
the contours of a "sobbing" voice, and sudden changes in the dynamic level also contribute to this impression.

Like the previous example, this one has a structure based upon
paired phrases, and the motivic form might be represented as
A A_1 B B_1 C C_1. Here, however, the pairs are somewhat more di-
vergent in character. The range of this song is extremely wide (an
octave and a major sixth), but in this instance the melodic motives
are not uniformly descending in contour. The tonality is also irregular; although it employs an anhemitonic pentatonic scale, there is
a shift of tonal center during the course of the song from g^1 (A motives) to b-flat (B and C motives).

In its overall character the song notated in example 7 seems
highly emotional or impulsive, and one might suppose that a song
so irregular in meter and dynamics would be sung differently from
performance to performance. This was not the case, however, as
I heard Frank Douglas sing this song more than ten times and it
was always done the same way.

Example 7. Jump Dance song sung by Frank Douglas (Yurok) and recorded by Richard Keeling in 1978.

Chapter Six

Rituals to Help Human Beings

*If the baby is sick or not doing well, that's why we
wave that fire over them. It scares away things. It
helps the baby to grow stronger. And then you use
sugar pine bark, and pound it up and put it in a little
cup. With water. That's what you give the baby to
drink. . . . It's supposed to be in the spring of the
year when you have this Brush Dance, so that the
child will grow up with all the leaves and the blossoms
and the grass. With everything that's growing. And
he'll grow up in that. He or she, whatever. And he'll
be just like that.*

> The purpose of the Brush Dance as explained
> by medicine woman Alice Pratt (Hupa) on
> August 24, 1979

The Brush Dance

The Brush Dance[1] is traditionally performed to cure a child who
is feverish or sickly. In the center of a pit, a medicine woman and
her helper work on the baby; they hold it in steam produced by
certain herbs, massage it, and wave burning sticks of pitchwood
over it. The duties of the medicine woman were described in chapter 2 and a more detailed account is found in Keeling (1982*a*).

Because of the use of burning pitchwood the dance is called *hont
naht weht* ("fire-waving dance") in the Hupa language. The Yurok
word for it is *meyli* or *melo-* and the Karok term is *hapish*.[2] The
English expression "Brush Dance" presumably derives from the
fact that the male dancers hold brush in front of them rather than
carrying regalia on the first night. Today they use salal brush for
this purpose, but Sam Jones (Yurok) mentioned that they used to
dance with blue spruce (February 5, 1979). The blue spruce is only

found at higher elevations and is less abundant today because of logging.

The public component of the ritual takes place during the night. While the medicine woman works on the child, males of various ages (and some younger girls) file into the pit and sing in order to help the doctoring. The singers are supposed to concentrate on the well-being of the baby, and this augments the prayers and good thoughts of the medicine woman. All of the songs are short, generally about one minute in length, and there are two types: heavy songs and light songs. Each set of songs begins with a heavy song, and these are more religious in character and slower in tempo than the light songs which follow. The heavy songs are always wordless and are sung only by men. After the heavy song is sung three times, any of the men or girls can sing a light song. A light song is also sung three times, and between each rendition there is a brief silence. After any song is sung three times, there is another, somewhat longer pause which lasts until another soloist is moved to begin. In all, a set of songs typically lasts about one half hour. Nowadays, two "teams" take turns in the pit, and they alternate through the night until morning.

The Musical Texture

At an actual dance, the listener's impression of Brush Dance singing is dominated by the unusual manner in which the male singers accompany the soloist. The soloist starts alone, and after a few phrases by him the others begin their rhythmic ostinato. This is done softly at first, but it becomes increasingly louder and more markedly rhythmic until toward the end they all but drown out the soloist because of the volume of their chanting.

This unusual vocal technique is rather difficult to describe in words, though Woodruff simply referred to it as "a weird grunt" (1892:59). In its most basic form, the ostinato consists of a series of forceful glottal stops that mark a regular one-beat rhythm. One singer might assist in this manner (sharply accenting each beat), while the man next to him softly murmurs vocables with resonant nasality and much tremolo or vocal pulsation. Yet another accompanist might add a soloistic part that trails the main part heterophonically. Thus the various accompanimental parts are often rather individualistic, but these differences are largely obscured as each man's voice becomes lost in the complex sound of the ensemble.

As in other dances, this accompanimental singing is called "rhythm" by the Indian singers themselves, and example 8 shows some patterns which are frequently used.

Although framed in repeat signs, these would not be repeated exactly but rather with considerable flexibility. Moreover (as mentioned previously) each would begin quite softly and grow louder throughout the course of the song. Many of the vocable patterns suggest 4/4 meter when sung by individuals in demonstration, but accent is uniform, and the collective effect in an actual performance is one-beat meter. The simpler patterns shown in the upper examples would occur in faster tempos, and the more irregular patterns shown in the lower examples would be used in slower songs.[3] Use of X's rather than note-heads indicates lack of pitch-focus, and parenthesized grace notes are meant to depict a sort of "glottal trill" which resembles sobbing.

In example 9 I have transcribed one phrase-group of a heavy song sung by soloist Fred Davis (Hupa/Chilula) accompanied by Herman Sherman, Sr. (Hupa).[4] Rather than using a conventional "rhythm" pattern throughout, Mr. Sherman chooses to accompany this part of the song by faintly trailing the descending melody of the soloist. He does so quite softly, as if he were humming rather than singing. Then toward the end of the phrase-group he and the soloist both employ more conventional "rhythm."

In an actual dance the accompanists sometimes take even greater liberties than this; the parts they add not only "echo" the solo part but loudly assert their independence. This is heard on a (light) Brush Dance song sung by Dorothy Moore (Yurok) and a group of men on a recording made by Margaret Woodward in 1953 (see appendix 1).

Heavy Songs

The heavy songs are wordless, and they are generally performed with a "sobbing" vocal delivery much like that heard in the Deerskin Dance or the Jump Dance. The solo part of a heavy song

Example 8. Typical "rhythm" parts chanted by male accompanists in the Brush Dance.

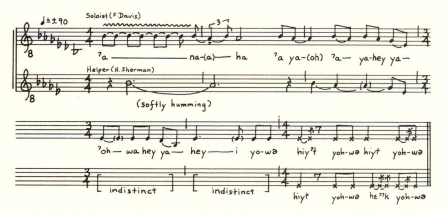

Example 9. Segment of a heavy song with accompaniment in heterophonic style.

by Elmer Jarnaghan (Hupa) is transcribed in example 10. The song is typical in beginning with a short intonation that establishes a tonal and rhythmic framework for what will follow. This bit of "rhythm"[5] also sets the tempo for the accompanists or "helpers." It also usually defines the tonic pitch of the solo part, and indeed it does so here though Jarnaghan has somewhat masked the fact by echoing the final note of each phrase-group (except X) with a measure or two of "rhythm" sung a minor third lower.[6]

Example 10. Brush Dance heavy song performed by Elmer Jarnaghan
(Hupa) and recorded by Richard Keeling in 1979.

Example 10. Brush Dance heavy song performed by Elmer Jarnaghan (Hupa) and recorded by Richard Keeling in 1979. (continued)

As in most Brush Dance songs, each phrase-group begins with a melodic leap to a relatively high pitch and descends gradually to cadence in the chanting of "rhythm." Thus each section typically ends with the solo singer allowing his voice to become absorbed in the glottalized ostinato of the group.

Most of these songs include a contrasting (B) section in which the singer moves up to a higher pitch level and delivers new melodic material in a climactic fashion. Thus the most typical structure is an AAB-type form, though note that the letters refer to phrase-groups rather than to motives as in previous analyses of other genres. The song in example 10 has an extra phrase-group (X) and a recapitulation which make its form AA(X)BA, but this follows the basic pattern and is only one of many possible variants that are heard.[7]

All of these Brush Dance songs are rhythmically exciting. Even though example 10 is rather slow in tempo and modest in its use of syncopation, the singer is constantly "stretching" the beat against that of the ostinato, much as a modern blues singer might. When Indian singers tap their foot to the music, they raise the toe on the downbeat and let it fall on the offbeat, thus producing a cross-accent like that produced by a jazz drummer when he strikes the ride cymbal on the weak beats of a 4/4 measure.

In the dance itself this cross-accent is particularly noticeable, as all the dancers rock their bodies in a similar counter-rhythmic fashion and wear heavy shell necklaces which rustle loudly in concert with the movement. The men heave their torsos up and down from the waist in a rather forceful way, and if there are girls in the pit they bob up and down on the balls of their feet in a more restrained way. All these songs have a duple feel, and 4/4 meter is the general rule.

The reader may have noticed that the pitch level of the song drops one half-step between phrase-groups X and B, and instances of "pitch drift" (in either direction) are common in the repertory as a whole. Adjusting for this, we find a scale that is anhemitonic and pentatonic, but here again (as in examples 3 and 7) the scale is irregular in that notes of the upper octave and lower octave do not correspond exactly. As mentioned previously, this is not the general rule but occurs often enough to be regarded as stylistic. Here again the melodic range is wide, and the overall contour is descending or perhaps terraced-descending. Finally, the ending of the song is signaled by a closing "flourish" shouted by the soloist, and this is a general characteristic of Brush Dance songs.

While the song in example 10 seems to have a relatively static or "fixed" character, others such as the one transcribed in example 11 are more spontaneous or improvisatory in nature.

In example 11 the formal structure is ABB_1, the B_1 phrase-group being drawn out into a rather lengthy improvisation. Thus the tension increases as the song moves toward an end. The songs are sung three times, and a superior singer often embellishes the last section of the song more and more each time, dramatically extending the climax of the music. Ewing Davis was a master at this, but other modern singers use a similar approach.

Having examined different versions of the AAB-type form in modern recordings, it is interesting to compare a Brush Dance song performed in 1906 by Domingo (Yurok), a famous singer from

Example 11. Brush Dance heavy song sung by Ewing Davis (Hupa)
and recorded by Frank Quinn in 1956.

Example 11. Brush Dance heavy song sung by Ewing Davis (Hupa)
and recorded by Frank Quinn in 1956. (continued)

Weitchpec. Generally speaking, the style is typical of that heard
on cylinder recordings collected among Yuroks around the turn of
the century.

   Like the modern songs discussed previously, the song in example 12 is wordless. The early song also resembles recent ones in
that its melody consists mainly of an alternation between motives
sung in the upper register and "rhythm" motives chanted in the
lower part of the singer's range. But instead of having the AAB-type
form, which has been postulated as a sort of norm in modern singing, this one has an irregular structure in which "rhythm" motives
are much more prominent. This occurs in other early recordings
and seems to suggest that the relatively common AAB-type form
in modern recordings could be a recent development. A similar
trend was noted with respect to Deerskin Dance songs.

The Light Songs

While the heavy songs are always wordless, light songs often have
meaningful texts or lyrics which reveal their secular character.
Example 13 is a transcription of a light song sung by Herman Sherman, Sr. (Hupa). Although many of the men's light songs are sung
entirely in vocables, this one has a text. Addressed by an older man
to the sweetheart of his youth, the words could be translated,
"Where we used to meet the grass is grown up high now." While
locals are quick to point out the humorous or sexually suggestive
character of Brush Dance lyrics, the tender sentiment in this text
shows the expressive range that they can cover.

Example 12. Brush Dance heavy song sung by Domingo (Yurok) of Weitchpec and recorded by A. L. Kroeber in 1906.[8]

Except for its use of a text and a somewhat quicker tempo, this light song is similar in style to the modern heavy songs considered previously. It begins with a measure of "rhythm," and in each phrase-group the musical interest centers upon the progress of the solo part as it first rises above the ensemble's ostinato, then gradually descends to merge with it. The use of a text in sections A and B makes this juxtaposition apparent, as words are used in the beginning of each phrase-group and vocables are used for the "rhythm" motives at the end.

Example 13. Brush Dance light song sung by Herman Sherman, Sr. (Hupa) and recorded by Richard Keeling in 1979.

Example 13. Brush Dance light song sung by Herman Sherman, Sr. (Hupa) and recorded by Richard Keeling in 1979. (continued)

Once again the postulated AAB-type form is interpreted quite freely, and the actual structure of this song is A X B B$_1$. Very seldom are phrase-groups repeated exactly in this style, but section X is clearly new material and seems to be improvised. Possibly (I feel) the singer began a new musical thought here and then decided against it for one reason or another. The style provides much freedom in this respect, for the soloist can chant "rhythm" motives virtually any time he wants to abandon one melodic idea and move on to another.[9]

As mentioned above, light songs in the Brush Dance may be sung by women as well as by men, and this is the main occasion for female singing in public ritual music today. In example 14 I have transcribed a light song sung by Aileen Figueroa (Yurok). Humorous and sexually explicit texts are common in this genre, and this text (set in sections V and VI) has been freely translated, "She was just an old woman, but she was a helper from the bottom." Lyrics like this often originate from spontaneous wisecracking at the dance itself, but then they might be used and remembered by local audiences for generations. This light song, for example, is still known by many today as "Grandpa Natt's Song," and it was first recorded as sung by Robert Natt (Yurok) himself in 1932.[10]

This example illustrates general characteristics of the female style, as opposed to that of the male singing in the Brush Dance: (1) the melodic contours tend to be undulating rather than descending, (2) the formal structure typically consists of one short phrase-group repeated several times with variation rather than using the AAB-type pattern,[12] (3) the motive at the end of the song is soft

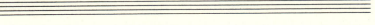
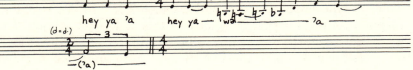

Example 14. Brush Dance light song by Aileen Figueroa (Yurok) recorded by Charlotte Heth in 1975.[11]

Example 14. Brush Dance light song by Aileen Figueroa (Yurok)
recorded by Charlotte Heth in 1975.[11] (continued)

and brief compared with the shouts or "flourishes" that men use
as a way of signifying conclusion,[13] and (4) elements of the glottalized ostinato accompaniment are not integrated into the solo part
of girls' songs, as they generally are in the men's solos.

The last-mentioned point is especially significant, for it illustrates how male and female soloists differ in relation to the ensemble. The male soloist interacts with the other male singers, his part
alternately rising above the ensemble and descending to merge
with it. By contrast, the girls' songs remain more independent of
the ensemble, dancing over the surface like a bubble in a brook.
Typically, however, the girls' songs include syncopations which
gently contradict the steady and emphatic beat of the ensemble.

Finally, the girls' singing differs from that of the men in vocal quality. Compared with the men's singing, there is much less glottalization, pulsation, and raspiness in the voice. In the men's songs there is a tense and nasalized vocal delivery in the upper registers alternating with diffuse and glottalized articulations on the lower notes. By contrast, Aileen Figueroa's voice has a light and tuneful quality throughout the song, and this is very typical of the style used by girls in the Brush Dance.

The Kick Dance or Doctor-Making Dance[14]

The Kick Dance has not been performed for many years. It was traditionally held in the sweathouse in order to help an Indian doctor control her power. This was considered necessary because the acquisition and use of power were believed to have a disorienting effect upon the female shaman. Pete Henry (Karok) specifically stated that the dance was used "for the curing of a new doctor" (Roberts 1926a), but from another perspective it seems clear that the dance also served to validate and confirm the young woman's new professional status in the eyes of the community.

The ritual begins at sunset, when wood is placed on the fire. After it has burned down once and night has fallen, several men enter the sweathouse and take their places around the fire. The Indian doctor then enters, seats herself, and begins to smoke tobacco. After a bit, someone sings a heavy song and the others help by singing "rhythm." The men are seated on stools, and they each kick one foot out in front of them so that it falls and strikes the ground on every beat of the music. This is the movement that gives the dance its name.

After the heavy song has been sung three times, someone else sings a light song, and the doctor rises to dance. After dancing through several songs she senses the presence of a "pain" in her mouth and begins to lose control. At this point, an attendant rises and grasps her by the belt from behind, holding her steady. Then, she is released and dances again as she withdraws the "pain," which is shown to the audience and swallowed again. After a rest, the singers begin again and the process is repeated through the night until dawn. In this manner, they dance for five nights.

The morning after the fifth night of dancing, the women prepare a feast of acorn mush. The doctor now appears in full regalia with her face and arms painted, and the men also are specially dressed as they enter the sweathouse to dance. In this phase of the ceremony, other women also enter the sweathouse to join in the dancing.[15] Meanwhile, the doctor has begun to dance within the circle of male dancers, who jump in place around her. By this time, she senses another "pain" and sings her doctoring song[16] as the men continue with their singing.

The men's singing reaches a new level of intensity at this point,[17] and as the doctor loses control of herself again an attendant steadies her once more by grasping her belt from behind. Her arms are then draped over one of the men's shoulders, as another man takes hold of her feet. In this constrained position she hops counterclockwise around the fire, circling it five times. Finally, after removing her "pain" for the last time, the Indian doctor lies down and goes to sleep. When the ritual is over, the others leave the sweathouse to have a feast and enjoy a general celebration.

The Musical Texture

Nearly all available recordings of this music feature a solo performer only, and the only ensemble recording that I have ever heard features Ewing Davis (Hupa) as soloist with an accompaniment by Jimmy Jackson (Hupa). Throughout the song, Jackson chants "rhythm" motives similar to those used in the Brush Dance but without the marked glottalization that characterizes the latter ritual.

The Solo Part

Like the Brush Dance songs considered previously, Kick Dance songs are relatively brief in duration (average 60–80 seconds) and are divided into two categories: heavy songs and light songs. The heavy songs are always wordless, while the light songs may or may not have lexically meaningful texts. Unlike the Brush Dance lyrics, however, these are not strictly secular. Sam Brown (Hupa) stated that many of the texts were based upon dream experiences and that the texts typically mentioned clouds, fog, birds, or other themes related to the sky (Golla 1984:141).[18]

Example 15. Kick Dance accompaniment chanted by Jimmy Jackson on
a recording collected by Mary Woodward in 1953.

The Kick Dance song transcribed in example 16 reveals a style
which is basically quite similar to that of the Brush Dance songs
considered previously. Here again, the song consists of several
phrase-groups arranged in what I have called an AAB-type form.
The actual form is A A_1 A B A_2 A_3. In each phrase-group the soloist
sings a series of motives that begin in a relatively high register of
the voice and gradually descend to cadence with the chanting of
"rhythm" on the tonic pitch. As in Brush Dance songs, the B section
involves a climactic rise to the upper part of the vocal range, and
in this example the increased intensity evidently causes the singer's
pitch level to sharpen by a half-step.

The style is also similar to that heard in Brush Dance songs in
other respects. A duple (4/4 or 2/2) rhythm characterizes both
styles,[19] but the meter is seldom very strict and most songs include measures with more or fewer beats than the meter dictates.
As in other genres described above, anhemitonic pentatonic scales
are the most common type, though others are often heard, and
the melodies are usually descending or terraced-descending in
contour.

In all of the genres considered thus far, we have found much
variation between songs, and this is also true of Kick Dance songs.
Example 17 is sung by Frank Douglas (Yurok) and is simpler in
structure than the previous example. Frank's song (and it was a favorite that he often sang while we were driving around) consists
only of a single phrase-group sung three times with slight variation.
It should also be mentioned that Frank never failed to speak a short
formula in Yurok at the end of every Kick Dance song.[20]

The Flower Dance

The Yurok did not conduct a public ritual for the occasion of a girl's
first menstruation, though the Yurok girl was subject to formalized

Example 16. Kick Dance heavy song sung by Ewing Davis and recorded by Mary Woodward in 1953.

Example 16. Kick Dance heavy song sung by Ewing Davis and recorded
by Mary Woodward in 1953. (continued)

isolation and fasting over a ten-day period (Kroeber 1925:45). The
Karok ritual seems to have been less elaborate than that of the
Hupa, but this impression may be due largely to lack of documentation on the ceremony.[21] Because the Hupa dance is more fully
documented, the following description focuses on this version of
the ceremony, which is now most commonly referred to as the
"Flower Dance." The ceremony has not been performed often in
recent years. I have never seen it, but I have been told that it was
conducted on more than one occasion during the 1980s.

A Summary of the Flower Dance Ritual[22]

Upon her first menses, the girl was placed in the care of her grandmother or another close female relative. For ten days, she under-

Example 17. Kick Dance song sung by Frank Douglas and recorded by
Richard Keeling in 1979.

went special training during the day and was the object of a ritual
held each night. During this period the girl was subject to many
restrictions, because it was believed that she was undergoing a
powerful process which was potentially dangerous for herself and
others. She was not allowed to look anyone in the face, for example,
lest that person might die.

It was also thought that her behavior during these ten days would influence her destiny throughout life, and this belief led to a number of specific restrictions. Touching her hair with her hands, for example, might cause it to fall out; eating hazelnuts would give her bad teeth; if she lied or acted cranky, she would always be an untruthful person or a mean one; and even just to stumble while walking was believed to cause bad luck in the future. Thus, the girl's behavior was highly circumscribed and closely attended by those around her. In this state of heightened self-awareness she endured the ten-day period without water and fasting on acorn soup taken once each day.

The ritual began with a ceremony in which the older woman blessed the bark skirt that the girl would wear for her ritual bathing.[23] On this first night only the women dance, and on this occasion they beat time using hazel sticks such as those used for making basketry foundations.[24]

The daily bathing routine was strenuous, and it has been described somewhat differently in our two main sources. Both state that the girl bathed twice daily (once at dawn and again towards evening), and both also note that she did not actually "bathe" but rather only threw water over each shoulder alternately in a certain manner. Sam Brown stated that this was done at seven different places along the river before running back up to the house (Golla, in press), and he also mentioned that the girl is teased by younger children throughout much of the ceremony. Goddard's account stresses the physical demands involved, stating that the girl had to run back and forth more than once between the river and the house, and also notes that she had to go for a load of wood after bathing (Goddard 1903–1904:53).

The public ritual was conducted on the second night, and the Hupa name for it means "first menses stick shaking." Goddard describes the ritual as follows:

The dance is held in the pit of the xonta.[25] The girl, covered with a blanket, is placed in the northeast corner. Six men sit about the fire facing it. The first one has the broad woodpecker head-dress (such as worn in the Jump Dance). The next has a row of sea-lion teeth around his head, with the close-knitted *kiseaqot* hanging down his back. These head-dresses alternate around the circle. These men hold in their hands curiously shaped flat pieces of wood. The other men wear caps of buckskin with large bunches of trimmed feathers at the top. Long bands of buckskin, painted in designs and terminating in a row of feathers, hang down the back. They carry in their hands sticks, five or more feet long and an inch and a half thick. These sticks are cut from syringa, *Philadelphus lewisii*. The top is split down about eighteen inches, making a number of parts which are worked down until they have plenty of room to rattle: the stick is painted in rings and has a fringe of bark left at some point.

Holding these sticks the men file in and stand in a close circle around the fire. The girl stands up but is covered with the blanket. The men sing a song, keeping time with their rattling sticks. When they have finished they march out, and the women, who have been sitting on the banks of the pit, sing songs of their own, tapping the girl with rattle sticks. The men return several times at intervals during the night and sing as at first. (Goddard 1903–1904:53–54)

Sam Brown's narrative corresponds rather closely to this description, but he also noted that the six men on the inner circle dance about the fire in a squatting posture, supported by short "walking sticks" that are held in their hands. They compete at this, mimicking animals; those wearing "hooks" imitate the movements of browsing deer,[26] and those wearing woodpecker "rolls" gesture like the woodpecker itself (Golla, in press).

On the tenth and final night, the ceremony is more elaborate and continues all night long. On all previous nights, the girl has stayed in the corner of the pit, but in this final ritual she is brought out to the middle of the dance area and is seated there, facing east. A blanket is held over her head and the men sing a special dance-ending song while tapping the blanket with their stick rattles. Finally, the girl emerges for one last session in the river followed by other concluding rituals held outside the family house.

Flower Dance Songs[27]

The musical style of Flower Dance songs is dramatically different from that of the other rituals described previously. The most obvious point of contrast is the musical texture, which is heterophonic and not polyphonic. This can be heard on two songs recorded by Margaret Woodward in 1953; in each of these examples, the accompanist (Jimmy Jackson) "trails" the soloist (Ewing Davis) and softly follows the line of the solo part with a sort of nasalized humming. This type of accompaniment was also noted as occurring in the

Brush Dance (example 9), but there it is only one of several options that occur and certainly not the most typical. In an actual Flower Dance, the accompanists would also mark each beat of the rhythm with their stick rattles, but this is not heard on the Woodward recordings.

Flower Dance songs are sung by men and women alike, and they are divided into two categories: heavy songs and light songs. The songs are said to have meaningful texts, often humorous or suggestive in character,[28] but the recorded examples available to me were sung mainly in vocables. All these songs are quite brief in duration (average 40–50 seconds) and the songs are sung rather softly in a relaxed voice lacking any trace of the "sobbing" delivery heard in other genres.

The song transcribed in example 18 is presumed to be a heavy song because Mr. Sherman sang it first in the group I recorded and because of its relatively slow tempo. It seems to be sung only in vocables.

This song is quite brief and the form is somewhat less complex than that of the other genres considered previously; here a single phrase is sung twice (section I), and then the first half of the phrase is repeated several times (section II).[29] In cantometrics terminology this would best be coded as a simple litany with moderate variation (Lomax 1968:58).

In other genres previously considered, the melodic range styles were generally quite wide, but the range of this Flower Dance song falls within a fifth. Moreover, the Flower Dance song is based upon a three-note scale, with much repetition of tones, and this tendency toward simpler scales is another characteristic that distinguishes the style from others described in chapters 5 and 6. Finally, one can always recognize a Flower Dance song by the ending pattern, which is sung softly in a falsetto voice.

The plain duple rhythm of example 18 is heard in other Flower Dance songs, but the one in example 19 is based on a sort of hemiola pattern. In this case melodic range (a major third) is even more narrow than that of the previous song, and again a three-note scale is used.

One example in this rather small corpus of Flower Dance songs was sung at a quicker tempo than the others. This presumably marks it as a light song, and the singer (Abraham Jack) identifies

Example 18. Flower Dance song sung by Herman Sherman, Sr. (Hupa) and recorded by Richard Keeling in 1979.

Example 19. Flower Dance song sung by Herman Sherman, Sr. (Hupa) and recorded by Richard Keeling in 1979.

it as a "hook-man's song" in a spoken cue on the tape. In other respects, example 20 is similar to the other men's Flower Dance songs notated above.[30]

In the demonstration recordings collected by Margaret Woodward in 1953, Lucinda Jack (Hupa) sang three Flower Dance songs. These may indicate a distinctive female style of singing in the Flower Dance, but it is entirely possible that the differences evident in these few examples are coincidental or a matter of personal style.

Like the men's Flower Dance songs, those of Lucinda Jack are brief (average 40–50 seconds) and sung rather softly in a relaxed voice. A basic 4/4 meter seems to predominate. In contrast, however, these songs each employ an anhemitonic pentatonic scale and a slightly wider melodic range. Moveover, the melodic form of these examples is clearly more complex than that of the other Flower Dance songs considered above. The one transcribed in example 21 has a melody which is strophic in form and rather intricate in the symmetry of its design.

The strophic song in example 22 is more complex yet. Here a two-part phrase is sung twice (section I), and this is followed by a contrasting motive and a sequential variant of it (section II). The opening phrase has an anacrusis of two eighth notes, the next anticipates the bar-line by one eighth note, and the last phrase begins right on the beat. Unlike the more spontaneous and impulsive style heard (for example) in Brush Dance songs, this Flower Dance song

Example 20. Flower Dance song sung by Abraham Jack (Hupa) and recorded by Mary Woodward in 1953.

Example 21. Flower Dance song sung by Lucinda Jack (Hupa) and
recorded by Mary Woodward in 1953.

Example 22. Flower Dance song sung by Lucinda Jack (Hupa) and
recorded by Mary Woodward in 1953.

gives the impression of being rather carefully calculated and precise in its delivery.

Finally, the song in example 23 is simpler and consists of two phrases standing in a sort of antecedent-consequent relationship. Still, there is a careful and static quality that distinguishes Mrs. Jack's Flower Dance songs from other forms of ritual music that have been discussed previously.

Example 23. Flower Dance song sung by Lucinda Jack (Hupa) and recorded by Mary Woodward in 1953.

Stone of Weitchpec. Photo by Kroeber, 1907. (Courtesy Lowie Museum
of Anthropology, University of California at Berkeley)

Hupa White Deerskin Dance. Photo by Ericson, 1890s. (Courtesy Lowie Museum of Anthropology, University of California at Berkeley)

Hupa White Deerskin Dance. From postcard dated 1912. (Courtesy Lowie Museum of Anthropology, University of California at Berkeley)

Hupa White Deerskin Dance. Photo by Ericson, 1890s. (Courtesy Lowie
Museum of Anthropology, University of California at Berkeley)

Hupa White Deerskin Dance. Photo by Ericson, 1903. (Courtesy Lowie Museum of Anthropology, University of California at Berkeley)

Robert Spott. (Courtesy Lowie Museum of Anthropology, University of California at Berkeley)

Hupa participants in the Jump Dance, held at the Yurok town of Pekwon. Photo by Ericson, 1893. (Courtesy Lowie Museum of Anthropology, University of California at Berkeley)

Domingo, with drum for gambling. Photo by Kroeber, 1906. (Courtesy
Lowie Museum of Anthropology, University of California at Berkeley)

Tree trimmed for firewood that was used in ritual sweathouse fire. (Courtesy Lowie Museum of Anthropology, University of California at Berkeley)

Part Three

Individual Use of Songs and Formulas

Chapter Seven

Making Medicine

*Hohohohoho! Alas, Person. You do that like me. I do
that, too. I'm like a wo'gey myself. I can go anyplace
and I feel like a wo'gey. Even if I bad. Now, you don't
want to say that, person. I always make medicine. I
like that medicine, person. I come tell you, person, to
be good luck. I'm a good one. I'm just like wo'gey.*

> Part of a deer medicine from Stone of Weitch-
> pec collected in 1902, spoken while burning
> angelica root on coals (Kroeber n.d.: Carton
> 6; Notebook 80, p. 29)

On Formulas

Spoken prayers such as the one quoted above have been identified
as "formulas" since the earliest period of research in this region. I
have continued to use the term, but readers should note from the
outset that it is not to be understood in its ordinary sense. The word
"formula" properly refers to a fixed set of words, often one that has
lost its original meaning, which is used as a conventional or ceremonial expression.[1] Perhaps the early collectors assumed that these
expressions were supposed to be recited verbatim, but this is almost certainly not the case.

A modern medicine man, the late Rudolph Socktish (Hupa),
once told me that the words of a prayer "just come to" him as he
speaks, and others I knew described such prayers as "talking" to
the spirits in a manner that suggests ordinary conversation rather
than formulaic speech in a strict sense of the word. A close look at
narratives collected around 1900 shows that this was also the case
in earlier medicine making.

Some relatively brief prayers were indeed recited verbatim, but
the present study focuses mainly on lengthier forms in which the
Indian actually carried on a dialogue with a being from the prehu-

man period. The person not only asked for help but also then proceeded to answer the appeal, letting his own voice utter words on behalf of the spirit-person who had been petitioned. It was this implication of transition in which the dialogue format found its main significance: when he answered his own prayer the formulist himself spoke as a *wo'gey,* and then his words had power.

More than any other figure in Yurok mythology, it was Wohpekemeu whom the men imitated in this way. But he was not the only one whose help the Indians sought, nor was wealth the only object of their prayers. Rather the number of spirit-persons who might be consulted in this manner was virtually limitless, and this sort of medicine making touched nearly every sphere of the aboriginal lifestyle. The next two chapters attempt to provide an overview of songs and formulas that were used for various purposes, but the summarized descriptions given there will only become meaningful after we more closely examine the general character of formulaic narratives and the actual context in which they were to be used.

Elements of a Medicine Ritual

> *Go get sweathouse wood. Then you will always have money, and no one can make you a slave. . . . Go at night to the top of the hill. Stay all night. Take angelica root and tobacco, and shout into the night. Perhaps you will say, "I am poor now, I should like to get money somehow! I wish you would help me you woge!" Shout like that all night and throw angelica into the fire.*
>
> Fundamentals of sweathouse training as taught
> to a boy on the verge of manhood (Kroeber
> 1976:292)

There are several components which are very prominent in various forms of medicine making, even though each is not necessarily present in a given case. These include the following:

1. Burning of angelica root.

   Angelica root is burned as incense in virtually all major ceremonies as well as used in personal medicine making. The root is crumbled up and dropped into a fire or placed on burning coals while a formula is spoken. The scent of the root is believed to attract the attention of the spirit-persons, and for Indians this fragrance marks the transition between the secular world and the sacred one.

2. Abstinence from food, sex, or water.

   Abstinence is a general prerequisite for medicine making. As noted previously, the human appetites are viewed as dangerous and degrading impulses that need to be controlled if a person wants to develop spiritual power. Thus a person has to be "clean" before attempting to make medicine. It should also be noted that fasting tends to heighten the sensibilities of the formulist and probably fosters a state of mind in which visions and other spiritual experiences are more likely to occur.[2]

3. Prescribed location for medicine making.

   In many instances location is a necessary component of the mythic archetype that the formulist seeks to duplicate. It seems clear from Waterman (1920) and other sources that Indian people interviewed earlier in this century understood the physical environment mainly in terms of mythic events which endowed certain places and various life forms with differing spiritual potentials.

4. Mythic incident from which the medicine was derived.

   Although each formula was originally derived from a mythic event, the spoken formula itself is a separate entity. This distinction is generally not explicit in published texts, which usually describe the mythic basis of a formula rather than containing the words of the formula as it would actually be spoken. The relationship between the two is somewhat complicated but will become more clear as examples are discussed in detail.

5. The spoken formula itself.

   The formulas themselves are often delivered in a stylized manner that differs from normal speech; this will be described in the section directly following this one.

6. An herb or other substance with miraculous powers.

   In some cases the plant is addressed as if it were a spirit-person, but in others it is used because a spirit-person used it. Usually the formula is spoken while gathering the plant substance, but it can also be spoken while mixing the medicine with water, dropping it into a fire, or applying it to the body of a person being doctored.

Substances used in this manner include the following: madrone leaves, fir leaves, hazel leaves, wild oat leaves, eel meat, sand from the riverbank, hazel buds, hazel twigs, myrtle leaves, alder bark, alder roots, willow roots, thimbleberry roots, water, ashes from the fire, tender shoots of buck brush, leaves of the redwood sorrel plant, white oak bark, tan oak bark, wild ginger, boughs from a small Douglas spruce, tobacco, body of water bug, sword fern, yellow pine bark, (human) mucous, (human) spittle, (human) blood, grape leaves, cottonwood leaves, pennyroyal plant, black oak leaves, and a number of other things that have not been identified in English.

7. A ritual action that duplicates something the spirit-person did.

Actions were sometimes as important as words in making medicine. In delivering a baby, for example, the formulist not only spoke but also took ashes from the fire, mixed them with water, and rubbed them on the woman's belly, just as Wohpekemeu had done when he invented childbirth.[3] In some cases a spoken formula was lacking entirely, and the ritual consisted only of a physical action. This would include things that the Indians were supposed to do "for luck" while traveling, some of which were mentioned in chapter 3. In doing these things one merely duplicated the actions of the *wo'gey* and no formula was required.

8. A song that the spirit-person used.

Medicine songs were likewise used in the context of a spoken formula or independently, but in either case they were mimetic and imitated the utterance of the spirit-person who originally sung them. Songs of this type were often delivered in a form of heightened speech rather than employing clearly focused tones as in other types of singing. Others seem to re-create the crying of spirit-persons as they hoped for things. Several examples are transcribed and analyzed in the chapters that follow.

9. An offering (generally tobacco) that the spirit-person requests in exchange for the medicine.

Finally, a formulist was often required to make some offering in return for using the spirit-person's medicine. The most common offering of this type was tobacco: not tobacco smoke but rather crushed leaves and stems of tobacco ready for smoking. At a certain point in their dialogue the spirit-person might ask for tobacco; then the formulist would make the offering by blowing dry tobacco off the palm of his hand.

The Style and Structure of a Spoken Formula

Though more than a hundred of these texts have been collected and translated, virtually all were recorded under artificial circumstances and do not directly reveal the manner in which formulas were spoken in actual use. In nearly every case, texts spoken for anthropologists or linguists should be viewed as explanations of formulas rather than spoken evidence of actual medicine making.

Interpreting these texts is all the more difficult because they were originally spoken in different languages and then translated into English by researchers whose interpretive and editorial approaches were not mutually consistent. And finally the element of regional and personal variation must be mentioned again: not only did Yurok formulas differ in style from those of the Karoks or the Hupa, but every village had its own way of doing things, and individual creativity was always a factor. Given these limitations, the following discussion focuses largely on general characteristics and allows that there are numerous exceptions even to these.

Style of Spoken Delivery

There is very little published evidence of the manner in which formulas were spoken in actual use, but one account of an Indian making medicine for deer hunting as witnessed by a white settler more than one hundred years ago was given in chapter 3, and a portion of this might be quoted again.

[The Indian] withdrew a few paces, fell on his knees, turned his face devoutly toward heaven, and prayed fluently and fervently for the space of full twenty minutes. Somes was so much impressed with the old savage's earnestness that he did not disturb him. Although able to speak the [Karok] language well, he understood nothing the white-haired petitioner uttered. (Powers 1877 [1976]:31)

From this account, it seems clear that the formula was spoken in a manner quite different from normal speech. The white settler was probably exaggerating when he states that the style was indecipherable even to one who knew the language, but Kroeber notes that the formulas were usually spoken quickly or muttered quite softly because they were regarded as valuable property and the Indian did not want to risk having a formula overheard and learned by someone else (Kroeber 1976:466).

Edward Sapir made a particularly interesting observation concerning this style of vocal delivery that was typical in the Hupa medicine formulas he collected.

Medicine formulas are traditionally recited in a shaking voice, each syllable staccato and breathy. If the reciter can't manage a shaky, quavery voice, he intersperses the formula with little coughs. This shaky voice notifies the spirit powers that medicine is being made. (Golla, in press)

Unfortunately Sapir did not produce recordings of these narrations. This distinctive delivery is not clearly apparent in Kroeber's recordings of Yurok formulas, but this may owe to the fact that his informants were actually explaining formulas rather than demonstrating them, as noted previously. The mannerism is clearly present in "animal" songs performed by Frank Douglas (Yurok) during the 1970s (see chapter 3), and similar "masked voice" techniques are noted in other personal medicine songs to be discussed in chapters to follow. In all such cases the gesture is basically mimetic, as the special voice is intended to represent the speech of spirit-persons or animals.

Formal Structure

In an introduction to a group of formulas that Gifford collected among the Karoks in 1940, an editor interprets some of Gifford's fieldnotes as indicating that the formulas were recited verbatim, "without missing a word" (Kroeber and Gifford 1980:263). This is almost certainly incorrect, except in the case of very brief prayers. Rather than being memorized, the formulas were loosely organized and permitted the speaker a great deal of freedom in carrying on his dialogue with the spirit-person who originated the medicine. The informal tone of these interactions is illustrated by the brief quotation at the head of this chapter. Kroeber also noted the loose construction of these narratives and addressed the issue in the following words:

It thus appears that formulas are not absolutely memorized as to content, even the framework of names and places fluctuating somewhat in the mind of the reciter. The change which a formula can undergo in a few generations of transmission is therefore considerable. It seems that the innumerable formulas known among the Yurok and their neighbors fall into a rather limited number of types, in each of which the idea is identical, but the skeleton as well as the precise wording individually different and unstable. Beyond this, there is a marked fundamental similarity of concepts, and even of stock expressions, extending to practically all formulas irrespective of their function. (Kroeber 1925:71)

Although the speaker might extemporize a great deal, the following basic elements are generally present in medicine formulas: (1) an *invocation* in which the formulist called upon the spirit-person by name, (2) a *narration* in which the formulist described the original miracle that the spirit-person accomplished, (3) an *appeal* in which the Indian states his needs and asks for help, (4) an *affirmation* in which the spirit-person grants use of his medicine, and finally (5) an *offering* in which the formulist expresses gratitude for the medicine.

The idea that the spirit-person must be addressed by name was very important and is evidently related to the general belief that use of a name was a means of exerting influence over the thing or person named.[4] This is illustrated in the formula spoken by Mack of Weitchpec (Yurok) circa 1901–1907 and translated by Kroeber:

If a person wants to tell me something, let him come up into the hills in the evening and stay all night. Let him take tobacco with him and angelica root, only those two. And he must be careful of himself before he does that: he must get sweathouse wood, and drink no water, and go with no women. Then I shall answer him if he calls my name; but if he does not do that, I shall not answer him. If I answer him he will have what he tells me that he wants. (Kroeber 1976:291)

Having called upon the spirit by name, the formulist recites an account of the original miracle upon which the medicine is based. In most published translations, this narration is cast in third person singular, which tends to obscure the sense of a dialogue taking place and makes the formula seem like an ordinary myth or story. In the context of a recording session or interview, the Indian narrator explains the spoken formula to a researcher rather than using it. In actual medicine making, the formulist addresses the spirit-person who had given the medicine, and this implies a different rendering of person when the text is translated into English.

Gifford solved the problem by including references to the spirit-person in parentheses. Thus for example a Karok formula narrated in English by Mary Ike in 1942 was notated as follows:

She was (You were) an old woman, the mother of ten children. She was (You were) lying down ready to die. She (You) could not make her (your) own fire. She (You) had no water to drink. All of the children had run out and would not wait on her (you). They gave her (you) no food or drink or fire. (Kroeber and Gifford 1980:14)

This device is very helpful in suggesting how a formula would be spoken in use, and published translations rendered in third person become much more vivid when imagined in this altered form.

Most published texts also fail to depict the dialogue that took place in actual medicine making, and this involved the elements of appeal and affirmation. The person needed to ask for help, and in practice the formulist probably bared his or her soul with some vehemence. Then he or she responded on behalf of the spirit-person, granting assistance and giving a guarantee that the medicine had worked before in prehuman times and would work again now. During this affirmation, the formulist spoke in the sacred voice of the spirit-person and possibly used his or her medicine song. Finally, following this climactic part of the ritual, tobacco was offered both as a tribute and in exchange for the medicine.

Conventional Expressions

Certain expressions were intrinsic to the dialogue format, and these deserve mention even though the present discussion does not attempt to analyze formulas from a linguistic perspective. Kroeber notes that the invocation portion in Yurok formulas often began with the formulist calling out *He'e'e'e'* (1976:363). This is elsewhere rendered *Huhuhuhu* (1976:246) or *Ha-a-a-a* (1976:248).

Commenting upon Hupa formulas, Sapir observed that the ex-

pression *Heng-heng-heng-heng* generally indicated a question being asked by the medicine maker. In answering, the spirit-person
would preface his response with *He-he-he-he . . . yang*. Sapir explains that this was a drawn-out version of the Hupa word (*he:yang*)
meaning "yes" (Golla, in press).

Two other mannerisms that tended to recur in Hupa formulas
were described as follows:

> One is the use of the exclamation *He:!*, spoken in a low tone of voice and
> held for several seconds. This exclamation indicates a long period of deep
> sad contemplation on the part of the originator of the medicine, just before
> he discovers the herb, song, or other thing with medicinal properties that
> he then "leaves" for the use of human beings. A second stylistic device
> of medicine formulas are the ritual phrases with which they nearly always
> conclude: "Whoever knows my body will do it this way," "Not many will
> know my body" . . . etc. In these phrases "my body" (*whiniste'*) refers not
> to the physical body of the medicine originator, but to his personality and
> deeds, specifically the ones recounted in the formula. (Golla, in press)

The Hupa translations in Golla (in press) are more carefully annotated from a linguistic standpoint than those collected among other
tribes, but it seems likely that standard expressions such as these
were used by other tribes of the area also.

Interpretation of Selected Texts

In this section the published translations of five formulaic texts are
revised and glossed in order to clarify how the narratives would
actually be used in making medicine. As readers will note, the
examples given here do not necessarily correspond in detail to the
structural model given above.

Moon and Frog Formula for Wounds[5]

The narrator of the published text (Billy Werk) begins by describing the mythic incident upon which the medicine was based. Moon
was traveling along at night, we are told, when he was viciously
attacked. The lizards, the crows, and other foul things cut him to
bits. Suddenly, the moonlight turned to darkness, and there was
blood all over the place. Grizzly Bear was one of his wives, and
she fought hard to protect him, seizing five of the creatures at once

and killing them left and right. In spite of her help they tore him apart and ate him. Finally, she gave up and just sat down in a heap, heartbroken.

Frog was his other wife, and she followed behind. The beasts were eating his flesh, his bones, and his skin. But Frog followed quietly after them, and wherever she saw a drop of blood she daubed it up with a frond of sword fern and shook it off into her fancy basket. After they killed him and went away, she continued to gather his blood, and when she finished picking it all up, she shook the blood from her basket onto a madrone leaf. Then, she took the pieces of his corpse and wiped them with the bloody madrone leaf until—somehow—he was alive again. He was completely restored.

In using this medicine a formulist[6] might begin by saying, "Huhuhuhu, I have come to see you, Frog. A person is hurt. They have hurt somebody. A person has gotten shot and wounded. That is why I have come to you, for your medicine. That is why I ask you to pity me."

"Use sword fern," Frog would answer (in the voice of the formulist). "Use it wherever he is wounded. This is my medicine. My medicine is good. They killed my man completely and ate him up. Even the bones. I could only find his blood, but still I made him better. This is my medicine. Sword fern. See how I use it to pick up the blood. Huhuhuhu."

While speaking thus the formulist also repeated the actions of Frog. She used the sword fern to gather drops of blood from the wound, then she took a madrone leaf and rubbed it around on the wound. While doing these things, she continued to speak (as Frog), pausing only to spit in the wound as she doctored it. She said, "This here is my other medicine, what human beings call madrone. You will not die. You cannot be killed. You will get well. Even though they always kill my man, he recovers. My medicine is good. Huhuhuhu."

After working for a while this way, she asks (as Frog) whether there is any tobacco around. Responding in her own behalf, the formulist says that she does have some tobacco. Speaking again as Frog, she says, "I want it. I am giving you my medicine and I want tobacco for it. It is not for me, it is for my man."

Then the formulist crumbles smoking tobacco into the palm of her hand and blows it off. She would conclude the talk with a final speech by Frog, who says, "Good. That tobacco is what I like, and it's hard to get. And I will help you because you give it to me. Now I use water with my medicine. But not too much. I put two drops of water where he is hurt and I rub it around a little bit." As previously the formulist matches actions to words as she tends to the wound.

Formula for Death Purification[7]

Here again the narrator of the published text begins by explaining the mythic incident upon which the formula is based. This involves a dispute that took place in the spirit world over whether or not human beings should have to die. He tells us that a certain group among the spirit-persons thought that human beings should be allowed to live forever. These (ten) said, "When they get old, let them lie down and go to sleep for a while. Then, when they awaken they'll be young again." Others disagreed, and among them was Wohpekemeu who noted that unless people died the earth would become too crowded. As they were talking, Wertspit (Jerusalem Cricket) lost his child. Hurt and angry over his loss, he buried the child straightaway. Since the baby was already buried, the group as a whole decided that they could do nothing about it. "Well, let it be so," they said. And thus it began that people died.

The ten spirits who had objected to death came to reside in rocks located at ten different places along the Klamath River. All of them were sorry that people had to die, but three of them (those at Kenek, Merip, and Kepel) were especially angry about it. "Have it your way," they said. "Let them die. But don't let them pass downriver in front of me. If I see a dead person, I'll make sure that they all die. Then the human beings will be gone for good."[8]

At the same time, the others wanted to do something to help people feel better again after a person had died. The one at Rekwoi thought, "What can I do?" and he decided to search for an herb which would help. Finally, he traveled to the sky and found a plant whose roots made people feel clean again. He gave some of this medicine to each of the other nine spirits who felt sorry for human beings (and this completes the description of the mythic event upon which the formula is based).

In actual use, this medicine is more elaborate than the previous one and was presumably quite expensive to have done. It would be spoken by a professional formulist in the sweathouse, and he began by lighting the fire in a certain way. He drops crushed sticks and fine shavings onto the coals, but he does not blow on them himself. When they burst into flame it is thought to be the Thunders who have blown on them, and this is taken as a sign that the spirits are paying attention to the medicine about to be made.

"Huhuhuhu," the formulist might begin, calling upon the spirit residing farthest upriver (at a place in Karok territory, probably Katimin). He would call him by name and stamp his foot while doing so. Then he asks for help, explaining that someone has died and that the other people feel bad about it.

"I also feel bad about it," the spirit might answer. "All of us *wo'gey* feel bad about it. We want to help you and that's why we gave you this medicine." Thus the formulist proceeds to dramatize a dialogue between himself and the spirit-person, offering him tobacco and accepting the offering on the latter's behalf. Finally the conversation touches upon the medicine (plant) which is supposed to make people feel better. The spirit-person states that he does not have the substance, and he tells the formulist to call upon the spirit-person who dwells just downriver from him.

The formulist then calls upon the next spirit-person and enacts a similar dialogue with him. Again they commiserate about the death and speak of the mythical dispute concerning death, but finally this one also reveals that he does not have the medicine himself. Once more the formulist is directed to next *wo'gey* downstream, and in this manner he speaks with all ten of the spirits, starting far upriver and proceeding downstream until he finally reaches the one at Rekwoi. There the last spirit gives him the medicine and instructs him to pound it up and mix it with heated water. And finally the formulist bathes the mourner with this infusion.

Formula to Make a Baby Stop Crying[9]

As in previous examples, this translation describes the mythic basis of the formula without indicating how it would be used in actual context. The story tells of a baby who lived at Dry Lagoon with his older sister. The baby cried constantly and annoyed all the people who lived nearby because of his incessant crying. They wondered what made him cry so much, and one day he said, "I am not crying. I am across the ocean where Kapuloyo lives and I am gambling.[10] You hear my gambling song and you think I am crying but I am not. I am singing."

This is interesting from a musicological standpoint because it shows that Yuroks themselves recognized the "sobbing" quality in their music. In actual use, the mother impersonates both the *wo'gey* baby and his sister. The story that unfolds is extremely interesting but is only summarized here for the sake of clarity.

The *wo'gey* baby explains that he has been gambling with Kapuloyo himself and that he has won Kapuloyo's sister from him. He tells his own sister that he must travel to where Kapuloyo lives in order to bring the latter's sister from there. "So do not rock me," he says. "Let me cry. For I am not actually crying but singing my gambling song and traveling across the ocean. I shall leave during the night. On the fifth day I want you to come and wait for me. Look northward up the coast and you'll see me coming home." Thus the narrative repeatedly plays upon the apparent contradiction between the visible *wo'gey* baby (continuously crying) and his wandering spirit, which journeys across the ocean and accomplishes miraculous things.

On his return, five days later, there was what seemed to be a wisp of fog traveling behind him, but this turned out to be Kapuloyo himself. Both her brother and Kapuloyo were beautifully dressed, and now the brother was no longer a baby but seems to have become transformed into a man. Then he says, "Hurry, sister! I have not come to stay long. I have come to take you along with us, back across the ocean. I am sorry for you, sister, because you have taken care of me for so long, and now I want you to come with me." Then, he told her to lie down and to cover her head.

He said, "Sleep, sister! We shall leave now. Sleep! You will not know how we go. Sleep! You will not wake up until we arrive." And truly she did not awaken until she arrived where Kapuloyo lived. In this closing speech, the human mother would speak these soothing words to her own (human) baby, and indeed throughout the text there are a number of dramatized speeches which (together with the singing and mock crying) would naturally tend to have a soothing effect on a cranky infant.[11]

Formula for Eel Medicine[12]

As in virtually all of these published translations, the narrator begins with an explanation concerning the mythological basis for the medicine. Here again the character of the translation (narration in third person) owes mainly to its context (a recorded interview). In actual medicine making, the story would emerge from a dramatized dialogue between the formulist and Yumantuwinyai, whom we have already identified as the Hupa equivalent of the Yurok super-hero Wohpekemeu.

Yumantuwinyai traveled across the ocean to the south and found a place where there were three lakes. There he saw the red eels that never come to this world. "They will come," he thought, and then the bank of the lake gradually slid away until it reached the seashore and its waters spilled into the ocean. After leading the eels across the ocean to the mouth of the Klamath River, he encountered a TimatciLtcwe.[13]

"You who stop the run of fish, you will go to sleep," he thought, and indeed the eels passed upstream while the fish-blocker slept. At Weitchpec he encountered another TimatciLtcwe and handled him the same way. Farther upstream, he caused a landslide that prevented the eels from moving up the Klamath River,[14] and then he walked along the Trinity River with the eels coming along behind him. "I don't want Otter to eat these eels," Yumantuwinyai thought to himself, "but even if she does they won't die. They will be good and many will be caught. Ten canoes will be filled with them."

And thus it was that Yumantuwinyai brought eels to Hoopa Valley. He also invented a ritual to assure that they would always be plentiful there, even when the Trinity ran shallow, and the formula described here was to be spoken in the context of this ritual. Before conducting this ritual, the priest had to fast for ten days. Then, early in the morning, he was to catch a load of eels at a certain place and cook them. He ate his fill, holding a medicine (unidentified) in one hand and dropping bits of eel flesh into the fire with his other. As the morsels burned he addressed Yumantuwinyai, extolling him for the deeds described above.

At certain points in the prayer, he impersonated Yumantuwinyai, and thus the story emerged through a rambling dialogue between formulist and *kixunai*. Instructions concerning the ritual it-self were spoken in the voice of Yumantuwinyai, and at one point he threatens the priest with a warning of what would happen if he failed to speak the formula or failed to hold the medicine in his hand correctly while doing so.

"You won't live," he said. "I hope you get bitten by a rattlesnake if you eat without holding the medicine in your hand. This is not a good thing. And you must talk about me. Even if you catch no eels you must talk about me. Then eels will be caught anyway. But if you do not talk about me you will die." Yumantuwinyai also lec-tured those in attendance by outlining various laws relating to eels and their consumption. These were stated in the form of proclama-tions, and the formulist probably held forth for some time, dictating (for example) whether it was acceptable for women to eat the eels, whether they could eat them while menstruating, whether they could hook eels themselves, and addressing various other questions such as these.

Formula for Internal Sickness[15]

The mythic context for this medicine concerns a pair of *kixunai* sis-ters who lived in the Yurok village of Merip. The narrator explains that these events occurred during a period of transition between the *kixunai* world and the human world. The older sister, we are told, wove baskets all day long and her door was seldom open. Once in a while she would open it very slightly, and when she did so a sort of wind would issue from the narrow crack in the door. The wind brought sickness, and that is why the door was seldom opened. The younger sister thought to herself, "This is how sick-ness comes. Cough, blood sickness, green vomit.[16] . . . This is why they happen."

She thought to herself, "I wonder how it's going to be when human beings come?" And with this in mind she looked at her sister and imagined that she was a human being. As soon as she did this, the elder sister fell to the ground—just like a trout that someone had thrown down. Her eyes just rolled around and around. Green matter and blood flowed out from one of her eyes.

Then the younger sister thought to herself, "It looks like it's going to be hard for people. If sickness does that to human beings, then what are they going to do when it happens? Now that I have made this sickness for people [by imagining or visualizing it], what can I give them for medicine?" Saying this, she went out. She looked all over the world, but she didn't find anything.

Finally, she looked down at the ground and then she saw it. "Hei:!," she thought. "I'm going to leave something nice for people." Then she pulled it up and took it back to the house. She put the medicine in a dipper basket and made a potion from it. She put a dab of this in her sister's mouth and laid her down comfortably. Then she thought, "People will do it this way when somebody gets sick. But not just anybody will do it. Not just anybody will know my medicine."

In actual use, this formula was spoken over the medicinal herb after it was placed in a dipper basket. The herb is identified only by a Hupa word meaning "its leaves-forked-little." The herb doctor would place it in the basket whole, and then she would call upon the *kixunai* younger sister and conduct a dialogue with her through which the story above would be disclosed. Toward the end of this conversation she would affirm the curative properties of the herb while speaking on behalf of the *kixunai* maiden. When she finished speaking the formula, the herb doctor would pound up the plant and pour water into the basket over it. Then, she warmed this mixture with a heated rock and gave it to the patient to drink.

Chapter Eight

Medicine Songs and Formulas, Part 1

*My cousin, they accused him of hitting a man from
downriver in the head, a long time ago. And they was
going to arrest him, I guess, and send him over the
road. So my Grandfather made medicine for him. He
says, "They won't bother you." And they never did.
I know the song he sang for that. I sing it sometimes
for myself.*

Hupa Man on Bald Hills Road (June 29, 1979)

In earlier times, medicine making was an important part of every-
day life, and a substantial body of information about it was collected
in the years between 1900 and 1942. Today these practices are
much less common, but the tradition is far from extinct and continues to be recognized as the foundation of the musical aesthetic
by Indians themselves. I can hardly count the times I was told that
songs had a practical function or that an Indian person proudly said,
"We used to have songs for everything."

This chapter and the next describe songs and formulas that were
used by individuals in earlier times. The survey includes both types
of medicine that would be used by "professionals" in a formal setting and other forms that were used by ordinary persons in private
or while engaged in practical activities such as hunting or gathering
acorns. A total of 216 items were located in published sources and
manuscripts, and these have been arranged into the following
categories (by application):

A. Birth and Child Rearing (23)
B. Sickness and Curing (28)
C. Hunting and Fishing (35)
D. Wealth (24)

E. Love Medicine (44)
F. Medicine for Use by Women (8)
G. Conflict or Revenge (20)
H. Safety in Travel (13)
I.   Sports and Games (6)
J.   Purification from Contact with a Corpse (7)
K. Miscellaneous Types of Medicine (8)

Not all of these examples will be discussed or even mentioned in this text. I have sought mainly to describe the general character of songs and spoken formulas used for various purposes and to illustrate the richness of the mythology on which these practices were based. Those who wish to obtain more detailed information about any specific example will find a complete inventory given in appendix 2.

Birth and Child Rearing

Spoken formulas to ease childbirth have been documented among every tribe of this region, and most of these texts call upon Wohpekemeu. Different versions of one very important formula were collected from seven Yurok persons between 1901 and 1907, and a particularly good explanation was given by Mack of Weitchpec (appendix 2, A–1).

The text begins by describing how it came about that Wohpekemeu invented childbirth. Originally, we are told, women always died giving birth to their first child because they had to be cut open to deliver. Wohpekemeu had wanted a woman (in some versions two), and somehow he managed to impregnate her through magical means, without her being aware of what had happened. Her ten brothers became angry about what he had done, so they threatened to kill him. But Wohpekemeu took ashes from the fire, mixed them with water, and rubbed the mixture on her belly. Because of this, the baby was born easily and the mother lived. A formula dramatizing this event was spoken during the delivery, and further information on Yurok methods of childbirth is found in Kroeber (1925:44–45).

Another childbirth formula involving Wohpekemeu was explained by Mary Marshall (Hupa) in 1901 (Appendix 2, A–7). Here again the superhero (identified by his Hupa name Yumantuwinyai) is portrayed as being obsessed with women and intercourse. While traveling past Willow Creek, he saw a hollow white oak tree and copulated with that. On returning from his journey he passed that way again, and standing near the tree he heard a baby crying. He remembered what he had done and stood facing the tree thinking, "How will it be?" Then he made a decoction from the bark and poured it on the tree. Thus he delivered a boy. In this case, the formula was to be spoken while preparing a medicine which was rubbed on the woman's belly before the delivery.

Two other formulas for childbirth were explained by Mary Ike (Karok) around 1940. One involves a man from downriver (a Yurok) who was getting sweathouse wood when he noticed his dog acting strangely. He took the bitch to a hollow tree and stayed inside there with her for ten days, during which time a flood occurred. She became pregnant and the man, looking for medicine, found only wild oats growing. He put these in water and gave it to the dog, who gave birth to ten human beings after drinking it. Only the blades of grass are used, not the seeds or flower of the plant. The formula is spoken while gathering the medicine, and the water is later drunk by the pregnant woman (appendix 2, A–22). The idea that humans emerged from the mating of men and dogs was mentioned often by Yurok persons I knew during the 1970s, and its currency among earlier Yuroks is documented in Kroeber (1976:331–332).

Mary Ike's other formula for childbirth was spoken while gathering a plant identified as *Lotus humistratus* or hill lotus. Its Karok name has been translated as "child without father plant" (Kroeber and Gifford 1980:284). In this text a young girl was gaining weight but did not at first know why. She gradually realized that she was pregnant and suffered greatly in this condition. Later she found a plant to use as medicine and she put it into a basket of water, which she drank. Then a strange man came to the door, spoke to her briefly in a mean voice, and left. Suddenly the baby was born and crying, almost without her noticing it (appendix 2, A–21).

Here one observes a clear tendency to disassociate the phenomena of pregnancy and childbirth from the father and from sexuality in general. This theme, also noted in the narrative in which Wohpekemeu impregnated a woman without her knowing, occurs repeatedly in formulaic texts relating to childbirth and child rearing.

In this context it not only reaffirms the belief that sexuality has a corrupting influence on spiritual things but also seems to reflect a broader tendency to characterize procreation in mythic terms rather than focusing on the worldly connection between a man and a woman.

In this connection, it is interesting to note that a Yurok formula for sterility was actually called "medicine for becoming alive" in the native language (appendix 2, A–2), rather than focusing on the problem from the parents' perspective. Another formula for sterility was based on the mythic story of a Weitchpec woman who was made pregnant by a creek spirit. Later she went into the brush to give birth while her husband decorated a cradle basket with dentalium shells (appendix 2, A–12).

Several formulas were intended to ease childbirth by making the fetus small, and two of these were explained by Mary Marshall (Hupa) in 1901. The first was spoken over an herb called buck brush (or wild honeysuckle) and called upon a pregnant female deer. All day and all night she feeds on this plant, the story goes, and yet she drops her young easily. By using this medicine, the formulist explained, humans could also avoid gaining weight in pregnancy. After the formulas had been spoken over the plant, its tender shoots were to be chewed by the expectant mother (appendix 2, A–4).

The other formula involved a female bear who ate constantly while she was pregnant and got so big that she could not walk. A plant spoke to her and said, "Put me in your mouth. You are in this condition for the sake of Indians." It was a single plant of redwood sorrel standing there. She put this medicine in her mouth, and the next day she found that she felt much lighter and was able to walk (appendix 2, A–5).

Three other formulas of the same basic type were spoken by Mary Ike (Karok) around 1940. One was spoken over hazel buds, which were then dropped into water that the pregnant woman was supposed to drink. The buds were addressed as if they were Mink, and the person using the medicine says, "You swim upriver, eating all the fish you can. When you come out of the water, you are so fat you can hardly move. But later, when you eat your medicine, you become so light that you could almost fly" (appendix 2, A–18).

Mrs. Ike's other two formulas were similar but called upon a snake (appendix 2, A–19) and a dog (appendix 2, A–20).

Formulas that were intended to hasten the maturity of children in various ways were also numerous and were collected among all tribes of this region. One example, collected from Emma Lewis (Hupa) in 1901, was simply intended to make an infant grow fast, and this text reveals again the tendency to disassociate pregnancy from males and sexuality and to focus instead on spiritual interpretations. The narrative involved a spirit maiden who lived in the sky. She stayed by herself and saw no one, but somehow she became pregnant. "From whom have I a child?" she wondered. While the baby was growing, she tried to pick it up, but it quickly dodged away from her. This occurred several times, and once when it evaded her the baby fell down from the world above and crawled to a certain beach. A certain medicine grew there (wild ginger). She picked some of it and steamed her baby in it, and the human mother was supposed to do the same thing (appendix 2, A–8).

Formulas to ensure the welfare of a baby in later life were also pervasive. One example spoken by Mrs. Emma Lewis (Hupa) concerned a man who lived all alone but found tracks of a baby in his sweathouse. He could tell from the tracks that the infant had been playing with his woodpecker scalps, but only after four days watching did he actually see the child. He then traveled all over the world looking for medicine that would help the child, but he found none. When he returned, however, he found good medicine growing right by the wall of the sweathouse. He put this under the baby and steamed him with it, and made him grow up fast. The baby became exceptionally strong as well. Later, the man was climbing up on the ridge and noticed that the skies were growing dark as the clouds came together. Then, suddenly, the baby ran up and the clouds withdrew. Sickness was afraid of him, the man thought to himself. The medicine he used was tobacco (appendix 2, A–10).

Finally, there were formulas to protect a child who might get lost or wander to a strange place. One example was collected from Emma Lewis (Hupa) in 1901. The formula called upon an old woman whose children were a flock of birds. They traveled everywhere but always came back safe. Once, however, they became imprisoned inside a mountain down by the coast. The old woman decided to make medicine and sat up all night long. She took a water bug and rubbed it against some incense root, then dropped the two things into the fire. When dawn came, the smell drifted to the place they were held, which resulted in their release (appendix 2, A–11).

Sickness and Curing

Spoken formulas for curing sickness or for treating wounds were very common and a few of them have been mentioned in chapters 3 and 6. In many cases the specific problem to be cured is not identified, and it seems probable that these formulas could be used for a wide range of problems. One such text was spoken by Jake Hostler (Hupa) in 1927. The narrative involved Big Cloud, whose children were taken away from him across the ocean. He became lonesome for them and started a sickness. After a while, his children were returned, but the sickness remained and his own children were stricken by it. As in many of these formulaic texts, the hero looked around for a medicine, and in this case he found (unspecified) parts of the Oregon grape and the tan oak. These were pounded up and fed to the children, who were then restored (appendix 2, B–16).

Similar formulas were also collected from Shan Davis (Karok) around 1940, and one was explicitly labeled "Formula for curing any sickness." This involved an upriver person who had traveled down the Klamath looking for trouble. He came to a place that was known to be dangerous,[1] and in a house there he saw an old man who seemed to be feeling around for something in a large basket. Suddenly, sparks came flying out of the basket and struck the upriver person, who dropped to the ground and died. Later, however, he revived himself using medicine made from madrone leaves, which he chewed and rubbed all over himself (appendix 2, B–26).

Several formulas were used for curing a thin and sickly person who had little appetite, and two good examples were collected from Mary Ike (Karok) around 1940. The first was specifically intended to help a person eat deer meat when recovering from a sickness. This concerned a man who had gotten deer meat for his sick wife.

At first, she was too weak to chew the meat, so he gathered fir boughs and had her chew a bit of the foliage. He also chewed some of it himself and rubbed the paste on her legs, arms, and head. Finally he cooked a bit of the chewed fir bough with the deer meat and fed her this. This made her feel so strong that she tried to pull up a tree by its roots (appendix 2, B–23).

Mrs. Ike's other medicine involved Wohpekemeu (identified by the Karok name Yeruxbihii). In this story, he sleeps with his ten wives, some of whom are pregnant, and breaks other serious taboos. Gradually he notices that he is becoming thin and weak, unable to eat. He finally locates a medicine that restores him, and the substance he used was thimbleberry roots. The formula should be spoken over the roots, which are to be soaked in water that the emaciated person drinks (appendix 2, B–20).

Spoken medicine was very important for treating wounds or other injuries, and a Yurok formula for this purpose was discussed in chapter 6. Another example, collected from a man identified as McCann (Hupa) in 1901, was specifically used for wounds made by a flint arrowhead. The text is about two *kixunai* who caught a water monster while fishing with a hook and line. One played a game by hiding and dressing himself in the skin of the water monster. He also removed the pith of an elder stick and put his vital organs inside it. Then, he entered a house where two women were sitting. They warned him to leave before their men returned home, but he stayed anyway. When they did come home, one shot him with a firelike arrow. He was saved because he had taken out his organs, but the wound was burning him. To ease the pain, he chewed on a frond of Woodwardia fern (appendix 2, B–8). A Chilula formula to prevent or heal fighting wounds was spoken by Tom Hill in 1905 (appendix 2, B–11).

Formulas for curing an upset stomach were also very common, and several were similar to the Yurok formula (mentioned in chapter 3) in which Buzzard had gotten sick from eating all sorts of things that were poisonous or taboo and was saved by a plant that he took as medicine. Texts based on virtually the same theme were also collected from Hupa and Karok speakers. In both cases, it is Wohpekemeu who has poisoned himself by eating dead bodies and other poisonous things. In the Hupa formula he cures himself by using an infusion prepared from the inner bark of the yellow pine (appendix 2, B–10), and in the Karok version he makes a similar medicine by mixing alder leaves in water (appendix 2, B–21).

It is most significant that some formulas were intended to cure sickness that was believed to have been caused by bad family relationships. One example was used to treat a person who had become sick from having neglected an elderly relative. The story involved an old woman, the mother of ten children, whose Karok name is translated "Poor Dead Person." Her children never helped her and never made a fire for her, nor did they even take time to talk to her. She went outside to die, cold and hungry, without even a drink of water. She traveled along the road of the dead, but her ghost returned whenever the children mentioned her name. Her ghost continued to trouble them until she herself returned and gave them medicine to drink and bathe in. The medicine she used was made with a type of goldenrod (appendix 2, B–24).

Another formula was used to cure sickness caused by an unhappy marriage. This involved a man and a woman who had ten children, but never spoke to each other. "They lived back to back," as the text itself explains, and this caused bad luck. One of their children died because of it, and when another was stricken the father decided to make medicine for him. The medicine he used was a sprig of fir, taken from a small sapling. The father dipped it into water, which the boy then drank (appendix 2, B–27).

Songs were also used for curing sickness and treating wounds, but these have not been documented so fully as they might have been. There are relatively few recorded examples, and these are more difficult to interpret than spoken formulas. The spoken narratives usually contain information about the problem being treated, the archetypal event being re-created, and in many cases even the way a medicine substance was to be used, but in itself a recorded song tells us little or nothing about such things. In some cases, the collector was careful enough to provide information about what a song was used for or what it represented from a mythic perspective, but the documentation is often inadequate. A survey of the few songs in this category that have been recorded will illustrate the type of problems that are encountered.

The song in example 24 was collected from Mary Grimes (Tolowa) in 1903 and was labeled simply "song used in doctoring (got-

Example 24. Song used in doctoring (gotten in a dream) sung
by Mary Grimes (Tolowa) in 1903 and recorded by
Pliny Earle Goddard (appendix 2, B–2).

ten in a dream)." There are no intrinsic qualities that identify this
as a doctoring song, and the style is similar in most respects to that
of other (especially Yurok) women's solo songs that are identified
as love songs or basketmaking songs. In all these songs the melodic
range is an octave or more, and melodic contours are descending
for the most part. Pentatonic scales are used in virtually every
example, and the tempo is generally slow. Typically, the singer
strikes a high note with moderate loudness and gradually descends
to the bottom of her range, singing more and more softly until she
can hardly be heard.

Generally, a short strophe like this would be repeated three times or more, but the song was sung only once in this early recording. The 12/8 meter is also somewhat unusual (most are strictly duple), but not much significance is placed on that. Whatever the song may represent in terms of its mythic significance is unknown, nor do we have evidence concerning the nature of the doctoring to which it pertained. The song seems to employ vocables rather than words, but the text could not be completely transcribed because the audio quality of the recording is rather poor.

A "song and formula to purify house after sickness" was collected from a man called Stone (Yurok) in 1907 (example 25). The formula precedes the song. It has not been translated, and the poor audio quality of the original recording makes it seem unlikely that a translation could ever be made. The song consists of a series of long-held tones that resemble the solemn foghornlike intonations heard in the Deerskin Dance or the Jump Dance.[2] Rather than being sung at one pitch level only, however, the tones in this song are strung together into a descending melodic pattern. The tempo is quite slow and the song is sung in free rhythm.[3] The diatonic (lydian-type) scale is rather unusual, but it has already been noted that the style is not at all uniform in this respect.

The other two songs in this category were not sung but performed in a type of heightened speech like that of other "animal songs" discussed in chapters 3 and 6. Both were sung by Pete Henry (Karok) in 1926, and one was identified as a "song for doctoring a sick dog" (example 26). There is no information concerning the mythic archetype behind the song, but the collector's notes give a translation and indicate that the song was used with a medicine made from some part (not specified) of the spruce tree. The song is sung ten times on the recording, and the Karok words are translated "spruce struck by pain, dog struck by pain" (Roberts 1926b). This type of (textual) parallelism is found in several of the Karok and Konomihu songs collected by Roberts during the 1920s.

The other song collected from Pete Henry (Karok) was for a person who got something stuck in his eye. This was the song that Bullfrog used when that happened (appendix 2, B–14).

Hunting and Fishing

This category includes various types of medicine for taking deer (22), salmon (4), bear (3), eels (2), fox (1), and for hunting in general (3).

Example 25. Song sung to purify house after sickness sung by
Stone (Yurok) and recorded by Weitchpec Frank for
A. L. Kroeber in 1907 (appendix 2, B–1).

Example 26. Doctoring song for a sick dog sung by Pete Henry (Karok)
and recorded by Helen Roberts in 1926 (appendix 2, B–13).

Deer Medicine

A formula and a song for deer hunting often belong together and derive from the same mythic incident. In most cases, the hunter would speak the formula while purifying himself in the sweathouse and then use the song while actually hunting. Whenever a medicine substance was involved, it was generally something that the hunter rubbed on himself in the sweathouse and that presumably also served to cover his man-smell.

The typical pattern is illustrated by a deer medicine collected from Domingo of Weitchpec (Yurok) shortly after 1900. The formula called upon a young man from Turip who hunted all the time and had ten dogs. The oldest dog gave him a song to use in hunting and also gave him certain instructions. He was to watch at a certain place along the river and allow ten deer to swim by. After ten had passed, then he should go after the eleventh one. "You must count them," the dog said. He did so, and the eleventh one was a precious albino deer whose antlers were covered with woodpecker scalps (example 27).

The song, which is very brief, was sung over and over again in a soft voice while the hunter walked around looking for game. As in most songs collected from Yuroks, the range is rather wide and the melody has a descending contour. There is much nasality, and in this transcription the parenthesized eighth notes are intended to indicate vocal pulsation as distinguished from repeated notes that are clearly articulated.

It is interesting to note that the (f to c) ending motive in example 27 could also serve as the cadential motive in a Brush Dance song, and in another deer-hunting song (example 28) the resemblance to Brush Dance singing was even stronger. The latter song not only has phrase-endings resembling those of a Brush Dance song but also includes a contrasting (B) section in which melodic material is transposed to a higher pitch level. Despite their being less complex in form (and more repetitive), it seems likely that both of these deer-hunting songs have been adapted from Brush Dance songs.

The song in example 28 is sung six times on the original recording. Although the verse transcribed here was sung entirely in vocables, words are also used in the song, and Kroeber's notes give the following translation: "Alas, eat grass. I will eat it fast. Eat grass.

Example 27. Deer medicine song taught to a hunter by his oldest dog sung by Domingo of Weitchpec (Yurok) and recorded by Kroeber circa 1901–1907 (appendix 2, C–9).

Alas, high up comes the fog." After singing, the hunter makes a blowing sound, as if making an offering of tobacco, and says (in Yurok), "I see you close by now. I'll catch you with this song" (Kroeber n.d.: Carton 6; Notebook 67, p. 37).

Not all of the Yurok deer-hunting songs had such a wide range, and Hawley of Meta (Yurok) had another one (example 29) that was based on a simple three-tone scale. We have no information concerning the mythic significance of the song, but like all of the others this was a song that was thought to have been used by a *wo'gey* for the purpose of deer hunting. Sung ten times on the original cylinder recording, this song has no words and the singer's voice is thick with nasality and glottalization.

While the Yurok deer-hunting songs considered above employ sung tones with relatively focused pitches, a speechlike delivery is evident in some examples. The song transcribed in example 30 uses a combination of sung and spoken tones. While performed here by a woman, this is originally a man's song and mimics the complaining of a toothless old (*wo'gey*) man who is never given his choice of deer meat but always just gets the liver, which is soft and boneless. The text has been translated:

(Sung)   (Spoken)
I am always told,   "Eat up your liver."

Example 28. Deer medicine song sung by Hawley of Meta (Yurok) and recorded by Kroeber in 1907 (appendix 2, C–20).

Example 29. Deer medicine song sung by Hawley of Meta (Yurok) and recorded by Kroeber in 1907 (appendix 2, C–18).

Example 30. Song of a toothless old man (for deer hunting) sung
by Florence Schaughnessy (Yurok) and recorded by
Robins in 1951 (appendix 2, C–34).

(Sung)   (Spoken)
I am never asked,   "Eat what you like."

There is undoubtedly a more extensive mythic plot that forms a
basis for this interesting text, but as in so many cases the entire
story has not been documented.

Although both Goddard and Sapir collected many spoken texts
among the Hupa Indians between 1900 and 1930, they did not
make many sound recordings. Therefore, we have comparatively
little evidence concerning the character of Hupa medicine songs
for deer hunting or any other application.[4] There is, however, a
Hupa deer-hunting song that was collected from Jimmy Jackson in
1953, and in the absence of other examples it becomes that much
more important.

Before singing the song (example 31), Mr. Jackson explains its
meaning—speaking in Hupa—as follows (translation courtesy of
Victor Golla):

Example 31. Hupa deer-hunting song performed by Jimmy Jackson and recorded by Woodward in 1953 (appendix 2, C–35).

Coyote said this at the time he was hungry for Deer's babies. He said this, sang this song [for a dance].

The first thing one notices about example 31 is the unusual half-step progression (three in succession) that occurs in the body and the coda of the song. This does not occur anywhere else in the entire repertory, but other anomalous scales have been noted previously. Perhaps more significant from a stylistic perspective is the relatively narrow melodic range (a perfect fifth) and the pendular contour of the melody. These features distinguish this song from the Yurok deer-hunting songs and apparently reflect a distinctly Athapaskan style that was noted previously in the Hupa Flower Dance songs (see chapter 5).

Deer-hunting songs collected among the Karok were virtually all quite brief and repetitive. Three-tone scales are typical, and the vocal delivery is very speechlike. As in most cylinder recordings, the phonology of the text is not clear. The collector's notes provide no information concerning the mythic significance of the song in example 32, but there is a transcription of the text and a rough translation. The same Karok words are sung three times in each verse, and they are translated "A doe. The deer's fat under the skin" (Roberts 1926*b*:38).

There is also no explanation concerning the mythic meaning of the deer-hunting song transcribed in example 33, though the text has been translated "A grown deer [va-ti-sa], it is playing [ni-fa-na-tu]" (Roberts 1926*b*:40).

It is unfortunate that these Karok deer-hunting songs are not so well documented as some of the other "animal songs" collected by Helen Roberts, because the texts of these songs are typically quite obscure and filled with hidden meaning. A song of the raccoon,[5] for example, has been translated "Top here, it is covered. Underneath here, it is rattling." But the meaning of the song only becomes clear through the following explanation (evidently in the words of the collector):

The raccoon is a great animal to steal acorns and the Indians put their acorns in a hole in the ground and put water on them and soak them there a year or so to extract the poison. Raccoon comes along and he knows they are there but they are covered with boards. He can hear the acorns rattling when he reaches in. (Roberts 1926*b*:44)

A song of the hummingbird provides another example.[6] The brief text is translated simply, "My mouth is too small," but the meaning of the song only becomes clear when the mythic context for the song is known. Roberts explains it as follows:

A long time ago they used to fish in the river with bait for trout and other fish. A sucker got hold of the bait and choked and was sick. The hummingbird was an Indian doctor and they got him to dance and after dancing a while he discovered that the sucker had the bait in his throat and it was choking him. He could not get it out, the doctor, because his mouth was too small. He could not grasp it. (Roberts 1926*b*:41)

Example 32. Deer-hunting song sung by Pete Henry and recorded by
Helen Roberts in 1926 (appendix 2, C–23).

Example 33. Deer-hunting song sung by Pete Henry (Karok) and
recorded by Helen Roberts in 1926 (appendix 2, C–24).

Thus, if the deer-hunting texts described above seem vague or
meaningless, it is only because they evoke a larger realm of understandings about which we have no information.

Spoken formulas used for deer hunting were impressively diverse in character, but sexual pollution and purification were central in many of the narratives. Such formulas were apparently used
so that a hunter could continue to be successful even though he
had not abstained from sex. A text spoken by Senaxon (Hupa) in
1901 is typical of the genre. In this narrative, one of the *kixunai*
wanted to spoil some other men's luck at hunting, so he had sex
and then went to visit with them. The next day, their dogs were

too lazy to hunt, and the *kixunai* were so worn out that they did not even get up until evening. Later, the one who had caused the problem decided to restore their luck. He made medicine with a certain herb, telling the others to rub it on themselves and on their dogs. The next morning they went out and the dogs barked wonderfully (appendix 2, C–4).

A formula spoken by Chester Pepper (Karok) in 1949 had the same basic theme (appendix 2, C–33). In this text, a being called Little Black Wolf in the Sky was hunting with his ten sons and they had killed many deer. Then, he wished them bad luck, so he had sex with his wife and ate deer meat. This spoiled their luck until he made medicine to restore it. In both this and the previous example, the men were supposed to rub an herbal medicine on themselves before hunting, and this was presumably done in the sweathouse.

Tom Hill (Chilula) had three formulas to counteract the polluting influence of sex. In one case, the hunter used to visit two women all the time, but he still got plenty of deer and money because he washed himself with a certain herb (appendix 2, C–17). The other two formulas involved hunters who had ruined their luck simply by having dreamed of women, and in both cases luck was restored by making medicine with certain herbs (appendix 2, C–13 and C–14).

Medicine for Salmon

Except for those used in World Renewal rituals, only four spoken formulas for taking salmon have been documented, and (probably by coincidence) all four were collected from Yurok speakers shortly after 1900.

A formula from Stone of Weitchpec (Yurok) called upon a *wo'gey* who had spoken with Nepewo (The Great Head Salmon). He asked him for salmon and other things. Although he held a spear, he did not attempt to strike Nepewo, who listened and then went on his way. After that, the spirit-person always found salmon and killed them easily. The *wo'gey* who is called upon in this formula instructs the fisherman to "talk to his harpoon" (that is, speak the formula over it) and dictates various restrictions that the fisherman had to observe in order to preserve his luck (appendix 2, C–7).

The second formula for salmon, collected from Billy Werk of Weitchpec, was used with a song. The narrative involved a story about Small Salmon (Tserhkr). He followed some other fish into a sweathouse, even though the owner told him that there was no room to lie down there. He found himself a place anyway and sang a certain song. This formula and song were to be used while the fisherman tied the webbing to the frame of his dipnet rather than after he had started fishing (appendix 2, C–8).

Another Yurok known as Lame Billy of Weitchpec had a formula for salmon involving Coyote, who pretended to be a Karok person traveling upriver. He disguised himself as an old man and persuaded some people to take him upstream in a boat. However, he got caught while passing by the fish dam at Kepel, because someone there accused him of being the one who had run off with his wife (appendix 2, C–5).

The last of these formulas was explained by Barney of Sregon (Yurok). This text calls upon Pigeon, who learned how to make a net by spying on White Duck. He copied how the net was attached to the frame and learned the names for various parts of the net. Later, he got caught watching and was beaten up. That is why his chest is so narrow now; they pushed him against the ground and injured him (appendix 2, C–11).

Bear Medicine

Only two songs for bear hunting were documented, and both were collected from Pete Henry (Karok) in 1926. One of the songs is transcribed in example 34, and its text has been translated as follows:

> At the clump of fir trees [where I live]
> Please let there be salmon for me.
> Please let there be salmon for me.
>
> At the rock shelter [my other place]
> Please let there be salmon for me.
> Please let there be salmon for me.
> (Roberts 1926*b*:37)

Each part of the text is repeated, so that the textual form is AABB, but the same melody is used for both the A and the B sections.

Example 34. Bear-hunting song sung by Pete Henry and recorded by Helen Roberts in 1926 (appendix 2, C–22).

Like the deer-hunting songs considered previously, the melodic range is narrow, and a three-tone scale is used.

A spoken formula for killing bear was collected from Mary Ike (Karok) when interviewed by Edward Gifford around 1940 (appendix 2, C–28). This text involved a woman who sought to avoid hearing anyone cry for the dead. She went to live at the foot of a mountain, but she heard crying there and had to move. Then she went to the top of the mountain, but there too she heard crying and had to move on again. She continued to move from place to place until finally she placed her basket upon the ground and a black bear came and fell into it. If a hunter calls upon this woman and repeats her story, then he too will take bear, but the hunter will always hear crying like the spirit woman did.

Medicine for Eels

A formula for taking eels was spoken by Georgia Orcutt (Karok) around 1940 (appendix 2, C–27). The text focuses upon the daughter of Wohpekemeu (identified by his Karok name Yeruxbihii). Even though it was taboo, she shared a dinner of eel meat with her brothers. Their luck at taking eel was not diminished, however, because she made medicine to counteract the harmful effects of this. This formula, whose purpose clearly resembles that of the deer-hunting formulas discussed previously, was supposed to be spoken over the eels while they were being cooked or prepared for drying. Similar formulas were also used by women who were menstruating in order to prevent causing bad luck for their husbands (see Medicine for Use by Women in chapter 9).

Wealth

The importance of crying in precontact spiritual life is dramatically illustrated by the style of songs that were used for money medicine, as the "sobbing" quality in these songs is even more pronounced than that heard in ritual singing. The song in example 35 is relatively unstructured from a melodic perspective, and indeed the "song" could be regarded as little more than a vehicle for crying at (five) different pitch levels. In examples such as this we sense a very unclear borderline between music and expressions that are actually nonmusical in nature.

A money medicine song sung by Tom Hill (Chilula) in 1904 gives virtually the same impression (example 36). Here again the singer seems to be "sobbing" as much as singing, and there is much nasality and heavy tremolo throughout. This song has an irregular and (apparently) improvised character, as if it might be sung somewhat differently from time to time. It is not repeated on the recording and the sequence of motives might be analyzed A B C B A C_1 B.

Other money songs by Julius Marshall (Hupa), Jim of Pekwan (Yurok), and Johnny Cooper (Yurok) give a similar impression, though the audio quality of these recordings is very poor (appendix 2, D–2, D–15, and D–18). In each case the singer's voice is tense, nasal, and glottalized, much as if the singer were actually crying instead of singing.

Since the anthropological literature describes Yurok civilization mainly from a male perspective (see chapter 4), it is very interesting to note that three of these money medicine songs were also collected from a Yurok woman identified as Weitchpec Susie in 1902

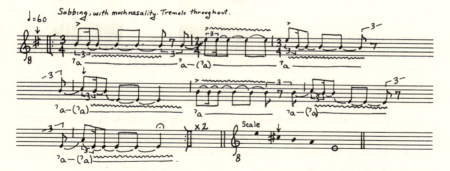

Example 35. Sweathouse wood gathering song. Sung by Umiits of
Kepel Creek (Yurok) and recorded by A. L. Kroeber in 1906
(appendix 2, D–16).

Example 36. Money medicine song. Sung by Tom Hill (Chilula) and
recorded by Goddard in 1904 (appendix 2, D–8).

(appendix 2, D–3, D–4, and D–5). One was labeled "Wetsqaaq Song" (example 37). Kroeber's notes (n.d.: Carton 6; Notebook 42, p. 48) do not provide a translation for the title, and the song appears to be sung only in vocables.

In this early recording, a single phrase is repeated seventeen times, with slight variations each time. Here again, the musical organization per se is very weak: the singer's intonation is inconsistent, so that some of the scale tones indicated here might more correctly be thought of as "scale tone areas." Relatedly, the meter is not at all clear, and this is why the 3/4 indication has been parenthesized. The song is sung with a heavy "sobbing" vocal delivery, and Kroeber's notes indicate that this and the other two songs were used much like the men's sweathouse songs.

The song in example 38 appears to be sung entirely in vocables, but Kroeber's notes mention a text and give the translation, "south along the coast, I am going there" (Kroeber n.d.: Carton 6; Notebook 42, p. 48). There was no explanation or translation of the title. The song is sung six times on the cylinder and has the same "sobbing" quality as other sweathouse songs considered previously. As in most Yurok songs, the melodic ambitus is rather wide, and the melody has a descending contour.

Another recording identified as "Maoxpir Song" was also collected from Weitchpec Susie and had a similar style (appendix 2, D–5), but Kroeber's notes reveal this was Susie's rendition of a man's sweathouse song rather than one that a woman would actually use.

Besides being prominent in the context of sweathouse practices generally (see chapter 4), crying was a recurrent theme in spoken formulas for wealth. In some examples, a spirit-person's crying produced some distinctive feature of the natural landscape, which then became a place where humans could make medicine (also by crying). Thus for example there is a rock formation at Trinidad Head which is identified by the Yurok name "He Sits Forever." This marks the spot where a spirit-person went to cry and ask for money. Gradually, he began to see dentalium shells swimming in the tidepools as if they were fish. He was mesmerized by this vision and sat there watching the money swim around until he turned into stone himself. This became a mythic event that humans could re-enact while making medicine at that spot (Waterman 1920:270). A

Example 37. Wetsqaaq Song sung by Weitchpec Susie (Yurok) and collected by A. L. Kroeber in 1902 (appendix 2, D–3).

Example 38. Meroctan Song performed by Weitchpec Susie and collected by A. L. Kroeber in 1902 (appendix 2, D–4).

similar formula involving Wohpekemeu was described at length in chapter 1 (appendix 2, D–11).

Crying was also an important element in other formulas that were not based on features of the landscape. A formula spoken by Henry Hostler (Hupa) in 1901 described the travels of a young man who always cried and gathered sweathouse wood (appendix 2, D–1). He was looking for water, but none existed in the prehuman world. Finally he went traveling in the upper world and found an old man without eyes. The old man showed him a basket of water, which he drank, but then the old man told him that it wasn't water at all. Instead, the basket contained all the tears that the young man shed in his life while praying. The old man also warned him against drinking water while training for wealth. "Many may pray, and even sweat themselves," he said, "but they will always remain poor if they drink water." The formulist would speak both parts of the dialogue in using this medicine.

The fact that crying itself could compel a change in luck is illustrated by a formula told by John Shoemaker (Hupa) in 1927 (appendix 2, D–22). The story involves two brothers (spirit-persons) who lived in Chimariko territory. The older one had set several fishtraps in which he could catch dentalium shell money. He would lie by his traps, singing as the money collected there, then take it and store it in one of his luck-basins. Every day, these would be filled with money by break of dawn. One day, the younger brother asked if he could tend the traps, and so he did. However, he began eating the meat of the dentalia that he caught. This caused the traps to drift away downstream. The older brother recovered them once, but they repeatedly floated away, finally going all the way down-river and out across the ocean. The older brother was broken up when he realized this, and he began to cry as he walked back from Rekwoi (at the mouth of the Klamath) to Hoopa Valley. Then, while crying, he found a piece of special quartz. He rubbed it against another rock and saw that it turned into money. He put this into the water at his old fishing hole, and his fishing traps became as they were before.

This medicine was to be used at a special "luck basin" that Shoemaker knew about. This term refers to a basinlike depression in a rock formation, and the Hupa word for it is translated into English as "rock bowl" or "rock basket" (Golla, in press [MS p. 214]). The use of a luck basin for success in gambling is described as follows:

When you find such a place you must "smoke" it with incense root and speak to it. You smoke it for ten days and talk to it about the people you're going to gamble with, and how many points you want to make in a stretch, and so on. Then you clap your hands to it, and leave some incense root in it. When you are ready to gamble, you go up to it and rub your hands with the incense root. (Golla, in press [MS p. 213])

The preceding discussion has focused mainly on the prominence of crying as a central theme in spoken formulas for wealth, but other

subjects were also important, as for example the story of the underdog who manages to come out ahead because of some miracle. Tom
Hill (Chilula) described two such formulas when interviewed in
1908. One involved a boy with nine brothers who was completely
covered with scabs and despised by all the rest of the boys in his
family. His younger sister fed him without their knowing. He used
to go fishing every night, until he had a good string of dentalia shell
money. Then, he presented it to his brothers and left home (appendix 2, D–19). The theme of "the scabby boy" is found in formulas
from various tribes of the region, and a Yurok version is published
in Kroeber (1976:292).

The other formula explained by Tom Hill (Chilula) involved a
spirit-person who was a bastard but nonetheless obtained money
from every direction because of a song that he used (appendix 2,
D–20). Formulas such as these reveal the "democratic" character
of medicine making among these tribes, expressing the (idealized)
belief that even the most wretched of persons could overcome his
fate through medicine making.

Chapter Nine

Medicine Songs and Formulas, Part 2

She cried when she realized there was no way to get home [from across the ocean]. After a time somebody came around and saw her sitting on sand. . . . The man said, "I can take you home if you want to go home. If you marry me I can go home with you." She married him and they came to Panamenik. When the woman cried, that man heard her and felt sorry for her. When they arrived at Panamenik, the woman said, "I never knew I was singing. I thought I was crying. I was crying because I had no way to come home. Now I find out I got a good song."

From a formula for love medicine as described by Georgia Orcutt (Karok) in 1940 (Kroeber and Gifford 1980:270–271)

Love Medicine

This is our largest category, and there are various explanations why songs and formulas for love medicine should be comparatively numerous. For one thing, this is a sphere of life that was not much affected by the economic and technological transformations that occurred in the period after contact, and it also seems likely that these songs and formulas were less guarded by secrecy than some other types of medicine, such as those for conflict and revenge. Indian persons interviewed between 1900 and 1942 were presumably less likely to share information about the latter or about other types of medicine that were considered quite valuable as property. In any case, the relative abundance and diversity of items in this category remind us that only a fraction of the songs and formulas that actually existed for any function were ever documented, and that the corpus considered here gives only a meager impression of the richness of the mythology on which Indian spiritual life was based.

Love medicine was used by a person in private rather than in the presence of the person who was its object. Typically, a formula and a song went together, but as in other types of medicine we do not always have complete information about both. In some cases a text of the formula was collected but no recording of the song associated with it exists, while on other occasions a recording was made but nothing was documented about its mythic significance. Despite these problems, a survey of the existing evidence tells us much about love medicine in general.

It is clear, for example, that crying was an important theme in love medicine, for it is mentioned in several formulas and evident in the "sobbing" timbre heard in many of the songs. The quotation at the head of this chapter formula is taken from the translation of a formula that was based on the story of a female spirit-person who had accidentally killed two "wind babies" (appendix 2, E–28). This caused a great wind that blew her house away and carried her all the way downriver and out across the ocean. She was lost there, and she had given up hope. Then a man heard her crying, and he fell in love with her, thinking that her crying was a beautiful song. As in other types of formulas, the woman using this medicine would re-enact these events dramatically, first calling upon the spirit-person and then acting out the dialogue between her and her suitor. The song could be used at various points in this conjuring or else just by itself.

The same speaker (Georgia Orcutt) also described a man's love formula that involved a crying (appendix 2, E–30). In this narrative, two wealthy women were being followed everywhere by a poor man from whom they wanted to escape. Later, they heard him crying as he traveled across a ridge in the high country and this made them change their minds so that they began pursuing him.

Similar texts were collected from another Karok woman, Mary Ike. One of the narratives involved the story of a young man who was frustrated by some girls who refused to speak to him and ran in the house every time they saw him coming (appendix 2, E–33). Later, one of them changed her mind and wanted him to stay with her, but he said, "No, I will not live with you. You did not like me. You did not want me." He cried as he said this and his tears created a big creek. He later became the mountain which is now called Preston Peak. In this example, a rejected (spirit) person turns the tables on the girl he desired rather than simply winning her heart. This vindictive element is present in many formulas, and another formula mentioned by Mary Ike is very similar in character (appendix 2, E–35).

Each of the formulas mentioned above involves using a song which represented (or consisted of) crying. Unfortunately, none of these songs was recorded, but there are several recordings of love songs in which a "sobbing" vocal quality is quite obvious. One example was sung by Tom Hill (Chilula) in 1905 and is transcribed below in example 39. The delivery is heavily glottalized, and the song is sung slowly in free rhythm. I have used tied quarter notes in order to indicate relative durations, but these are only approximations as there is a halting and irregular quality to the rhythm from beginning to end. The range is extremely wide (an octave and a fifth) and the singer can barely reach the lowest note, which is quite unfocused in pitch. The song is sung only once on the recording, and thus it is not clear whether it would be sung the same if repeated. There is little sense of symmetry in the phrasing, and the song has an aimless quality, much as if the singer were moaning in grief.

A love song collected from Weitchpec Henry (Yurok) in 1906 has a similar character (example 40). Here again the song is in free rhythm and the phrasing is rather unsymmetrical. A formal structure ABB₁ can be discerned, but the B sections differ significantly from each other and it is not clear to what extent the song is improvised. The singer begins quite softly, as if he were moaning, but at various points he sings quite loudly. These dynamic contrasts produce a "sobbing" quality that seems somewhat more urgent or dramatic than that heard in the previous example.

Other love songs collected from Yuroks identified as Weitchpec Nancy (appendix 2, E–9) and Blind Bill (appendix 2, E–18) could not be notated, partly because of the poor audio quality of the recordings but also because these "songs" were closer in some respects to actual crying than to singing.

Not all of the love songs in the corpus had a "sobbing" quality, and one that was collected from Tom Hill (Chilula) in 1905 is very different indeed. This song (example 41) has a vigorous quality and

Example 39. Love song performed by Tom Hill (Chilula) and collected by Pliny Earle Goddard in 1905 (appendix 2, E–12).

even includes vocal pulsations reminiscent of Plains Indian singing. It is sung loudly and the pitches are clearly focused. As in so many songs of this region, the range is very wide and the melodic contour is descending, but here the use of pulsated notes produces a more terrace-shaped melody. This vigorous style is also heard in a love song performed by Frank Douglas (appendix 2, E–44).

The love songs used by women were very diverse in character. Even more prevalent than the "crying" type is a more lyrical style of love song such as that sung by Aileen Figueroa (Yurok) in the next example. Here a sense of meter is clearly discernible, though the tempo is very slow and there is much rubato, and the singer's intonation is very precise. The construction is simple but elegant, as the song seems to be composed of five short units that fit together neatly and descend through an octave. The type of pentatonic scale observed here is very common in these songs. Even to the modern, non-Indian listener this song seems very "musical" indeed, yet it has a mournful character, perhaps largely due to the repeated use of the glottal stop (with much aspiration and nasality) in a manner that suggests crying.

A love song collected from a woman identified as Minnie (Yurok)

Example 40. Love song performed by Weitchpec Henry (Yurok) and
collected by Alfred Kroeber in 1906 (appendix 2, E–6).

Example 41. Love song performed by Tom Hill (Chilula) and collected by Pliny Earle Goddard in 1905 (appendix 2, E–13).

Example 42. Love song performed by Aileen Figueroa (Yurok) and recorded by Charlotte Heth in 1975 (appendix 2, E–43).

in 1909 and notated in example 43 fits the same general profile and shows that the style has changed little during this century. Both songs employ vocables rather than words, and both are very slow in tempo. The song in example 43 uses another anhemitonic pentatonic scale (1-2-3-5-6) which is fairly common. The tonal structure of this song is somewhat obscured by the use of e natural (330 hz), but this only occurs as the singer is trying to find her pitch level and not in the body of the song itself. As in the previous example, the ambitus of the song in example 43 is very wide and the lowest tones are sung so softly that they can barely be heard.

A third love song in this lyrical style was collected from Weitchpec Nancy (Yurok) in 1906 and has been notated in example 44. The melody has an arched contour rather than a descending shape, but a similar effect is achieved. Most listeners would agree that the song seems very "musical" to modern ears and is perhaps even more "pretty" than the previous two examples. Still, the early recording date makes it quite clear that these three songs belong to a style that existed prior to any Euro-American musical influences. The audio quality is rather poor, and the text could not be transcribed where the performer was in her lower register and singing quite softly.

An altogether different style is heard in love songs collected from a Wiyot woman named Molly Brainerd (Wiyot) in 1923. Each of her songs has words that are sung repeatedly in a simple melodic pattern based on three tones or less. The texts refer to the loved one in various ways, and the songs all have a brooding and hypnotic character. The song in example 45 is sung thirty times on the recording, and the mantralike text has been translated "He travels the hills [hunts]." She sings in a low register, and the dark quality of her voice is enhanced by use of tremolo throughout much of the recording.

Another love song collected from Molly Brainerd (Wiyot) refers to two different men, as if the singer were trying to choose between them. The words of this song have been translated "Tall, lean man [or] delicate pitiful one." The song is sung eighteen times on the recording, with slight variations in the B section.

A love medicine song sung by Sara Frank (Yurok) and recorded by Kroeber in 1907 is somewhat more melodic but basically quite similar in character. This song (example 47) is sung fifteen times

Example 43. Love song performed by Minnie (Yurok) and recorded by Weitchpec Frank in 1909 (appendix 2, E–8).

Example 44. Love song performed by Weitchpec Nancy (Yurok) and recorded by A. L. Kroeber in 1906 (appendix 2, E–7).

Example 45. Love song performed by Molly Brainerd (Wiyot) and recorded by A. L. Kroeber in 1923 (appendix 2, E–16).

Example 46. Love song performed by Molly Brainerd (Wiyot) and recorded by A. L. Kroeber in 1923 (appendix 2, E–17).

Example 47. Love song performed by Sarah Frank (Yurok) and recorded by A. L. Kroeber in 1907 (appendix 2, E–11).

on the recording, and the musical form is AABB. The text seems to be based on an alternation between two parallel expressions, but unfortunately there is no translation.

A love song collected from Mary Grimes (Tolowa) in 1903 is rather unusual in that each note is articulated very crisply, and staccato (or perhaps mezzo-staccato) markings could have been placed over nearly every note in example 48. Presumably this distinctive vocal delivery relates to some mythic characterization in a spoken formula, but unfortunately we have no information concerning the archetypal event upon which this or any of the other love songs considered here were based.

The style of example 48 is similar to that of the Hupa Flower Dance songs that were discussed in chapter 5. One can hardly escape noticing that songs used for love medicine were quite diverse in character, as at least four distinct styles have been transcribed here. This multiplicity of styles is addressed in the next chapter, which moves away from specific examples to describe the musical tradition from a more general perspective.

Returning to the subject of spoken formulas, we find that the theme of the underdog who manages to prevail is prominent in love medicine just as it was in medicine for wealth, and some of these texts actually involve dogs. One such formula was collected from John Shoemaker (Hupa) in 1927. This is about a dog that was so ugly people would ridicule him when passing the place where he lived. He took the foreleg bone of a deer, and painted it red and black in a certain way. Then, after breaking the bone in two, he painted a black line and a red line across his face. Finally, he sang his medicine song. This made all the women want him.

As usual, the formulist impersonates the dog at various points in making medicine and states at the end that even a homely man can have women if he knows this medicine (appendix 2, E–25). Two other formulas involving dogs who managed to get women even though they were homely or aged were collected from Mary Ike in 1940 (appendix 2, E–31 and E–32). Both were associated with songs, but unfortunately the songs were not recorded.

In other cases a female spirit-person is the underdog, as in a formula collected from Georgia Orcutt (Karok) around 1940 (appendix 2, E–34). This story is about Sun Young Man and his wife Frog.

Example 48. Love song for woman to use performed by Mary Grimes (Tolowa) and recorded by Goddard in 1903 (appendix 2, E–14).

He was always gone, so Frog said that she wanted to travel with him. While they were traveling through the sky, he threw her into a fire which consumed her. It turned out that he had another woman across the ocean all along. Later, he felt so guilty about Frog that he stopped visiting the other woman. Frog assembled her bones together and came back to life. Toward the end of the texts Frog states that her song will make a husband return to a wife he has left.

As noted in this example, love medicine used by women was usually intended to hold on to a man or to make him return after he was gone. By contrast, men's love medicine was typically used in order to make initial contact with a woman (or frequently with two women). The idea that a man using love medicine might also obtain dentalium shell money as a bonus is also rather prominent, as for example in two formulas collected from Tom Hill (appendix 2, E–2 and E–3). Indeed, there seems to be much affinity between men's formulas for wealth and for success in love, and several Yurok formulas collected by Kroeber shortly after 1900 were evidently intended for money or for women without differentiation.[1]

Medicine for Use by Women

In the years between 1900 and 1910, Alfred Kroeber made 372 wax cylinder recordings among the Yurok Indians. Of these, 349 feature male narrators or singers, and only 23 cylinders contain evidence expressing the female side of things. Hardly any of this material was documented in Kroeber's published writings, and there is a distinct male gender bias pervading the literature as a whole. Today we realize that women once had a separate spiritual life, parallel to that of the men, which was never adequately documented, but it seems unlikely we will ever have a full understanding of these practices given the evidence that is available today.

We do know that there were formulas designed to counteract the effects of menstruation, and these texts are most revealing. A woman's monthly isolation meant her domestic duties had to be deferred, and this posed additional burdens on the whole family. For this reason, women made medicine in order to purify themselves and shorten the menstrual period. To let her husband and others know that she had protected them in this manner, a woman would mark a cross on her right arm with a charred acorn (appendix 2, F–1).

One such formula was collected from Weitchpec Susie (Yurok) in July 1902 (appendix 2, F–3). The formulist begins by calling upon a spirit named Sky Girl. She asks for help, stating that she has been ostracized and that everyone avoids her for fear of pollution. Sky Girl answers:

Indians you will be all right. I also never come on the trail. They fear me. You see me standing here. I have lots of blood. Too bad. I can't go on the trail. I can't use what they use. Indians look over here. Sky middle lake. You can see white scratches. That is the trail. I pity you Indians. Better hurry up. I have gone about long in the middle lake. Okego. That is the one. That's where they drink. Deer, elk, ducks. You can go in any-place. You need not be afraid. Money will stay in the house. Now you look here. You will see white scratches along the trail. Because that's where they drink. Money and arrows. That's why the lake is there. The white marks are saliva from their mouths. That's where you will wash. The lake is saliva foam from money and arrows. That's where you are going. Because they fear you so. That's where I come for ten days. Then you will come home. There will be money in the house. No one will fear me. You will be thus also. Only sink yourself once in the water. Now go Indian. (Kroeber, n.d.: Carton 6; Notebook 42, pp. 42–48)

Whether there is actually a lake that was called Okego or whether this medicine would be spoken while bathing in the Klamath River is not clear. The only mention of the word in Waterman's "Yurok Geography" relates to a spot in the Klamath near Kenek. There, the placename "okego" is translated as "rapids" or more literally "where it goes over, or pours over" (Waterman 1920:250). Other Hupa formulas to shorten the menstrual period were quite similar to the Yurok example described here (appendix 2, F–1 and F–5).

Another distinctly female domain that involved use of medicine was basketry, and one such formula (with song) was collected from Emma Dusky (Hupa) in 1901 (appendix 2, F–2). This text involved a *kixunai* maiden who used to sit and weave baskets down by Humboldt Bay. One day the wind gusted strongly and blew her basket out to sea. The next morning, she was surprised to see that it had returned, and that the hazel ribs were covered with sucking dentalia. Her basket always left home like that and returned with money. This spirit-person also grants long life to those who remember her deeds (that is, who use the formula) and sing while they weave, as she did. Another formula for wealth, used while weaving baskets, was collected from Georgia Orcutt (Karok) in 1940 (appendix 2, F–6).

These examples and other songs and formulas discussed previously under the heading "Wealth" (chapter 8) make it clear that the female tradition of spiritual practices surrounding the wealth quest was no less developed than that of the men, even though we do not know much about it today.

A song for basket making was collected from Aileen Figueroa as recently as 1975. This song (example 49) is sung in a lyrical style such as that of several Yurok love songs discussed above. The melodic range is quite wide (an octave and a fifth), and again the melody descends in brief phrases that dovetail together neatly. As in so many of these songs, the notes in the upper register are sung rather loudly while the lower notes barely can be heard. The song is sung three times on the recording, twice using vocables and once

Example 49. Basket song as sung by Aileen Figueroa (Yurok) and recorded by Charlotte Heth in 1977 (appendix 2, F–8).

using words. The words describe a basket that was thrown into the Klamath River and floated all the way downriver to Rekwoi; thus the descending melody and supple rhythms of the song tend to mirror its textual meaning. Mrs. Figueroa stated that the song was used in order to make sure that somebody would buy the basket being made.

Finally, another medicine song was to be sung while gathering acorns, traditionally a woman's activity. This example was sung by Phoebe Maddox (Karok) and recorded by Helen Roberts in 1926. The collector's notes state that this was the song of the little white worm who lived inside so many acorns. When he was a person, the singer explained, he also loved acorns, and the song text is translated, "Lots, lying around." The song is sung twelve times on the recording, sometimes using words and sometimes only vocables (as in the segment transcribed here). The irregular meter seems unusual, but such anomalies are not altogether unexpected in songs that mimic the speech of particular animals or spirit-persons.

Conflict or Revenge

This section covers medicine to be used in at least three distinct contexts: (1) for fighting or war, (2) for causing death or sickness, and (3) for escaping revenge or resolving conflicts by payment. Most of the examples documented are songs or formulas with songs, rather than formulas that were only spoken. None involved the use of plant substances or herbs as a medicine.

Songs and formulas for fighting or war were the most numerous and a surprising number involved (the spirit-person) Chickenhawk, evidently because the bird itself was observed to be a good fighter. A typical formula was collected from Henry Hostler in 1901. In this text, Chickenhawk is described as a girl who always remained a child and who never menstruated. She told her brother that a group of men were coming to fight, and then she made medicine to kill them. She had her brother throw a bundle of twigs at her, pulling away the knot that bound them so that none struck her. Then, she used her song, which she sang morning and night, and she entered the battle wearing a skirt of black oak bark (in strips). Thus, she killed a hundred men and was not struck herself, for she

Example 50. Acorn gathering song sung by Phoebe Maddox (Karok)
and recorded by Helen Roberts (appendix 2, F–4).

had made herself invincible. Toward the end of the text, Chickenhawk speaks herself, telling men to use her song and to put twigs
and strips of black oak bark in their hair before they fight (appendix
2, G–1).

Goddard (1904:335) provides a musical transcription of the song,
but it seems to be notated incorrectly[2] and should probably be written as in example 51. It seems likely that the song is supposed to
imitate the voice of Chickenhawk, as its character is similar to that
of other "animal songs" described previously.

Another song of Chickenhawk was collected from Johnny Cooper
(Yurok) in 1907, and this gives the clear impression of a birdcall
(example 52). The singer stated that the song was sung by him before a fight to ensure that he would not be hit, which suggests again
that Chickenhawk's medicine is largely defensive. The bird seems
to have been regarded as a mercurial fighter and a target that was
difficult to hit.

Another medicine song from Chickenhawk was collected from
Phoebe Maddox (Karok) in 1926 (appendix 2, G–15). The original
cylinder was broken, but the singer's comments about the song are
described in unpublished fieldnotes of the collector, Helen Roberts
(1926b). Mrs. Maddox said that she had learned this song from her
uncle, who was born around 1826 and died in 1906. According to
her, Chickenhawk was considered a mean bird that killed any other
bird that came near its perch. The song was to be sung over a gun
or an arrow, which would always kill an enemy when the song was
used. Mrs. Maddox said that she was always afraid when she heard

Example 51. Chickenhawk's song for going to war as sung by Henry Hostler (Hupa) in 1901 (appendix 2, G–1).

Example 52. Song of Chickenhawk for fighting as sung by Johnny Cooper (Yurok) in 1907 (appendix 2, G–6).

the song as a girl, and that one could tell it was a mean song by the way the voice "kind of goes back down [low]."

A fighting song collected from Stone (Yurok) in 1907 employed the "sobbing" style of vocal delivery (example 53). The medicine involved both a spoken formula and a song that were used over bullets, and Stone stated that he got the medicine from a man named George of Rekwoi, who could kill his enemies with a single bullet after using it. No translation of the narrative could be located

Example 53. Song used over bullets before fighting performed by Stone (Yurok) and collected by Kroeber in 1907 (appendix 2, G–3).

among Kroeber's fieldnotes, and the song sounds very much like crying. This musical transcription tends to make the song appear more focused in pitch and more regular in meter than it actually sounds. It is sung (very slowly) three times on the recording and varies slightly each time. The impression of "sobbing" is achieved through a very nasalized vocal delivery and use of tremolo throughout the song.

Other fighting songs had a vigorous character and were more strictly metrical. It seems likely that these were used just before fighting, either to build up one's own aggression or to intimidate an adversary. An example collected from Johnny Cooper (Yurok) in 1907 is labeled "Song sung by person wishing to meet and succeed in killing enemy" and consists of a single phrase spoken (not sung) twenty-two times (example 54). The tempo is very quick and centers mainly on the tone f (175 hz). There is no translation among Kroeber's notes, and the audio quality was so poor that the text could not be transcribed.

Four other fighting songs of the same general type were collected from a man named Ira Stevens (Karok) during the 1920s (appendix 2, G–9, G–10, G–11, and G–12). One was labeled "song to put an enemy off his guard" and its vigorous style makes the song seem very intimidating indeed (example 55). Here again a single phrase is sung more than twenty times on the recording, though in this case the song seems to employ vocables rather than words. The ending pattern, a downward glissando of unfocused pitch, is typical in many types of ceremonial singing.

Although documented examples are quite rare, it is clear that

Example 54. Fighting song from Johnny Cooper (Yurok) collected by
A. L. Kroeber in 1907 (appendix 2, G–8).

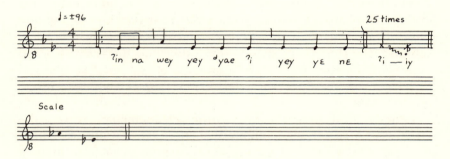

Example 55. Fighting song from Ira Stevens (Karok) collected by
Derrick Lehmer in 1923 (appendix 2, G–11).

spoken formulas were also directly used to cause death, sickness,
or bad luck. There were professional "doctors" who were paid in
advance for making medicine of this type, and Frank Douglas
(Yurok) informed me that there were special places on Red Mountain where they worked. These specialists were also described by
Mary Ike (Karok) in 1940; she said that such a person was called
an *eim* in Karok and that the *eim* spoke his formulas at sundown
(Kroeber and Gifford 1980:267).

One formula for working evil was described by Georgia Orcutt
(Karok) in 1940 (appendix 2, G–19). The text involves a man and
his wife who lived just upstream from Happy Camp. She told him
never to go up on the ridge above there. He did so anyway, and

discovered several nice young girls digging potatoes. He stayed there with one of them for some time. Later, he tried to return to his wife, but she would not take him back. She turned herself and her son into two rocks, and her husband was transformed into a wolf. This medicine was to be spoken over water, such as the river.

The formula is particularly interesting in light of a song that was collected from Phoebe Maddox (Karok) in 1926 (example 56). The recording is labeled "medicine song for anger (about two rocks at Katimin)," but a spoken cue on the tape itself indicates the song was used to ask for help from the two rocks in order to work evil against someone. The song is sung five times on the recording and seems to employ vocables only instead of words. There is a hint of "sobbing" in the singer's voice, and the delivery is quite unfocused in pitch. The song gives the impression of speaking or mumbling rather than singing, especially because the tessitura is rather low (for a female).[3] Here again, the singer adds a brief ending pattern like those heard in ceremonial singing.

Medicine for escaping revenge was also important, and a formula (with song) involving the familiar character Chickenhawk was described by Mary Marshall (Hupa) in 1927 (appendix 2, G–17). Although he kills people frequently, the narrative states Chickenhawk himself will never be killed because he prays like this and burns roots all night. "My enemies will melt away from me," he says. Then he sings his "melting away" song to protect himself from his enemies. Unfortunately, the song was not recorded.

Another formula of this type was described by Mary Ike (Karok) in 1940 and is labeled "formula to protect a person who has committed murder or theft" (appendix 2, G–20). The narrative involves a long-nosed creature that was probably either the mouse, shrew, or mole. Men were waiting everywhere for him. They wanted to kill and eat him, but he dodged them by traveling under the ground. As long as a person calls upon this animal, the formula states, that person can always travel without being seen.

Johnny Cooper (Yurok) had two songs for escaping revenge. Notes at the Lowie Museum of Anthropology indicate that the song in example 57 could also be sung to ward off sickness from the house. The song is sung only once on the brief recording, and it has a spontaneous or aimless quality that suggests it is at least par-

Example 56. Song used to work evil against a person (addressed to two rocks near Katimin) as sung by Phoebe Maddox and collected by Helen Roberts in 1926 (appendix 2, G–14).

Example 57. Song to enable murderer to escape when pursued by the relatives of his victim. Sung by Johnny Cooper (Yurok) and recorded by A. L. Kroeber in 1907 (appendix 2, G–4).

tially improvised. The vocal delivery is more speechlike than sung, but the song employs vocables rather than words. There is no information concerning its mythic origin.

Johnny Cooper's other song for avoiding revenge (example 58) is closer to the basic style that I have called "animal songs." Narrow in range and delivered in a speechlike voice, this brief song is sung thirteen times with slight variations throughout. Here again the rhythm is somewhat unusual. The song seems to be sung in vocables and again no information concerning its mythic source or significance could be located.

The last item considered in this section is a Yurok song that was sung when settlement was paid for a slain person (example 59). In this ritual, dentalium shell money was smoked over a fire while the song was sung. According to Yurok law, this payment by the murderer to the family of the victim wiped the slate clean, and no further grudge could be nurtured (Kroeber 1925:50). Use of this song ensured that if the recipient of the blood money continued to harbor thoughts of revenge, his evil wishes would recoil upon him.

This unusual song is sung eight times on the recording. The bracketed portion consists of Yurok words, but the rest of the song is in vocables. The words are not the same each time, and the text seems to be improvised. Unfortunately, no translation is available, and the poor audio quality makes it impossible to produce an accurate transcription of the Yurok text. There are also some variations in the music, but these are not shown in the transcription given here.

Safety in Travel

Documented examples in this category include a formula for safety in general and others to protect against rattlesnakes or to prevent drowning while traveling by canoe. The former was spoken by Tom Hill (Chilula) in 1905 and is labeled "eagle's medicine for protection from enemies" (appendix 2, H–10). The narrative explains that Eagle traveled far to the north into enemy territory, but he remained unharmed because he carried a certain (unidentified) herb with broad, gray leaves. Later he also traveled to the south, protected by the same herb. The narrative closes with a statement to

Example 58. Song to ward off approach of those seeking revenge for slain relatives. Sung by Johnny Cooper (Yurok) and recorded by A. L. Kroeber (appendix 2, G–7).

Example 59. Song sung when settlement is paid for a slain person. Sung by Sarah Frank (Yurok) and recorded by A. L. Kroeber in 1907 (appendix 2, G–5).

the effect that humans can also travel without fear if they carry the medicine that Eagle used.

Rattlesnakes are common in this area and formulas to protect against them were used by all tribes of the region. An example collected from a Hupa man named McCann in 1901 called upon Wohpekemeu (identified by his Hupa name Yumantuwinyai). In his time, the narrative explains, rattlesnakes had wings and flew about at night, so he needed a medicine to protect him. He saw a bush (identified as *Philadelphus*),[4] broke off a shoot, and used it as a cane. When crossing a prairie, he would whip the air with it, and because of this he never saw any rattlesnakes at all (appendix 2, H–2).

Mary Ike (Karok) also mentioned a formula to keep rattlesnakes away and stated that the text consisted of words that conjure the presence of Hawk, an enemy of the snake (appendix 2, H–11). A similar Yurok formula was described by Joy Sundberg (Yurok) during the 1970s.

Travel by water was also perceived as a significant danger. Formulas to protect a person while traveling by canoe were collected among the Hupa (appendix 2, H–1) and Karok (appendix 2, H–12 and H–13), but most of the documented examples were collected from a single Yurok person, Captain Spott of Rekwoi, on various dates between 1901 and 1909. Each of these is discussed below, as the variety of medicines for water travel known by one individual seems truly impressive and reminds us once again of the richness of the mythology on which these practices were founded.

The first example called upon the Pleiades, who were regarded as a group of sisters who repeatedly fall into the water from the sky,[5] and upon a group of sea monsters who lived in the water at the mouth of the Klamath River (example 60). Kroeber's notes reveal that the sisters and the monsters were both thought to be "bad friends" and dangerous (Kroeber n.d.: Carton 6; Notebook 67, p. 46). The speaker seeks to identify with these beings in what seems to be a rather ingratiating manner, saying, "You won't eat me. I am very mean, too [just like you are]. Let the sea be smooth now. It can get rough again after I return to the river."

These words are spoken in Yurok at the beginning of the recording and again after the song has been sung. The song itself seems perfectly suited for a person who is frightened on rough water. The delivery is very tense and nasalized as the singer hums two short

Example 60. Medicine song used in boat when water is rough. Sung by Captain Spott of Rekwoi and recorded by A. L. Kroeber circa 1906–1909 (appendix 2, H–4).

phrases in a very forceful manner. The tempo is quick, and the song is given five times on the brief recording. Musicians will note that the melodic ambitus is a tritone.

Another medicine described by Captain Spott took a more aggressive approach (example 61). As noted previously (in chapter 3), it was the Yurok deity Pulekukwerek who originally made the estuary at the mouth of the Klamath safe for water travel. In some accounts it is said that he killed these monsters (e.g., Waterman 1920:228), but other texts state that he used a song to make them stop causing the water there to churn. This formula calls upon Pulekukwerek and repeats the story of how he accomplished this. Unlike the previous song, which seems to reflect the singer's nervousness or fear, this one imitates the bold voice of Pulekukwerek as he commanded the sea monsters to be still. Here the psychology of the song seems somewhat different, as it is evidently more of a confidence builder, but both songs appear to be well-suited to the situation.

Example 61. Medicine song from Pulekukwerek for use in boat when water is rough. Performed by Captain Spott of Rekwoi and recorded by A. L. Kroeber circa 1906–1909 (appendix 2, H–5).

Though longer than the previous example, the song in example 61 is not so different in its musical structure, as both songs involve a single melodic idea that is sung at two different pitch levels. In Pulekukwerek's song each part consists of a single tone, first intoned in a long-held note and then attacked from a major second below using vocables in an alternating pattern. As in some of the other notations, relative durations of the long-held notes are indicated through use of tied quarter notes.

The third medicine from Captain Spott resembles the biblical story of the flood (appendix 2, H–6). In this text, the world became covered with water, but two men and two women were saved because they had a boat. Sky Owner gave them a song to sing, and this caused the water to recede.[6] Another formula reminiscent of the biblical flood story was later collected from Karok speaker Mary Ike (appendix 2, H–13).

The fourth of Captain Spott's formulas involves a girl who always went out on the ocean alone (example 62). The words ask that she look after the formulist until he gets back to shore. The text has been translated, "You must look after me. I always get lonesome on the ocean. You must handle me good and help me get back to the shore" (Kroeber n.d.; Carton 6; Notebook 17, p. 47). The song used with this formula is repeated several times on the recording and sung loudly with much tremolo.

Next was a formula which called upon Seagull (example 63). The text merely states that the singer is afraid and doesn't want any trouble on the ocean. It is also noted that Seagull learned the song from the ocean and that Seagull and Ocean were born at the same place, somewhere far across the sea. The song seems to have words but these could not be transcribed owing to poor audio quality.

Finally, Captain Spott (Yurok) had a set of eleven songs for rough water which were originally composed by each of eleven brothers (appendix 2, H–9). There is no information concerning the mythic story behind the songs, but Kroeber's notes indicate that the formula and songs would be used in two situations: (1) launching and beaching one's boat and (2) emerging onto the sea from the mouth of the river and entering the river again. The texts are very similar to some of the others noted previously, including phrases such as, "Take it easy. Handle me good. Take me back on shore. I want to be alive and have a good time. I don't want trouble on this ocean."

Most of these are similar to previous examples in musical style as well (i.e., narrow in melodic ambitus and sung with a speechlike delivery), but two of them are quite different. These have a relatively wide melodic range, descending contours, and a "sobbing" vocal quality. One of them is notated below. The song has no words, only vocables, and there is great dynamic contrast between

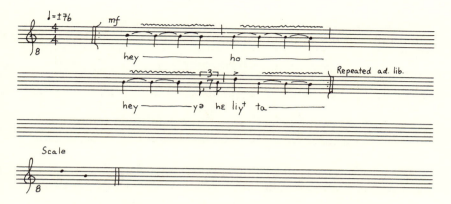

Example 62. Medicine song for rough water from The Girl Who Traveled the Ocean. Sung by Captain Spott and recorded by A. L. Kroeber circa 1906–1909 (appendix 2, H–7).

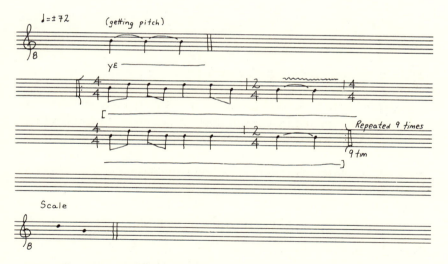

Example 63. Medicine song for rough water from Seagull. Sung by Captain Spott of Rekwoi and recorded by A. L. Kroeber circa 1906–1909 (appendix 2, H–8).

Example 64. Medicine song for rough water from the seventh of eleven brothers. Performed by Captain Spott of Rekwoi and recorded by A. L. Kroeber circa 1906–1909 (appendix 2, H–9).

notes in the upper register (loud) and those in the lower part of the singer's range (soft).

Sports and Games

Examples in this category include types of medicine for (1) a gambling game, (2) a rugged form of field hockey, and (3) wrestling. The most prominent form of gambling in this area is a guessing game that is played by men only, and Kroeber describes it as follows:

A bundle of 25 or 50 slender rods is used, one being painted in the center. These sticks are shuffled, in sight of the opponent, with a peculiar rolling twist, divided behind the back, and then shown, the middle portions concealed in the hands. After some deliberation, and frequent false or pretended starts, the opponent guesses for the hand containing the one marked stick, indicating his decision by pointing past the other hand. If he is right, he wins nothing but the opportunity of playing [dealing]; if wrong, one counter goes to the player [dealer], who shuffles again. (Kroeber 1925:849)

This game was frequently played while relaxing between events at major ceremonials such as the Deerskin Dance or the Jump Dance, and at least three of the elders I interviewed during the late 1970s could remember games played for stakes well in excess of one hundred dollars. Today, the game is played mainly for demonstrations but many young men know how to play and are skilled at singing the songs.

The gambling songs are not covered in this study, but a few comments seem necessary. To begin with, the singing is considered integral to the game and it is the dealer who sings, mainly in order to develop power so he will not be "guessed out" by his opponent. It is also believed that the player guessing can see right through a person who has had sex or alcohol within the last three days. While the dealer sings he beats a five-beat pattern on a frame drum, and (according to expert singers) the solo part is supposed to mesh neatly with this unusual meter and with a bass part sung by others who sit behind him. This is the Indians' explanation; however, it should also be noted that the solo part does not always mesh with drum and bass parts, so that a complex polyrhythm is frequently heard. These quasi-secular songs present some interesting descriptive problems and need to be considered in a separate essay.

Spoken formulas for gambling were undoubtedly known among all tribes of the region. One example that involves crying was explained by Tom Hill (Chilula) in 1905 (appendix 2, I–1). The text involves Mink, who had traveled south to go gambling. He camped one night and sang, feeding the fire all night with limbs from a Douglas spruce. His tears were dropping as he thought about himself and his power. The next day he gambled with his hair wrapper as a stake. He won constantly, and took home a large pack of money after playing for four days straight.

Another formula emphasizes fasting, and this was collected from Georgia Orcutt (Karok) in 1940 (appendix 2, I–2). The text calls upon a poor man who sought to improve his luck at gambling by eating nothing but bulbs, so he went without fish or other fresh foods for a long time. In gambling, he used a song that described his poverty and his abstinence from food. In using this medicine, Mrs. Orcutt states, the gambler must drink no water and eat nothing but acorns and bulbs for about three months.

The Indian field hockey game in this region is a rough sport which combines elements of Lacrosse and wrestling. Three formulas, or possibly versions of the same formula, were collected from three different Karok persons, and each is the story of a pitiful character who was scrawny and covered all over with scabs. It is interesting to consider all of these together, as they illustrate a flexibility that undoubtedly permeated the mythology as a whole, and they also show the role of personal creativity in originating variants of the same idea.

The first two were gathered around 1940. In the text collected from Georgia Orcutt (appendix 2, I–3) there was to be a big game, and two girls were going to marry the winner. Somehow, a weakling covered with scabs got involved in the competition, along with his emaciated dog. Just before the match, the boy and the dog were miraculously transformed. Suddenly the boy was covered with beautiful woodpecker scalps; he then outplayed the competition on the field and married the eldest of the two girls. This formula was to be spoken over the water in which the player bathes before the game.

A similar text was collected from Mamie Offield (Karok) around the same time (appendix 2, I–4). The text involves ten brothers who lived up on the mountain behind Weitchpec. The youngest was small and scabby, and he spent all his time with his dog, which was also sickly. The oldest brother went to play the stick game, but he was beaten. Then, each of the others went to play in turn, according to age, and each was beaten, until it came time for the scabby one to try. He dived into the river and had his sister cover him with a basket, whereupon he became transformed into a handsome man whose hair was tipped with woodpecker scalps. He and his dog won easily.

Several years later (circa 1949–1950) Mamie Offield (Karok) described what seems to be another version of the same formula (appendix 2, I–5). There was a game between a family living at Burrill

Peak and another team from Baldy Peak. The smallest child from the Burrill Peak family grew up with his hands closed. He and his dog were both covered all over with scabs. The family was being beaten in the game, so the scabby boy told his sisters to weave big seed baskets. He bathed, and then covered himself in one of the baskets, from which he emerged miraculously transformed. Then he entered the game and won easily.

A very similar theme is involved in a formula for wrestling described by Mamie Offield (Karok) during the same year (appendix 2, I–6). In this narrative, ten brothers were talking about wrestling with a giant who lived nearby. The smallest sat in the ashes by the edge of the fire. Only after all the others had tried and lost did he get his chance. Then the smallest one stepped up and beat the giant, throwing him into a nearby lake.

Purification from Contact with a Corpse

These formulas were used mainly to purify a person who had handled a corpse, but might also be used to terminate a period of mourning for a close relative who had died. They were spoken in the sweathouse by a specialist who owned the medicine in question and who charged a fee for the service.

Five different versions of one formula for this purpose were collected (e.g., appendix 2, J–1, J–2, and J–3), and an interpretation of the formula is given in chapter 7. Basically, these texts all refer to an argument between several spirit-persons as to whether human beings should die or be allowed to continue living forever. Death became the rule, but ten spirit-persons[7] objected to this and went to live in rocks located at ten different locations along the Klamath River. The one farthest downriver (at Rekwoi) found an herb that would make a human feel better again if he had contact with a corpse or was in mourning, and he gave some of this medicine to each of the other nine spirit-persons. In using this ritual, the formulist called upon each of the ten spirit-persons by name, beginning with the one farthest upriver, and each referred the formulist to the next one until finally the spirit-person at Rekwoi was addressed. He finally provided the medicine[8] and instructions as to how it should be used. After speaking the formula the medicine man bathed the mourner (or contaminated person) in an infusion prepared from the roots of the plant.

A related formula was also collected from John Shoemaker (Hupa) in 1927 (appendix 2, J–5). The setting for this lengthy text is an evil place down on the coast in Yurok territory; this place is along the road that corpses travel on their way to Hell. There was a cannibal who lived there, but he did not get sick because of the medicine he knew. Thus, in spite of his eating the corpses who passed by, he did not get sick because of the herbs he chewed. A mourner comes to him seeking to be purified from corpse contact, but rather than curing him directly, the cannibal directs him to consult another spirit. This one sends him to yet another one, and the mourner thus needs to consult several different spirits, following a trek that takes him from the coast to places far upstream along the Klamath River.

Two quite different formulas were collected from Mary Ike (Karok) around 1940. One called upon Spider,[9] who was born across the ocean (appendix 2, J–6). Spider was often invited to eat while visiting with people during his travels, but he had to decline because he has so much contact with corpses. At one place, he agreed to eat deer meat if he could make medicine first. This not only allowed him to eat but also improved his luck at hunting deer. Madrone leaves are used, and the formula is spoken while these are collected.

The other formula is about a hunter who had killed a deer and returned home to find relatives crying over a baby who had died (appendix 2, J–7). He assisted in burying the corpse, and because of this and other contaminating things he became unable to see any deer tracks while hunting. After making the medicine, his luck returned. The formula is to be spoken over a few sprigs from the bough of a fir tree, and these are placed in water that is drunk by each person attending a funeral.

Miscellaneous Types of Medicine

There are a number of songs and formulas that do not fit neatly into the categories above. Songs intended to drive away rain (or bring sunshine) were collected from three different women. One sung by Phoebe Maddox (Karok) in 1926 (example 65) was said to

Example 65. Song to drive away the rain as sung by Phoebe Maddox (Karok) and recorded by Helen Roberts in 1926 (appendix 2, K–2).

have a text that refers to the bluejay or more specifically to its color. The following translation was given in the collector's fieldnotes (Roberts 1926*b*):

Blue jay tail. Bring it down from upriver. Let's clear it up on top down at the [downriver] end of the world.

On the recording itself, the song seems to be sung only in vocables, but it is delivered in a clipped and harpy voice perhaps intended to resemble the call of the blue jay.

A similar song performed by Mrs. Brigmore (Karok) in the same year refers to the underside of a lizard, presumably to the "bluebelly" lizard that is found locally in countless numbers during the spring and summer (example 66). The following translation was given in the collector's fieldnotes (Roberts 1926*b*):

Lizard breast bring it downriver. Other side clear it up. Sunshine sack open.

Here again, however, the recording does not seem to include all the words given in the translation, and both of these songs (examples 65 and 66) are similar in style to numerous other "animal songs" collected from Karok speakers by Helen Roberts during the 1920s.

A song collected from Ella Norris (Yurok) in 1975 has a distinctly different style (example 67). There seem to be words in the song, but no translation is available. The tonality is rather unusual, as the scale consists basically of an augmented triad. The song is sung only once on the recording, and the pitch level drifts downward

Example 66. Song to drive away the rain (or bring sunshine)
as sung by Mrs. Brigmore (Karok) and recorded by
Helen Roberts in 1926 (appendix 2, K–3).

Example 67. Song to stop the rain sung by Ella Norris (Yurok) and
recorded by Charlotte Heth in 1975 (appendix 2, K–8).

toward the end so the expected major third interval widens to a perfect fourth. A simplified transcription is given in example 67, but sound registrations produced by a melograph provide a very close analysis in Keeling (1982a:413–420).

Although she was Yurok by descent, Ella Norris lived near the border of Tolowa territory and knew several Tolowa songs, among which this one should almost certainly be counted. The melodic contour in example 67 is pendular, and the song has a certain symmetrical quality that is noted in other Tolowa songs (examples 24 and 48) and in Hupa songs for the Flower Dance.

A comparable symmetry of phrasing is also observed in a "song for a young man to improve his looks," collected from Ernest Marshall (Hupa) in 1956 (example 68).

A formula to make tobacco grow quickly was collected from

Example 68. Song for a young man to improve his looks as sung by Ernest Marshall (Hupa) and recorded by Frank Quinn in 1956 (appendix 2, K–7).

Georgia Orcutt (Karok) in 1940 (appendix 2, K–5). This lengthy narrative concerns Tobacco, who was living with a younger brother for whom he provided. The boy adopted a "pet" that grew up into a monster and abducted him. Tobacco followed him across the ocean and rescued him from a bunch of cannibals who were going to cook and eat him.

Georgia Orcutt (Karok) also knew a formula to give self-assurance (appendix 2, K–6). The medicine was originated by a female spirit who was a plant and who had once been ignored by people all the time. This is identified as a form of mint called pennyroyal. "I am going to live alongside the road," the plant said, "so that all the money that travels at night will touch me. I'll always be lucky. I'll be like the sunset glow, which everybody looks at because it is nice and red." When using this medicine, which also makes a person more popular, a person must not drink water for five days.

Part Four

Interpretations

Chapter Ten

Music and Culture History

It is not uncommon to find in the possession of a single group a number of styles, represented in different categories of songs; specific styles that do not seem to have any organic reason for co-existing. . . . In order to characterize the music of an ethnic group, it is necessary to separate the strains that are obviously due to the intrusion of foreign elements or to the survival of old forms from those which make up the bulk of the musical lore. The latter will be more apt to range themselves readily into the picture of a prevalent "style."

Herzog 1935*b*:24

Musical Analysis

When taking a broad view of the world's music, there is a temptation to assume that each culture has a single style. This presumption is very prevalent in ethnomusicology, particularly in studies relating to the music of indigenous or tribal peoples, but in most cases the idea is overly simplistic. Far from being unusual, a multiplicity of styles usually becomes apparent once the music of a given people becomes known in some detail. As applied to North American Indian music, Herzog's model of the musical tradition as a composite has particular validity for culture areas such as the Plains or the Eastern Woodlands, where centuries of cultural interaction led to the formation of truly "international" repertories, but even in northwestern California, where Indian cultures were considerably more isolated before the white invasion, the musical corpus is found to be a complex amalgam comprised of several distinct elements or substyles.

For present purposes, the following styles can be distinguished in the total corpus of recordings collected among the Yuroks and neighboring tribes in the years since 1900: (1) a predominating style of ensemble singing in modern ritual music performed by men, (2) a related but distinct style of female singing in songs for the Brush Dance, (3) an unrelated style of ensemble singing by males or females in the Flower Dance, (4) a type of personal song that seems closely related to the predominant style of male ensemble singing, (5) a type of personal song that borders on actual crying, and (6) a style used in personal songs that imitate the speech or singing of animals or spirit-persons.[1]

Musical transcriptions of examples representing each of these styles have been discussed in previous chapters, where various song types were described in relation to their function or performance context. This chapter characterizes each of the styles in more abstract terms and makes some preliminary assertions about their significance for local culture history and within the broad sphere of North American Indian music. For comparative purposes, cantometrics coding for each of the styles have been provided in appendix 3.

Ensemble Singing by Males in Modern Ritual

The three main dances in modern ceremonial life are the Deerskin Dance, the Jump Dance, and the Brush Dance, and male singers dominate in each of these contexts. The musical style for each dance is immediately recognizable because each has relatively distinctive vocable patterns, characteristic musical textures, and certain other aspects of melody and rhythm that serve as markers. Despite these differences, however, the various genres can also be viewed as variants of one basic style. This is what Herzog calls the "prevalent" style (1935*b*:24) or what Lomax more precisely labels "the core public performance style" (1976:160). The same basic style is also heard in gambling songs and in archival recordings of Kick Dance songs, and there is no significant differentiation between Yurok, Hupa, or Karok versions of it. The following are its basic characteristics (though subject to many exceptions):

1. The vocal delivery often resembles "sobbing," and there is much tension, tremolo, nasality, and glissando.
2. Song texts generally consist of vocables rather than words.

3. The musical texture involves a solo part plus some type of bass part sung by the group.

4. The melodic ambitus is extremely wide (always more than an octave, and often as much as a twelfth).

5. Melodic phrases are typically descending in contour.

6. The solo part typically includes melodic motives of the bass part, especially at the end of phrases, and there is a general tendency for the solo part to begin in a high register, then descend gradually so as to merge with the bass part at the end of phrases.

7. The soloist may chant motives of the bass part ad libitum, and the melodic phrasing of the solo part is generally asymmetric.

8. The melodic form may be strophic or through-composed, but in either case the song typically includes a contrasting (B) phrase or phrase-group sung at a higher pitch level than the (A) section at the beginning.[2]

9. Scales are predominantly anhemitonic and pentatonic.

10. The overall impression is that of an emotional and unrestrained style, often with a strong element of improvisation in the solo part.

While I have focused mainly on vocal quality as the hallmark of this style, the musical texture is probably its most remarkable characteristic from a comparative perspective, as this is perhaps the only style ever documented among North American tribes that can truly be described as polyphonic and contrapuntal. The rarity or nonoccurrence of polyphony in Indian music was the subject of an essay by Bruno Nettl, who reviewed the published literature and concluded that "Indian polyphony, if indeed it exists or existed at one time, has been an extremely elusive phenomenon" (1961:354). Shortly thereafter, Lomax reported that polyphony clearly did occur among the tribes of California (1968:168), but it should also be noted that part singing among Indians of the region was previously mentioned in less well-known sources such as Angulo and d'Harcourt (1931:210–211) and Kroeber and Gifford (1949:68–69).

Different styles of multipart singing have been documented among other California Indians, and to this extent polyphony represents a general characteristic of the region as a whole. In other

traditions, however, the multipart texture seems to be more sporadic or inconsistent,[3] but here the use of counterpoint is absolutely integral and occurs in virtually every genre of ensemble singing by males. The bass part can and does stand alone, musically
speaking, in each of the dances, and it is on this basis that the music
is considered true counterpoint by contrast to drone polyphony
or other forms of multipart singing in which the parts are not so
independent.[4]

Nettl assumed that polyphony was most likely to occur in more
highly developed societies, and scattered evidence of drone polyphony among tribes of the Pacific Northwest prompted him to
speculate that these cultures were on the verge of developing true
polyphony before they were disrupted by whites (Nettl 1961:361–
362). By contrast, Lomax found that counterpoint is typically an
archaic coding that occurred mainly among gathering peoples, particularly those in which females shared equally in food production
(Lomax 1968:166–168). In the western hemisphere, for instance,
he showed that counterpoint was far more prevalent among the
root-gardening tribes of South America than among the hunters and
maize cultivators of North America, and similar findings emerged
from Asia and Oceania, where counterpoint was noted among tribal
peoples but not in more complex societies (Lomax 1968:168).

Generally speaking, the present study confirms Lomax's theory
about polyphony, both in regard to the female contribution in traditional economy and because the counterpoint seems to derive
from a relatively ancient layer of North American culture rather
than a modern one. There is more to be said about the significance
of polyphony in local culture history, but this is best reserved for
a separate discussion to follow.

Female Singing in the Brush Dance

While males tend to dominate in public performance of ritual
music, young unmarried women may perform "light songs" in the
Brush Dance, and this is the main context for public singing by
females nowadays. A girl performs only as a soloist in the Brush
Dance, while men sing the bass part much as they would if a man
were the soloist. This style is closely related to the previous one;

despite the connection, however, it differs from the male performance style in the following ways:

1. There is no trace of the "sobbing" delivery, but rather the voice is clear and more focused in pitch.
2. The girl sings more softly.
3. She performs only as a soloist, and her song does not include motives of the bass part at phrase endings.
4. The melodic range is narrower (an octave or less).
5. The melodic form is less complex, typically consisting of a single phrase-group repeated several times with slight variations.
6. The song often has words, and humorous texts are common.
7. The tempo is more strict.
8. Compared to the more emotional men's songs, the female style gives the impression of being more controlled and more artful or clever; the songs typically include syncopations that gently contradict the emphatic rhythm of the bass part.

Like the predominant male style, this one is shared equally by Indians of Yurok, Hupa, and Karok descent, and its basic characteristics are not differentiated by tribe.[5]

Singing of Males and Females in the Flower Dance

The style of Flower Dance songs is strikingly different and comprises a "foreign" element when viewed in relation to the predominant style. The Yuroks do not have a public ceremony for girls' puberty; thus, their public vocalizing is always in the predominant style or its feminine counterpart. The following composite is based principally on recordings of Hupa singers,[6] but a similar style is heard in Karok recordings[7] and in other girls' puberty dance songs collected among the nearby Nongatl Indians.[8] By comparison with the predominant male style, this one has the following characteristics:

1. The vocal delivery is relaxed, but there is still much nasality and glottalization.[9]

2. The volume is rather soft.

3. The songs are often wordless, but many songs do have words.

4. The musical texture is heterophonic, consisting of a solo part and ancillary parts which are sung more softly and "trail" the lead of the soloist.

5. The singing is always accompanied by a pair of stick rattles which are struck in unison and mark each beat of the music.

6. The melodic contours are undulating rather than descending.

7. The range of the melodies are quite narrow, generally less than a fifth and always within the octave.

8. Pentatonic scales are noted, but three-tone scales are equally common.

9. Both simple meters and complex meters are found, and tempo is rather strict.

10. The enunciation is rather slurred.

11. The songs usually consist only of one or two short phrases, but strophic forms do sometimes occur.

12. There seems to be a preference for symmetrical melodic designs in the Hupa Flower Dance songs; this may include sequential movement, mirror-image relationships, pendular motion, or antecedent-consequent relationships.

Because of their melodic symmetries, the Hupa Flower Dance songs are easy to distinguish from the (more impulsive and irregular) predominant male style and from the simpler "animal songs" to be described later. This tendency toward melodic symmetry is also noted in some of the personal medicine songs that were collected from Hupa persons[10] and from other nearby Athapaskan speakers such as the Tolowa.[11] It is much less evident in Yurok medicine songs[12] or in those collected from Karok speakers.

Personal Songs in a Style Resembling That of Ritual Music

These personal songs are monophonic, but the melodies are otherwise quite similar to those of the solo part in male ensemble singing. The general profile could be summarized as follows:

1. The voice has much glottalization and nasality, whether the singer is male or female, and men's songs often have a "sobbing" delivery.
2. Song texts consist mainly of vocables but may include words.
3. The musical texture is monophonic.
4. The melodic ambitus is extremely wide (always more than an octave, and often as much as a twelfth).
5. Melodic phrases are typically descending in contour.
6. The melodic form may be strophic or through-composed.
7. Scales are predominantly anhemitonic and pentatonic.
8. In contrast to the predominant ensemble style, tempo is usually very slow, and songs in free rhythm are common.

In some cases, these songs have phrase-endings or cadential figures identical to those heard in ensemble singing, and then it seems likely that the personal song was simply conceived in the mode of a ceremonial song or directly influenced by the ensemble style. Thus, for example, a deer medicine song sung by Domingo of Weitchpec in 1906 (example 27) has a cadential figure which is identical to the bass part in a Brush Dance song. Songs in this category were sung by men and women both, which seems particularly significant because this is not a style that females would use in public ensemble singing. Among the examples transcribed here are eight men's medicine songs of this type, and all but two were collected from Yurok singers.[13] Similarly, the present study includes five examples of women's songs which fit into this category, and four of them were sung by Yuroks.[14] This distribution reflects that of the corpus as a whole (see appendix 1), though it must be noted that very few recordings of Hupa personal songs were ever collected. Among the medicine songs collected by Helen Roberts among the Karoks in 1926 there are many examples in the "animal song" style, but virtually none in this style.

Personal Songs That Border on Actual Crying

These songs are primarily associated with wealth medicine and related sweathouse practices, but they were also used in medicine for love, for deer hunting, for safety in rough water, and for making bullets more lethal. Nearly all of the recorded examples were collected from men, but a few recordings performed by a woman named Weitchpec Susie (Yurok) make it clear that the style was also used by women.

Several recordings seem to consist of true crying rather than singing with a "sobbing" delivery. This pertains to recordings collected from Johnny Cooper (Yurok),[15] Jim of Pekwan (Yurok),[16] Julius Marshall (Hupa),[17] Weitchpec Susie (Yurok), and Blind Bill (Yurok). None of these could be effectively transcribed using standard musical notations. Others which could be transcribed, though never quite accurately, include songs collected from Hawley of Meta (example 29), Umiits of Kepel (example 35), Tom Hill (example 36), Weitchpec Susie (examples 37 and 38), and a man called Stone (example 53). These have the following basic characteristics:

1. The vocal delivery clearly resembles "sobbing," with much tremolo, nasality, and glissando.
2. The songs are sung in (unstructured) vocables rather than words.
3. The melodic range is wide (typically an octave).[18]
4. The melodic contour is descending.
5. Although pitches are unfocused and intonation is inconsistent, most songs have scales that are anhemitonic and pentatonic.
6. The tempo is very slow.
7. A sense of meter is quite vague (some songs have changing meters and others border on free rhythm).
8. Phrases are very short.
9. Melodic forms are classified as strophic, through-composed, or litany.
10. The songs give a general impression of being highly emotional and very unstructured or inconsistent from a musical perspective.

Our first observation is that, like the solo songs discussed previously, these crying songs also have a close relationship to the predominant (male) ensemble style. Except for two recordings—those collected from Tom Hill (Chilula) and Julius Marshall (Hupa)—all were collected from Yurok persons. There is little doubt that "sobbing" songs were used in sweathouse training by all tribes of the area, but it may be significant that other types of medicine songs in this style were only collected from Yuroks, even though this may be merely coincidental or an accident of sampling.

Personal Songs That Imitate the Speech of Animals or Spirit-Persons

These songs have been described in chapters 3 and 8, where they are loosely referred to as "animal songs." Most of the recorded examples were collected from Karok speakers,[19] but the corpus also includes Yurok examples[20] and others from persons of Hupa,[21] Tolowa,[22] and Wiyot[23] descent. The basic characteristics of the style are as follows:

1. The vocal delivery is speechlike, but besides having more pitch inflection it often differs from normal speech through presence of nasality, glottalization, or other special mannerisms intended to signify the speech of spirit-persons or animals.
2. In some cases, this "masked" voice is so speechlike that it cannot be transcribed effectively in musical notations.[24]
3. The songs usually have words rather than vocables, though the enunciation is typically rather slurred.
4. The song typically consists of one or two short (symmetrical) phrases that are repeated several times (ten or more on most recordings).
5. The melodic range is very narrow (a fifth or less).
6. The melodic contour is undulating.
7. Songs in which pitches can be discerned usually have very simple scales with only two, three, or four notes (though exceptions occur).
8. Duple meters tend to be most common, and the tempo is usually moderate or slow.
9. The songs have a simple and repetitive character, giving the clear impression of an incantation rather than a "song" as such.

Although songs of this general type were used by every tribe in the region, those with exaggerated raspiness and glottalization were mainly collected from persons identified as Yurok or Wiyot. Those of other tribes typically employed a more "clear" vocal delivery, but were basically similar in purpose and character.

By contrast with the unique polyphonic style discussed previously, these "animal songs" were used throughout much of northern California. In published sources they have been noted among the Yuki (Herzog 1935*b*), Modoc (Hall and Nettl 1955), Yahi (Nettl 1965), and various other tribes of northeastern California (Angulo and d'Harcourt 1931), but there seems to be little doubt that their actual distribution was much wider.

In northwestern California, these songs were eclipsed in the repertory by songs in the predominant ceremonial style, and a similar subordination occurred in areas where the Kuksu religion became important (that is, among various divisions of the Maidu, Miwok, Wintun and Pomo). Thus, these "animal songs" have mainly been noticed and collected among the Sierran groups and among other tribes whose ceremonial life was considerably less specialized.

Fortunately, the musical tradition described here was documented quite thoroughly, and it is mainly due to this that we know so much about these "animal songs" and their use. In other areas, "survivals" such as these were not collected in great numbers, but they probably existed quite late among all the tribes of northern and central California, and from this perspective they might be regarded as the most characteristic type of song in the California region as a whole.

Historical Interpretations

Now and then it seems permissible for the student to leave off his daily association with specific facts and rise above them on the gyroscope of his imagination to discover if a broader view may not give him insights into their relations or alter his conception of their setting in the larger landscape of nature as a whole. . . . The present essay is such a soaring of hypothesis. While it starts from the solid ground of twenty years

of inquiry into the culture and speech of the Califor-
nia aborigines, it pretends no greater validity than
any summary, undocumented, historical reconstruc-
tion may claim.

Kroeber 1923:125

Kroeber's Reconstruction of
Local Culture History

This is the introduction to an early essay in which Alfred Kroeber
tries to produce a summary of California Indian history mainly
through interpreting the geographical distributions of ethnographic
and linguistic data. He relies largely on guesswork, seeking a level
of detail which seems overly ambitious today, and he made several
assertions that we now consider incorrect. Nonetheless, the paper
provides a very useful background for separating comparatively
modern and ancient elements in the musical tradition described
here.

After discussing some of the specific problems involved in this
sort of reconstruction (1923:126–130), Kroeber presents a model of
California Indian history in four stages, summarized here mainly
as they apply to the northwestern part of the state.

In the First Period (2000–1500 B.C. to 500 B.C.),[25] Kroeber en-
visioned a relatively simple and uniform culture throughout the
California region as a whole (1923:130–131). The people of this era
were presumed to be ancestors of the modern Hokan-speaking
tribes (including the Karok), and they subsisted primarily on the
gathering of seeds, especially the acorn, and to a lesser extent on
fish and small game. Besides the war dance (of triumph), the principal dance throughout the whole California region during this era
was the girls' puberty ceremony. Kroeber judges that the sweathouse was probably known during this era, and that religion was
"influenced largely by shamans who derived their power from actual or fabulous animals or celestial phenomena" (1923:131).

The Second Period (500 B.C. to A.D. 500) brought populations
and important cultural influences from areas to the north. Kroeber
estimates that the proto-Algonkian ancestors of the Yuroks and
Wiyots probably appeared in northwestern California during this
era, as did the early Athapaskan speakers whose modern counter-

parts include the Hupa, Tolowa, and Chilula. Shamanism and society were acquiring a different character during this period as is
described by Kroeber.

The shaman's power was no longer derived so much from animals as from
intangible spirits of localities. The novice in the art was aided by older
men in a shaman-making dance. Shamanistic food-supply rites were
slowly being elaborated, especially in connection with the salmon run.
Society remained unorganized as before, but possession of property and
public influence were beginning to be correlated, and marriage was by
purchase. (Kroeber 1923:132)

Most important, Kroeber felt that the new populations entering northern and northwestern California did not bring dramatic
changes in culture but rather had much in common with the various
Hokan-speaking peoples they encountered, particularly because
their migrations were conceived as being very gradual and intermittent processes (1923:132).

It was during the Third Period (A.D. 500 to A.D. 1200), in
Kroeber's view, that Indian cultures of various subregions of the
California area began to become sharply differentiated or specialized. There were continuing influences from the cultures to the
north during this period, and Kroeber summarizes local developments in these words:

In the northwest this local differentiation seems to have been most rapidly
consummated, and to have become quickly established and correspond-
ingly limited in geography. Consequently it is difficult to distinguish this
period and the next in northwest California. The pure type of plank house,
the high esteem of property, exact valuations and laws connected with
property, the use of compulsive formulas in religion, the attachment of
rites to particular spots, the belief in a prehuman race in place of a creator,
all must have evolved to an appreciable degree during the third period.
(Kroeber 1923:134)

Finally, Kroeber describes a Fourth Period (A.D. 1200 to recent
times) in which Indian cultures in various parts of the California
region were consummated or acquired the basic character that they
had when first encountered by whites. In northwestern California,
there were continuing influences from the north Pacific, but in
Kroeber's view the developments during this era were mainly local

in character rather than mere reflections of northern prototypes. This was the era during which the carving of redwood canoes and other technologies were perfected, and various aspects of society and religion were attaining their finished character. As Kroeber writes,

> Treasures or money as such assumed a larger part in life, as compared with merely useful things: dentalium shells from the north, obsidian from the east, ornaments of woodpecker crests obtained at home. The dances, whose esoteric portion remained formulistic, afforded opportunities for the display of much of this wealth, thus rendering unnecessary a potlatch or credit system and perhaps even preventing an introduction of this northern institution which might otherwise have taken place. The wealth in turn gave an added dignity to the festivals and enabled them to take on more definitely their ultimate character of world renewing or new years rites. The intensive localization of ritual, myth, magic, and custom was no doubt fostered in some measure by assignment of economic and legal values to fishing places and nearly all tracts or spots that were specially productive. . . . The idea of spirits as guardians diminished to the vanishing point; disease and cure were thought to be concerned mainly with self-animate pain objects; and shamans of importance were now always women. (Kroeber 1923:137)

This sort of highly detailed analysis of trait distributions has not been prominent in anthropology since the 1930s, and indeed the approach taken in this paper seems more intuitive and much less systematic than Kroeber's later culture element studies as described by Stanislaus Klimek (1935). Nonetheless, the larger outlines of this history are confirmed by more recent research in archeology and comparative linguistics as summarized by Albert Elsasser (1978), though certain corrections or qualifications need to be mentioned.

The archeological evidence deals only with elements of culture that can be surmised from relatively imperishable material remains, and it contradicts Kroeber's reconstruction only to the extent that it seems to imply that the superimposition of northern cultural patterns was more dramatic and not so gradual as Kroeber suggests (1923:132). Excavations conducted during the past fifty years at more than ten different sites revealed ample remains of a marine-adapted culture not so different from that of ethnographic

Yuroks and Tolowas, and radiocarbon analysis suggests that the same basic culture existed continuously in the region since at least A.D. 900. This tends to suggest that the bearers of this culture arrived in northwestern California with their subsistence patterns more or less established. It should be noted, however, that these assemblages yielded certain objects that did not survive into historical times, and Elsasser describes them as follows:

Some aspects of this culture, so far as it is known without excavation in pertinent cemeteries, did not survive into historic times: animal-form clubs and other ground slate artifacts; baked clay objects such as female (fertility?) figurines; and a type of olivella disc beads. For the rest, there is no mistaking a continuity, dating probably from about A.D. 900. (Elsasser 1978:52)

Evidence of an earlier culture was discovered by Richard Gould (1966) in a lower level at Point St. George in modern Tolowa territory. These deposits contained crudely chipped tools markedly different from those found in upper levels at the same site, and they did not include fishing equipment and other woodworking implements that were typical of later assemblages. This earlier toolkit apparently reflects a more ancient, nonmarine-adapted culture and was dated by carbon 14 analysis at 300 B.C. (Elsasser 1978:50). Presumably, these objects might well belong to one of the seed-gathering, Hokan-speaking peoples who populated California during the earliest period in Kroeber's history. To this extent, archeology confirms his speculations, though (as noted) the evidence as a whole tends to suggest that northern populations arrived somewhat later than Kroeber had estimated.

Evidence of comparative linguistics also contradicts Kroeber's notion that the Algonkian- and Athapaskan-speaking peoples both entered the region between 500 B.C. and A.D. 500 (Kroeber 1923:132). Elsasser seems to allow that the ancestors of the Yuroks and Wiyots may have entered the area toward the end of this period, but he strongly denies that Athapaskans could have come so early. Citing Harry Hoijer's lexicostatistical analysis of the Athapaskan languages (1956), he states that this group was probably not present in California or southern Oregon before A.D. 900 and perhaps did not arrive until several hundred years later (Elsasser 1978:50).

The Religious Complex of
the Northern Hunters

*The Indian, whatever his origins, was not one single
people. It can be said that the beginnings lie in a two-
fold ecological adaptation—a sub-Arctic and Arctic
hunting pattern, and a temperate, tropical, and sub-
tropical seedgathering adjustment. There are those
groups which retained the hunting base, and there
were those seed-gatherers who found their way into
agriculture, controlling nature instead of being controlled by it.*

(Spencer, Jennings, et al. 1965:2)

In order to best interpret the northern elements in music and
culture of northwest California—and to describe the special place
of this civilization in the overall sphere of Native American
studies—it seems necessary to take an even broader perspective
on North American prehistory. This requires a summarized
chronological framework that recognizes at least the following basic
periods or divisions:

Paleo-Indian Period (30,000 B.C. through 1500 B.C.)[26]   This is
the period during which the Americas were populated by immigrants who originally came across a land bridge that existed between Siberia and Alaska during later phases of the last (Wisconsin)
glacial period. These paleolithic nomads spread southward over the
American land masses, and two basic ecological patterns gradually
became distinguishable in North America during this phase: (1) an
Arctic and sub-Arctic pattern based primarily on hunting and (2) a
southern adaptation based on seed gathering. In many instances,
the northern hunters retained much of their Asian heritage, and
this was passed on to later cultures, so that not only the Eskimos
but also many Indian tribal groups of the northwest coast, the
Plateau, and even northwestern California show some dramatic
parallels with indigenous cultures of northeastern Asia.[27]

The Aboriginal Period (1500 B.C. through A.D. 1540)   The inven-
tion of agriculture, perhaps by seed-gathering Paleoindians in the
Valley of Mexico, marks the advent of a new period, one that saw
the emergence of distinctly American cultural patterns as opposed

to older Asian ones.[28] Gradually, the cultivation of maize spread northward, so that the Anasazi of northern Arizona had probably developed a settled economy based on maize cultivation as early as the second century A.D. The new lifestyle reached Indians of the southeastern and Woodlands areas at approximately the same time.

Maize cultivation supported the development of the Mayan and Aztec civilizations in Mesoamerica, and these radiated a continuing progressive influence on Indian cultures to the north until around A.D. 1300 (Spencer, Jennings, et al. 1965:286). Meanwhile, a great many Indian tribal groups, particularly those of the northern and western regions, retained a basically paleolithic hunting pattern and associated religious concepts throughout the entire Aboriginal Period.

Historical Period (A.D. 1540 through A.D. 1870)   During this period, Indian cultures in nearly every region of North America were much altered through contact with Euro-Americans. For Indians north of Mexico, the beginning of the period occurred when Coronado and de Soto marched into the southwestern and eastern regions of North America. The presence of whites in North America not only displaced and destroyed aboriginal societies but also stimulated culture growth in various ways. Thus, to give one example, the presence of Europeans and later Americans on the Atlantic seaboard during the seventeenth and eighteenth centuries tended to foster indigenous sociopolitical adaptations such as the creation of large tribes and confederacies (Spicer 1969:11–44).

Similarly, the Spanish introduction of the horse during the 1500s proved to be an important element in the subsequent development of Plains Indian cultures. Before the advent of this technology, the region was barely habitable, and only because of the horse did it become feasible for larger groups of people (many of which had been agriculturalists) to move out onto the Plains and survive there through buffalo hunting. Without the horse (and other more destructive influences), the Plains Indian lifestyles might never have come into existence, and from this perspective one might regard many elements of Plains civilization as relatively recent innovations, even though a distinct connection to the northern hunter complex seems apparent.

Indians of Alaska and the Pacific Northwest were also greatly affected by external contacts that first occurred during the latter half of the eighteenth century (Drucker 1965:189–204), but the Yuroks and other tribes of the northern California region remained isolated for another one hundred years and were among the last in all of North America to be affected by contact with whites.

*The Ethnographic Period (*A.D.* 1870 through* A.D. *1950)*   Our image of North American Indian culture is based largely on information collected during this period. Indians had certainly been described in earlier literature, but some very important sources begin to appear during the 1870s, mainly in the form of diaries and other writings by government agents, travelers, journalists, and other amateurs.

Systematic anthropological research began in the 1890s, stimulated in large measure by a general belief that Indian cultures were disappearing and needed to be documented before they were completely extinct. The Edison phonograph had been patented in 1877, and this not only marked the beginning of research on Indian music but also revolutionized the study of ethnography and linguistics. In many cases, the anthropologists used information gathered during this period to construct images of "traditional" Indian cultures as they existed somewhat earlier in time, but the cultures portrayed in such studies had already been greatly transformed by historical events.

From this chronology it becomes clear that our whole knowledge of North American Indian cultures is biased by historical parallax to an extent that cannot be overemphasized. When we compare the musical traditions of different culture areas, we are actually considering expressions which reflect different historical layers as much as geographical divisions per se. Wax cylinder recordings collected circa 1900 among Indians of the southwest or eastern Woodlands reflect cultures which had received progressive influences throughout the Aboriginal Period and had also been affected by three hundred years of contact with European and American presence. On the other hand, the songs that Kroeber collected from elderly Yuroks around the same date emerged from a culture that had remained relatively isolated throughout the Aboriginal Period and had only recently been disturbed by whites.

It is for this reason that there is such a clear connection between Yurok religious practices and those of other indigenous peoples to the north. Similar beliefs and customs are documented among Eskimos; in various Indian cultures of the sub-Arctic, the northwest coast, and Plateau regions; and even among tribal cultures of northeastern Asia. I refer to a distinctive set of customs and ideas relating to hunting and use of game animals for food. While it takes different forms, a listing of its basic elements from a cross-cultural perspective might include the following:[29]

First salmon ceremony (or seasonal ritual for other game animal)
Propitiation of game (including spoken prayers or other offerings)
Concept that animals are immortal and only lend flesh for humans
Concept that animals are conscious of human intentions
Ritual disposition of unused parts and offal
Sexual and other restrictions to avoid offending game animals
Fear of menstruation and ambivalence toward female sexuality
Institution of the sweathouse for purification

The elements listed above (along with other traits such as facial tattooing of women, the semisubterranean house design, the sinew-backed bow, and shamanism involving extraction of "pains") seem to comprise a relatively unified trait-complex, and from its geographic distribution we can probably state with some confidence that this first emerged among northern hunters of the Paleo-Indian period.

This is not to assert that the music or culture described in the present study dates back to Paleo-Indian times. Rather, influences from the north or northeast probably did not reach northwestern California much earlier than A.D. 500, when ancestors of the Yuroks and possibly the Wiyots arrived in the area. While elements of the northern hunting complex as outlined above have a huge Amerasian distribution, Yurok religion has its most dramatic parallels in much nearer cultures such as those of the Sanpoil and Nespelem tribes of the middle Columbia River as described by V. F. Ray (1932).

Despite these important influences from the north, it is important to recognize that the civilization that took shape in northwestern California during the period between A.D. 500 and A.D. 1500 was also in many respects a local development. It was decidedly Californian in character, and a strong imprint from the early population of Hokan-speaking seed gatherers has persisted to the present day. This local element is very apparent in the musical corpus, and having established this basic historical context there is much to say about each of the vocal styles represented here.

Modern Ritual Music and Related Monophonic Styles

The locally specialized character of Indian civilization in northwestern California is nowhere more apparent than in the predominant style of ritual singing. This highly evolved use of counterpoint is not heard in other styles of California Indian music (though polyphony seems to be an ancient tendency in the region as a whole), and to the extent that it is associated with a distinctive ceremonial system we can probably surmise that it developed rather late. According to Kroeber's chronology, specific elements of the World Renewal complex did not take shape until after A.D. 1200 (Kroeber 1923:137), and there is not much reason to believe that this specialized brand of polyphony developed before that time.

Other elements of the predominant vocal style (wide melodic range, descending contours, nasal delivery, and heavy glottalization) are found in other vocal traditions of the Plateau and northern Plains regions. This style is related to the very forceful vocalizing that would later become dominant in Plains singing as defined for example by Nettl (1954:24–33), and it survives as a subordinate strain in many of the northern repertories. The style can be heard in (for example) some of the Flathead Indian songs collected by Alan Merriam[30] and it may once have been widespread among northern hunters on this side of the Pacific Ocean.

Monophonic songs in this general style and the more exaggerated "sobbing" version were mainly collected from Yurok individuals, and this is especially significant because of the strong likelihood that the ancestors of the Yuroks may have entered northwestern California from the northeast (Elsasser 1978:50). As noted previously, there is a close resemblance between Yurok religious practices and that of some middle Columbia River tribes as described in Ray (1932), and thus it is tempting to speculate that proto-Algonkian ancestors of the Yurok may have migrated along the

Columbia River to its mouth and then proceeded southward along the coast until they came to reside on the lower reaches of the Klamath.

This may have been one of the styles that ancestors of the modern Yuroks brought to the region with them, though the specific symbology of crying in Yurok spiritual life was almost certainly a local development that took shape much later.[31] This was not the only style connected with the northern hunting complex, however, nor was it the oldest.

Songs of Animals and Spirit-Persons

> This [animal song] style represents no doubt one of the oldest layers that survive in present-day Indian music. Cycles of animal stories are common and old in the entire Old World; they must be old in North America too, to judge from their wide spread in the Western hemisphere. The extreme simplicity of songs in such stories suggests that the songs are old also, at least as old as the stories themselves. The technique of singing these songs is, with most of them, startlingly different from that commonly employed in [other types of] American Indian music.
>
> Herzog 1935b:30–31

The ancient character of these songs was first noted in print by Herzog (1935b), and his comments are in general agreement with the conclusions of cantometrics analysis as stated by Lomax (1968: 82–85, and 102–105) and elaborated upon in Erickson (1970:105–117). These later writers move closer than Herzog toward the dramatic assertion that these may have been the type of songs that the ancient Paleo-Indians brought with them from northeast Asia when they originally populated North and South America.

Commenting on the cantometrics coding for Arctic Asia, Lomax writes:

This style is remarkably consistent all the way across Siberia to the camps of the Norwegian Lapps. In most respects it can be viewed as an ancient, worn-down prototype from which Amerindian style could have developed. It is certainly closer to the South American profile than to that of (ethnographic) North America. (Lomax 1968:107)

It is interesting to compare the cantometrics profile for animal songs collected in northwestern California (see appendix 3) with the Arctic Asian profile given by Lomax (1968:107). Generally speaking, the correspondence is very close, but Yurok animal songs are distinctly closer to the Arctic Asian profile than Karok ones. As a group, the Yurok animal songs were found to be more glottalized, lower in vocal pitch, wider in vocal width, and somewhat raspier than their Karok counterparts. The presence of much glottalization strikes me as the most important point of contrast, and it confirms the remote but unmistakable connection between Yurok singing (or heightened speech) and that of other northern hunters.

The Karok animal songs more closely approximate the South American profile as given in Lomax (1968:83). This profile is not only less glottalized than the Arctic Asian one, but it also allows for the presence of polyphony, which we know to be a general tendency in California Indian music. In other respects, the Arctic Asian and South American profiles are rather similar, and they may be interpreted as comprising two different aspects of a single expressive style whose distribution reaches (though not continuously) over the entire New World.

The distinction between these two profiles may well correspond to the ancient split that divided northern hunting cultures from more southerly seed-gathering ones in Paleo-Indian times. From this viewpoint, glottalization can be understood as the single most important signifier of the northern hunting complex. Taking a more local perspective, it seems reasonable to hypothesize that the Karok profile reflects a vocal style that ultimately derives from the seed-gathering, Hokan-speaking Indians who populated California in the earliest period of Kroeber's history (1923).

Finally, it is important to note the mimetic character of the animal songs wherever they occur in the Americas or in northeastern Asia.[32] The northern hunters relied mainly on glottalization in producing different types of masked voice, but various southern styles also serve to signify the speech of an animal, spirit-person, or deity in a similar way. Thus, the different animal songs that survive in many modern repertories provide a glimpse—however partial and obscure—of the earliest religion in the New World.

Hupa Flower Dance Songs and Personal Songs in a Similar Style

We have already noted that these songs comprise a "foreign" element when viewed from the perspective of the predominant style, and it may also be useful to remind the reader that the Flower Dance is performed among the Hupa and Karok, but not by Yuroks, though the latter do have rigorous private rituals that the adolescent girl must observe.

While Flower Dance songs have been collected from Hupa and Karok singers, the following discussion focuses mainly on recordings that were collected from Hupa individuals. Personal medicine songs in a very similar style were collected from Hupa persons and among other Athapaskan speakers such as the Tolowa. The distinctive style heard in these songs is much less evident in medicine songs used by Yurok or Karok persons.

There is a certain disagreement over the history of the girls' puberty ceremony in northwestern California and the Far West, and it seems useful to discuss this style in relation to that issue, particularly insofar as it applies to the local culture described in our study. As mentioned previously, Kroeber considered the girls' puberty ceremony (and the War Dance) to be quite ancient in California. Indeed, he called it "the principal dance" celebrated by the Hokan-speaking seed gatherers who occupied the region as a whole before the ancestors of the Yuroks and Hupas arrived in northwestern California (Kroeber 1923:131).

Driver examined the literature on this subject from a much broader geographical perspective and produced a more detailed, though still admittedly speculative, history of the customs surrounding girls' adolescence in various Indian cultures of western North America (1941). He concludes that some of these observances (food and drink restrictions, scratching taboo, seclusion, and a belief that the girl is unclean) must indeed be extremely ancient and were probably brought to North America by the first immigrants (Driver 1941:60).

Despite the archaic nature of some of these customs, Driver argues that the public recognition of girls' puberty was a relatively late development and one that originated among tribes of the north Pacific coast. Going on the presumption that tribes of that region placed relatively great emphasis on publicization of individual crises or changes of status, Driver hypothesizes that the public girls' puberty ritual originated there and then spread southward. His concluding statement on the subject reads as follows:

> The predominant type of public puberty ceremony originated on the Northwest Coast and proceeded southward mainly by migration, perhaps entirely in the custody of Athapascans. Subsequent diffusion took place in both Northern California and the Southwest. Although the intruders seemed to have been rather successful in imposing their new ideas on the earlier occupants of these areas, they also seem to have absorbed a great deal from the latter. (Driver 1941:62)

The musicological evidence is hardly conclusive, but there is little to suggest that the Flower Dance style is an import from the north. Without attempting a broad comparison of Athapaskan vocal styles, it is worth noting that public songs associated with girls' puberty rituals among the Navajo and Apache are indeed performed in a wide-ranging style that the present study generally identifies with northern hunting peoples. This is perhaps a clue to the comparative recentness of the Athapaskan migration into the southwest region.

By contrast, the Hupa Flower Dance songs (and personal songs in this style) have none of the northern characteristics and indeed closely resemble the animal songs described previously, except for a distinct tendency toward melodic symmetry. This type of singing is probably best viewed as a rather recent Athapaskan elaboration of a style that was present in California since the earliest period.

Chapter Eleven

Crying and Singing

Hakananap-manan grew far downriver across the ocean. He cried constantly. . . . He thought, "When people live here they will remember my tears as long as anyone is alive." He camped at the lower end of the [future] upriver ocean, still crying. His tears began to make a little lake there. He looked at it. He said, "I cry because I want to know how dentalia are to come into being." Then, there were things like fish jumping in the water: they were dentalia; Hakananap-manan had made them. His tears made the upriver ocean Kayurash.

How tears created the upriver ocean
Kayurash, as told in 1902 by a Karok man
identified only as Dick Richards's father-in-law
(Kroeber and Gifford 1980:48–49)

The "Sobbing" Quality in a Modern Song

In previous chapters I have often mentioned a "sobbing" quality that is conspicuous in ritual singing and certain personal songs among the Indians of northwestern California. The sound is difficult to illustrate through musical notations, but its presence is obvious in recordings, and it can be described well enough using words. Typically, the voice is tense and pulsing with tremolo. The pitches are not separately articulated, but slurred together with much glissando. Melodic phrases are mainly descending in contour. The singing is quite nasal, and there is considerable glottalization, by which I mean that the epiglottis is prominent in vocal production. In short, this singing has many of the same phonological characteristics as actual crying, and the resemblance to crying is usually reinforced by the facial gestures of the singers.

This is not a widespread characteristic in California Indian music, but rather it is limited to tribes of the northwestern part of the state. Songs in which the mannerism is present have been recorded mainly among the Yurok, Hupa, and Karok tribes. This is not the only style documented among the three tribes, but recordings in which the "sobbing" quality occurs can reliably be identified as belonging to one of them or to a close neighbor such as the Chilula or the Tolowa. Thus, the mannerism marks the boundaries of the musical tradition and of the distinctive civilization that these tribes came to share.

Modern Indian people do not explicitly mention this subject in talking about their music. The singers and other knowledgeable people whom I knew as friends or interviewed during the late 1970s often described the circumstances under which they received a song, or spoke of what a song meant to them personally, but the "sobbing" quality itself seems to be something that was simply taken for granted, and the importance of it was never apparent to me until several years after I had left the rural Indian community.

The musical symbology described here occurs along a continuum in which highly explicit representations shade by degree into relatively subtle ones. Thus, many early recordings seem to consist of actual crying, while by contrast more modern ones typically reveal a very attractive musical style in which the "sobbing" is little more than a nuance. In concentrating on this mannerism, I do not mean to imply that it suffices to describe the musical tradition as a whole. This is but one of many paths that might have been taken in describing an expressive complex of extraordinary richness.[1]

A Survey of References to Crying in Earlier Writings

As I focused more closely on this aspect of the music, I became more aware of references to crying in the existing literature and even found some very explicit references I had somehow glossed over or missed entirely in earlier readings. It seems useful to begin by reviewing these passages, both to assure the reader that we are not dealing only with my own subjective impressions and to provide some background for discussing the interpretive approach taken in this study.

The earliest writer to mention crying explicitly was Stephen

Powers, who may be remembered as a journalist who traveled through northern California in 1871. Powers was impressed by the intense emotion that typified Indian spiritual practices among the northwestern tribes, and he left this poignant image of a Karok man crying while he gathered wood for the sweathouse fire.

All this time he is weeping and sobbing piteously, shedding real tears, and so he continues to do while he descends, binds the wood in a fagot, takes it upon his back, and goes down to the [sweathouse]. . . . When asked afterward why he weeps when cutting and bringing in the sacred fuel, if he makes any reply at all, it will be simply, "For luck." (Powers 1877 [1976]:25)

This description points up the difficulty of distinguishing actual crying from singing that resembles crying. Powers clearly implies that this was real crying that he witnessed, but some of the sweathouse songs discussed in chapter 8 (see "Wealth") sound very much like crying, even though they were recorded during interviews with white anthropologists. From a descriptive viewpoint, there is no clear border between songs and what appears to be actual crying in these early recordings (and the boundary between singing and speech in animal songs is equally blurred).

The first to mention "sobbing" in relation to Indian music was Jaime de Angulo (Angulo and d'Harcourt 1931), who described the vocal quality of Indian music in northwestern California as follows:

The Yurok, Hupa, and Karok tribes form this cultural province. They do not sing at all like the others. The auditory effect is totally different. The rhythm is quite marked. At the end of each phrase, they breathe the air noisily, exactly as if they were sobbing. The women sing in an incredibly high and flutey voice. The men often make use of their head voice. (Angulo, in a recent translation from the original French version by Garland [1988:15–16])

Although Angulo clearly mentions sobbing, he also seems to be referring to some sort of cadential figure rather than to a general in the singing,[2] and for this reason the exact meaning of his remark has never been clear to me. It seems possible that he is commenting upon the bass pattern which becomes particularly conspicuous at the end of phrases in Brush Dance songs.

A few years later, Kroeber also describes the music by reference to its distinctive vocal quality and affective characteristics. His impression clearly coincides with my own, even though he does not mention "sobbing" or "crying" explicitly.

A relatively uniform style seems to prevail over most of California and probably Nevada. . . . In the northwest, however, a different style is patent: the voice is held whiningly plaintive, the volume swings back and forth between forte and piano instead of being kept relatively constant, and there are long descending pitch glides. The effect is that of a deliberate endeavor to express a mood or feeling tone, and there can be little doubt that analysis will show a structure different from that of the music of most of California. (Kroeber 1936:113–114)

The last comment reveals Kroeber's presumption that statements about vocal quality were somehow less reliable or less meaningful than what could be shown through analysis of scales, rhythmic units, formal structures, and other elements of musical style that can be schematized or quantified in a relatively direct fashion. As noted in chapter 1, this type of thinking was very prevalent in ethnomusicology of the 1930s, and it was perhaps not until the advent of the cantometrics methodology (Lomax 1968) that vocal quality began to receive due weight in cross-cultural music analysis. As the present study hopes to show, this aspect of vocal music also has much promise for modern interpretive works following the generalized sort of semiology advocated by Geertz (1973, 1983), and (personally speaking) it strikes me as rather ironic the extent to which modern thinking in ethnomusicology has become so closely aligned with the "gut feelings" that Kroeber distrusted as unscientific.

Kroeber's assertions relating to actual crying in Yurok religion form an important element in his characterization of Yurok culture in opening chapters of his *Handbook of the Indians of California* (Kroeber 1925) and other writings. Like Powers before him, Kroeber saw crying mainly as a product of emotional intensity, but Kroeber probed more deeply into the purpose and character of this medicine making. As the following passage shows, he viewed it mainly in relation to the quest for wealth.

The persistence with which the Yurok desire wealth is extraordinary. They are firmly convinced that persistent thinking of money will bring it. Particularly is this believed to be true while one is engaged in any sweat-house occupation. . . . Direct willing, demanding, or asking [for dentalia shell money] are a large element in all the magic of the Yurok, whatever its purpose. Saying a thing with sufficient intensity and frequency was a means toward bringing it about. They state that at night, or when he was alone, a man often kept calling "I want to be rich," or "I wish dentalia," perhaps weeping at the same time. (Kroeber 1925:41)

This passage also makes it clear that Kroeber distinguished this type of weeping from "natural" crying (as an expression of grief or pain) and regarded it as a gesture that was purposefully cultivated by the Yuroks.[3]

If Kroeber's words on the wealth quest seem somewhat disparaging, the interpretation of crying in Erikson's psychoanalytic study of the Yurok (1943) is even more offensive from an Indian perspective. Basically, Erikson argues that there is a direct causal relation between early childhood experiences and salient elements of Yurok culture and personality. He focuses mainly on actual crying in private medicine rituals, but also makes the following comment about Yurok singing:

Yurok songs, too, in their content as well as in their phonetics seem to be cries of desire and longing and in this are quite different from the martial cries of the Sioux. (Erikson 1943:293)

Erikson describes crying in Yurok religious life as regressive behavior and regards it as a deliberate activation of infantile crying (1943:281). He notes that the Yurok child is nursed for a maximum of one year, which Erikson says is rather brief by comparison with most other American Indian peoples, and he also states that the Yurok child is also encouraged to creep at a particularly early date (1943:285).

According to him, these and other infantile crises have traumatizing effects on the child, and it is due to this that the adult Yurok interacts with the spiritual world much as an infant relates to its mother. Thus Erikson views the crying in Yurok spiritual life as a gesture that is derived from and directly parallel to infantile feelings of helplessness and frustration. In his words,

Institutionalized crying . . . can only be explained in connection with Yurok child training. . . . A deliberate activation of infantile crying, it is, like all regressions, full of ambivalence. (Erikson 1943:281)

The range of Erikson's other conclusions concerning the cultural effects of early weaning are perhaps best illustrated in the following passage, though he touches on other subjects not mentioned here.

The "object" relation to the mother or both parents, as built up during the oral stages, contributes the following relations of the Yurok to the beings surrounding him: (1) ambivalent avoidance of women and their houses, possibly with . . . a fear of being held and weakened; (2) a displacement of preambivalent trust into substitute parents behind the visible world from whence an eternal supply is flowing; and (3) anarchic mistrust of earthly parent substitutes, such as political officials. (Erikson 1943:294)

It is truly impressive what a symphony of interpretation could be generated from Erikson's limited acquaintance with Yurok people, but not at all surprising that—when all is said and done—his conclusions so closely match the subjective impressions which Kroeber seems to have had toward these people. To begin with, Erikson's analysis was based mainly on Kroeber's portrait of the Yurok in opening chapters of the *Handbook of the Indians of California* (Kroeber 1925) and on interviews conducted with Kroeber's contacts during a brief visit to Yurok territory. Moreover, a comment in the preface of Erikson's paper states that the essay was indeed written under Kroeber's continuing guidance (Erikson 1943:iii).

Thus, one might say that what Erikson produced was actually a psychoanalysis of Kroeber's image of the Yuroks, rather than of the Indians themselves. Even in the brief quotation above, there are distinct traces of Kroeber's response in each of the assertions, specifically: (1) a male-biased interpretation that is evident throughout Kroeber's writings, (2) a distrust of sacred concepts in favor of secular (particularly economic) explanations, and even possibly (3) a resentment that was felt by Kroeber because some of the Yuroks did not accord him the respect to which he was accustomed.

Crying and Transcendence

Looking at Erikson's essay in retrospect, the dangers of imposing an overly determinant style of cultural interpretation become embarrassingly clear. In the present study, I have tried mainly to interpret the "sobbing" quality in contemporary songs by showing its relationship to the larger sphere of medicine making from which it emerged. The narratives reviewed here have shown much about its meaning, and here I want to recapitulate this information in a more focused manner.

To begin with, let us consider the contexts in which crying occurred. Crying as a textual motive is mentioned most often in formulas for wealth, particularly in texts relating to use of the sweathouse or the high country. The same may be said for songs in which the "sobbing" quality is evident; these are mainly prominent in wealth medicine or in the collective rituals for World Renewal, even though they do occur often in other, more directly functional types of medicine making.[4] To this extent, we can say that crying belongs to a relatively abstract sphere of the religious life, rather than occurring in those areas where the sacred touches the practical sphere more directly. Thus, the gesture operates on a different level from other symbols and representations in the mythology of medicine making. We might even regard this as an archetypal symbol: rather than conjuring a specific mythic event, this one represents the empowering principle on which the entire system of medicine making depends.

Every medicine formula or song described in this study is basically symbolic in character. Each is a reenactment of something that an animal or spirit-person did in the period before human beings existed, and taken collectively they comprise a matrix through which nearly every element of the natural environment becomes imbued with some sort of mythological significance. This forms the basis for all native science and technology.

The imagery is very rich, especially when one considers that the 216 items mentioned here probably represent only a small fraction of the medicine formulas and songs that actually exist or existed. Most important, the human contribution to this imagery is categorically denied, and the belief that the songs and formulas (and rituals) were only "given" to human beings, rather than invented by them, is fundamental.

The matrix supports a continuing connection between human beings and the mythic (prehuman) world, and the natural landscape is the physical locus of this symbology. The high country has a special importance in this relationship, and during the late 1970s an elderly Yurok woman named Ella Norris described its signifi- cance in these words:

Red Mountain? Doctor Rock? That's our Holy Land. Everything we done, we went there, for prayer. They'd go there for different things. If you wanted to be a good stick player, or a gambler, [or whatever]. Different places, too. Not just right on Doctor Rock. Doctor Rock is just a place for Indians, for a woman or man that wants to be a doctor. Just like a white man doctor [there are different kinds of doctor]. Some of them is for surgery, [and] some of them is for something else. Well that's the same thing. They go there [to Doctor Rock], and they get their degree. Not only for Indian doctor. Some of them got a special prayer for boils, or for choke, and some of them used to get poisoned. Their stomache would swell up. They got a special song for that. Or a prayer. Or your eyes get sore. Or just a million things. They learn that up there. (interview at Cres- cent City, November 13, 1979)

The relationship between early medicine making and modern Indian thought concerning the nature of singing was still very ap- parent during the late 1970s. Singers I knew virtually never stated that they had composed a song themselves. Sometimes a song was said to have been learned from another singer, but otherwise it was usually described as something that came miraculously, from out- side the person, in a relatively complete form.

A typical set of comments were those given by Elmer Jarnaghan (Hupa), after I had asked the (purposefully) leading question "How do you make up all these songs, anyway?" First he said,

I would dream about a dance somewhere. That's the way I make up a song. I would dream they were having a dance, and I would hear a song. I'd learn the song from that. (June 29, 1979)

He went silent for a while—remembering something—and then he said,

Once, when they were having a Brush Dance, I went up to the summit. Me and my son. We went up to salt cattle. We were coming back. I was walking down the trail, leading my horse, and a song came to me. A Brush Dance song. So I sat down next to the trail and sang. I sang that song down there that very night. A lot of people used to tell me, "You must make them songs up all the time." I says, "No. They just come to me."

Later during our talk, Jarnaghan told me how he received a certain Brush Dance song when he was down in the pit with Abraham Jack (Hupa), and they were running out of fresh songs to use in a dance. This was obviously an experience he treasured greatly.

Abraham says "I got just one song left, and I'm saving that for the last dance." So we started dancing, and we sang. And he sang the one he was going to save. And the song I was going to sing for the last dance, after a while I sang that too. I had no more songs. I was done. Then, the Matilton side came in, and I was sitting there under a locust tree. I was thinking to myself, "What am I going to say?" Then—to tell the truth—I could actually hear a song. It sounded like singing from way up in the air. Then Ike Spencer come along and says it's time to get ready. And I went down, and I started getting ready, and I sang. (June 29, 1979)

Sometimes, a person might even regard the question of personal creativity as an insult to the ancient pedigree or genuineness of a song. Once when I was careless enough to ask my friend Frank Douglas (Yurok) whether he had made up a certain animal song he had just sung, the old man looked at me like I was a fool and said,

Well Jesus Christ I didn't make songs a million years back. That song been going on a million years probably. You see, this damned continent wasn't made yesterday. (June 14, 1979)

Statements about the sacred provenance of songs were also given by younger singers in the community. For example, during an interview conducted by Charlotte Heth at the University of California at Los Angeles, Loren Bommelyn (Karok and Tolowa) performed a song and then said,

That song came to me when I was sitting by the riverbank. I used to have a favorite place that I used to sit by the river. It washed away now, but it was up on a high bank. . . . And I would sit up there, and I'd think. And I'd look across the river, and I'd look up on the mountain, and at the redwood trees, and watch the river go by. And these deer would come down—very seldom, but they do. And they would come down so gracefully. And [the song] says that the deer walk so graceful, and when he listens his ears go just like this. And the rhythm [of the song] is just like the rustling of the river when I was there. (Bommelyn et al. 1977)

While this statement seems to allow a certain element of personal creativity, the song is clearly conceived as a representation, and the key phrase here is "That song came to me." The idea that a song is something composed or crafted in the western sense is utterly foreign to the tradition.

Returning to the specific question of the "sobbing" quality in modern songs, we find that its meaning is much illuminated by looking more closely at references to crying and how it occurs in some of the early narratives described previously. To begin with, it was clearly regarded as a method for initiating contact with the *wo'gey,* and this is illustrated nicely in the formula in which Wohpekemeu explicitly tells humans to cry and think of him if they want his help (Kroeber 1976:308). Other narratives show that crying was a medium through which the spirit-persons themselves obtained power to transform and create things. Thus, in the quotation cited at the head of this chapter, the Karok deity Hakananap-manan created an ocean that was filled with dentalium shells, simply by crying and visualizing it (Kroeber and Gifford 1980:48–49). Similar instances of crying with fabulous results are mentioned in other formulas collected from Yuroks (Waterman 1920:270) and from Hupa speakers as well (Golla, in press).

In chapter 4, we saw that crying played a very similar role in the medicine making of a male aristocrat (Sregon Jim's ancestor) and a female shaman (Fannie Flounder). In both cases, crying served to intensify their ecstatic experiences, preparing them to receive whatever vision or sign of sacred contact would be given. But perhaps even more important from the standpoint of crying as a collective symbol it tended to validate their experiences in the eyes of others. When people saw them coming down from the high country in tears, they knew that authentic spiritual contacts had taken place.

Even normal crying had magical properties in this belief system, a fact that was perhaps best illustrated by the text in which a female spirit-person began to cry because she was lost, then discovered that her crying was a powerful love medicine (Kroeber and Gifford 1980:270–271).

Thus while any song or medicine formula can be considered to be symbolic or representational in character, crying represents the connection between humans and spirit-persons in a more general way. This is the act that somehow came to symbolize the very miracle upon which the entire system of medicine making depended.

We have previously talked at length about the placatory spirit which permeated the World Renewal rituals and even the medicine making of individuals. The Indians were apologetic toward the animals whose flesh they borrowed, and they were sorry for corrupting the world in general. They saw themselves as the weakest and sole polluting element in a world that was otherwise "perfectly clean." But crying is not a gesture of weakness nor even of shame, so much as a movement toward ecstasy. And if you ever have the chance to see a Deerskin Dance or a Jump Dance in person, and the men seem to be crying, this is what it means: The singer is not only asking for help, but also being transformed. For the brief duration of a song, he is becoming more like a spirit-person himself.

Appendix 1
List of Recordings Considered
in this Study

A. Tape duplicates of wax cylinder recordings at the Robert H. Lowie Museum of Anthropology (University of California, Berkeley).

Tribe	Collector	Date	Catalogue Numbers
Yurok	Kroeber	1902	24–545 through 24–555
Yurok	Kroeber	1906	24–800 through 24–909
Yurok	Kroeber	1907	24–974 through 24–1034
Yurok	Kroeber	1907	24–1132 through 24–1151
Hupa	Goddard	1900	24–1699 through 24–1703
Hupa	Goddard	1901	24–1722 through 24–1731
Whilkut	Goddard	1908	24–1773 through 24–1794
Chilula	Goddard	1908	24–1795 through 24–1855
Tolowa	Goddard	1905	24–1856 through 24–1870
Yurok	Waterman	1909	24–1871 through 24–1980
Yurok	Kroeber	1909	24–1891 through 24–1905
Wiyot	Kroeber	1923	24–2518 through 24–2544
Karok	Lehmer	1926	24–2709 through 24–2719
Yurok	Lehmer	1927	24–2720 through 24–2742

B. Tape duplicates of wax cylinder recordings of Karok songs collected in 1926 by Helen Roberts and obtained from the American Folklife Center, Library of Congress (377 items).

C. Tape recordings collected by Frank Quinn at the Robert H. Lowie Museum of Anthropology (University of California, Berkeley).

Tribe	Date	Catalogue Number
Yurok and Hupa	1956	24–112
Yurok and Hupa	1956	24–113
Tolowa	1955	24–117
Hupa, Karok, Tolowa	n.d.	24–120

D. Tape recording of Yurok songs collected in 1951 by R. H. Robins and partially described in Robins and McLeod (1956).

E. Tape recording of Hupa songs collected in December 1953 by Mary Woodward and available at the University of California (Berkeley) Language Laboratory (MA 022).

F. Yurok and Tolowa songs recorded by Charlotte Heth in 1975 and available on the commercial disk entitled *Songs of Love, Luck, Animals, and Magic* (Heth 1978).

G. Thirty tape recordings collected by Richard Keeling between 1978 and 1980 and featuring the following individuals: Frank Douglas (Yurok), Herman Sherman, Sr. (Hupa), Elmer Jarnaghan (Hupa), Alice Pratt (Hupa), Ella Norris (Yurok), Fred Davis (Hupa/Chilula), Georgina Trull (Yurok/Karok), and Alberta Sylvia (Yurok) and other members of the Indian Shaker Church at Johnson's.

Appendix 2
Inventory of Formulas and Songs for Use by Individuals

A. Birth and Child Rearing

A–1. Formula from Wohpekemeu for use at childbirth, spoken by Mack of Weitchpec (Yurok) between 1901 and 1907 (Kroeber 1976:281–283). See chapter 8.

Note: Kroeber (1976) also includes or mentions other versions of the formula as spoken by Jack of Saint's Rest (1976:327), Charlie of Murek (1976:353–354), Jack of Murek (1976:360–363), Opn of Sregon (1976:375–376), Billy Werk's wife (1976:474), and Captain Spott of Rekwoi (1976:424).

A–2. Formula for a woman unable to give birth, spoken by Opn of Sregon (Yurok) between 1901 and 1907. A literal translation of the original Yurok title is "medicine for becoming alive" (Kroeber 1976:370). See chapter 8.

A–3. Formula for baby with cramps, spoken by Wets'owa of Pekwan (Yurok) between 1901 and 1907 (Kroeber 1976:410). See chapter 3.

A–4. Formula for pregnant woman to make fetus small, spoken by Mary Marshall (Hupa) in 1901 (Goddard 1904:275). See chapter 8.

A–5. Formula for pregnant woman to make fetus small, spoken by Mary Marshall (Hupa) in 1901 (Goddard 1904:276–277). See chapter 8.

A–6. Formula to ease childbirth, spoken by Mary Marshall (Hupa) in 1901. This is another version of the formula in which Wohpekemeu impregnates a woman and invents childbirth in order to escape revenge from her brothers (see also A–1). He uses ashes from the fire to make the birth easy. These are placed in the woman's mouth and rubbed across her abdomen (Goddard 1904:278–279).

A–7. Formula for birth of first child, spoken by Mary Marshall (Hupa) in 1901 (Goddard 1904:280–285). See chapter 8.

A–8. Formula to make an infant grow fast, spoken by Emma Lewis (Hupa) in 1901 (Goddard 1904:286–287). See chapter 8.

A–9. Formula to make a baby grow up strong, spoken by Emma Lewis (Hupa) in 1901. This formula invokes an old woman who lived with her grandson. He was working on arrows, and threw little scraps of deer sinew into a spoon basket. A small baby came out of the basket and the old woman steamed it using medicine made from small Douglas spruce trees (Goddard 1904:288–291).

A–10. Formula to ensure long life for an infant, spoken by Emma Lewis (Hupa) in 1901 (Goddard 1904:292–298). See chapter 8.

A–11. Formula to protect children in strange places, from Emma Lewis (Hupa) in 1901 (Goddard 1904:299–304). See chapter 8.

A–12. Formula for childless woman to have child, spoken by Billy Werk's wife (Yurok) in 1906 (Kroeber 1976:474). See chapter 8.

A–13. Formula to make baby stop crying, spoken by Ann of Espeu (Yurok) between 1901 and 1907 (Kroeber 1976:456–460). See chapter 7.

A–14. Song to make small child walk soon, from Phoebe Maddox (Karok) in 1926. This is the song that Deer sang to her children so that they would walk around as soon as they were born. The words have been translated: "Something [is] up on the hill; something [is] up on the hill" (Roberts 1926*b*). The original recording is at the American Folklife Center,

Library of Congress (HHR 46d); however, the wax cylinder was broken and no tape duplicate could be prepared.

A–15. Formula for steaming a child so that he will grow up wealthy and brave, spoken by Emma Frank (Hupa) and written by Edward Sapir in 1927. Thunder discovered a baby who had been living under the wall of his house. This was a plant that could be used for making children strong and protecting them against sickness or curses. The substance is only identified by its Hupa name (Golla, in press: MS pp. 179–182).

A–16. Formula for mother whose milk ceases to come, from Georgia Orcutt (Karok) between 1940 and 1942. The formula is only mentioned and not explained. It is spoken over medicine from a plant that exudes white juice, but not milkweed (Kroeber and Gifford 1980:263).

A–17. Formula used when baby eats acorns for the first time, spoken by an unidentified Karok person between 1940 and 1942. The formula is only mentioned and not explained (Kroeber and Gifford 1980:265).

A–18. Formula from Mink to make fetus small, spoken by Mary Ike (Karok) between 1940 and 1942 (Kroeber and Gifford 1980:282). See chapter 8.

A–19. Formula from Absunkarax to make fetus small, spoken by Mary Ike (Karok) between 1940 and 1942. This formula addresses a large snake or water monster who eats great quantities and gets fat but manages to feel light after making medicine with a small black rock. The formula is spoken over a cup of water into which sand has been poured, and the water is then given to the pregnant woman to drink (Kroeber and Gifford 1980:284–285).

A–20. Formula from Dog to make fetus small, spoken by Mary Ike (Karok) between 1940 and 1942. The formula calls upon a female dog who eats much but always stays thin and gives birth easily. It is spoken over a cup of water into which wild oat leaves have been added, and the water is then given to the pregnant woman to drink (Kroeber and Gifford 1980: 283–284).

A–21. Formula to ease labor pains, spoken by Mary Ike (Karok) between 1940 and 1942 (Kroeber and Gifford 1980:284–285). See chapter 8.

A–22. Formula for childbirth, spoken by Mary Ike (Karok) between 1940 and 1942 (Kroeber and Gifford 1980:285–286). See chapter 8.

A–23. Formula to enable baby to eat the juice from deer meat, spoken by Mary Ike (Karok) between 1940 and 1942. A couple had a little son who was constantly crying, so they decided to look for medicine. The man found myrtle leaves, pounded them up, and mixed the paste with juice from cooked deer meat. This mixture was fed to the child and rubbed all over him, after which the baby was relieved. Later he was fed the juice of the deer meat, and finally the meat itself (Kroeber and Gifford 1980:287).

B. Sickness and Curing

B–1. Formula and song to purify house after sickness within, collected from Stone (Yurok) in 1907. Formula not translated. Recording at the Lowie Museum of Anthropology (24–1147). See chapter 8, example 25.

B–2. Song used in doctoring (gotten in a dream), collected from Mary Grimes (Tolowa) in 1903. Recording at the Lowie Museum of Anthropology (24–1863). See chapter 8, example 24.

B–3. Formula for curing a person who is thin and sickly, spoken by Tskerkr of Gold Bluff (Yurok) between 1901 and 1907. An herb doctor is traveling along the coast and following someone. He finds the person at Sumig (Patrick's Point) and doctors him in one of three houses that have since become rocks. The formula is spoken while steaming the sick person using parts of a plant with white flowers found growing in the coastal sand (Kroeber 1976:193–195).

B–4. Formula from Frog for wounds, from Billy Werk of Weitchpec (Yurok) between 1901–1907 (Kroeber 1976:246–249). See chapter 7.

B–5. Formula from Buzzard for stomach sickness, spoken by Domingo of Weitchpec (Yurok) between 1901 and 1907. Buzzard ate anything he found, and after a while he became weak and sickly from this. A plant spoke to him as he traveled on Bald Hills, and he used this as medicine to doctor himself (Kroeber 1976:313–314).

B–6. Formula of the Rattlesnake woman for curing, spoken by Wets'owa of Pekwan (Yurok) between 1901 and 1907. A person from Wohtek was sleeping in the sweathouse and noticed something on his belly. Later, two children came and said that they wanted him to come and meet their mother. He went and learned that these were his children, conceived when their mother was resting on his belly. She was Rattlesnake (Kroeber 1976:408–409).

B–7. Formula for stomach sickness and vomiting, spoken by Wets'owa of Pekwan (Yurok) between 1901 and 1907 (Kroeber 1976:409). See chapter 3.

B–8. Formula for wounds made by flint arrowhead, spoken by McCann (Hupa) in 1901 (Goddard 1904:328–331). See chapter 8.

B–9. Formula for green vomit sickness, spoken by Emma Duskey (Hupa) in 1901. This formula was given by Sun, whose wife was Earth. While pregnant, she got sick and began vomiting green stuff. He made medicine with a cup of hot water into which alder roots had been dropped (Goddard 1904:340–345).

B–10. Formula for spoiled stomach, spoken by Emma Duskey (Hupa) in 1901. Yumantuwinyai (a Hupa equivalent of Wohpekemeu) traveled all over the world and ate anything he found along the river, even dead things. He got sick and died because of this. Later he used yellow pine to make a medicine that restored him. He scraped off the inner bark and prepared an infusion that he drank and rubbed on his arms and legs (Goddard 1904:346–350). See chapter 8.

B–11. Formula to prevent or heal fighting wounds, spoken by Tom Hill (Chilula) in 1905. This concerns a woman who made medicine to protect her brother. Others came to fight him. She cut his hair wrapper and tied it with something else.

She threw ashes from the fire outside. When they came, she prayed to a flint that nothing would penetrate him. She also makes medicine for those who have been shot. She uses ashes to make a mark across their upper arm and speaks the formula over the mark (Goddard 1914*b*:346–347).

B–12. Formula for nettles, spoken by Jerry James (Wiyot) in 1922. This formula concerns a child named He-Grows-Slow. His mother left him with his father, and the baby would not stop crying. Frustrated, the father placed nettles in the baby basket and ignored the crying. When the mother returned, she blew her nose and rubbed mucous all over the baby, and this made him stop crying (Reichard 1925:143).

B–13. Song for doctoring a sick dog, collected from Pete Henry (Karok) by Helen Roberts in 1926. Notes and translation in Roberts (1926*b*). Recording at the American Folklife Center, Library of Congress (HHR 13b). See chapter 8, example 26.

B–14. Song sung if one gets anything in the eye, collected from Pete Henry (Karok) by Helen Roberts in 1926. This was the song that Bullfrog sang when he got something in his eye (Roberts 1926*b*). Recording at the American Folklife Center, Library of Congress (HHR 17e). Not transcribed. See chapter 8.

B–15. Formula for internal sickness, spoken by Emma Frank (Hupa) and written by Edward Sapir in 1927 (Golla, in press: MS pp. 171–173). See chapter 7.

B–16. Formula for sickness, spoken by Jake Hostler (Hupa) and written by Edward Sapir in 1927 (Golla, in press: MS pp. 174–175). See chapter 8.

B–17. Formula for person who became sick from having neglected an elderly relative, spoken by Georgia Orcutt (Karok) between 1940 and 1942. The illness comes whenever the deceased person thinks about how he or she was neglected while living (Kroeber and Gifford 1980:268).

B–18. Formula to ease suffering when choking on fish bones, spoken by Mary Ike (Karok) between 1940 and 1942. This formula calls upon an old woman who ate the dirt that collected when people sweep the ground. The user says, "I guess you are mad because they are not feeding you enough. I guess that is why you made this person choke." This was spoken over a cup of plain water, which was then drunk by the sufferer (Kroeber and Gifford 1980:287–288).

B–19. Formula to ease suffering when choking on deer bones, spoken by Mary Ike (Karok) between 1940 and 1942. This formula calls upon Wolf. He eats the deer quickly, bones and all, and they come out whole without hurting him a bit (Kroeber and Gifford 1980:288).

B–20. Formula for thin person to restore appetite, spoken by Mary Ike (Karok) between 1940 and 1942 (Kroeber and Gifford 1980:288–289). See chapter 8.

B–21. Formula for upset stomach, spoken by Mary Ike (Karok) between 1940 and 1942. This formula also calls upon Yeruxbihii (see also B–20), who traveled around eating poisonous things such as frogs, lizards, snakes, dogs, and even human flesh. From this he became sick, but he restored himself using alder leaves in water. He drank the water and rubbed it all over himself (Kroeber and Gifford 1980:290).

B–22. Formula for upset stomach, spoken by Mary Ike (Karok) between 1940 and 1942. Duck was traveling upriver and visited several houses where he was fed poisonous things such as rattlesnake, semen, and menstrual blood by people who sought to kill him. He got very dizzy from this but restored himself by drinking water containing willow roots that were gathered from the riverbank (Kroeber and Gifford 1980: 291–292).

B–23. Formula to enable person recovering from illness to eat deer meat, spoken by Mary Ike (Karok) between 1940 and 1942 (Kroeber and Gifford 1980:292–293). See chapter 8.

B–24. Formula for person who dreams about the dead, spoken by Mary Ike (Karok) between 1940 and 1942 (Kroeber and Gifford 1980:314–315). See chapter 8.

B–25. Formula for curing any sickness, spoken by Shan Davis (Karok) between 1940 and 1942. There were ten brothers, and all but the youngest one went hunting constantly. The youngest just sat there and never ate. He went downriver and organized a group of men who went around killing people. Finally he had enough of that and he went up to the high country. He broke off some madrone leaves and threw them behind him. This became a medicine that humans could use for curing (Kroeber and Gifford 1980:320–321).

B–26. Formula for curing any sickness, spoken by Shan Davis (Karok) between 1940 and 1942 (Kroeber and Gifford 1980:321–323). See chapter 8.

B–27. Formula for sickness caused by an unhappy marriage, spoken by Shan Davis (Karok) between 1940 and 1942 (Kroeber and Gifford 1980:323–325). See chapter 8.

B–28. Formula to cure boils, spoken by Mary Ike (Karok) between 1940 and 1942. An old man lived with his granddaughter. She found a little glowworm and kept it in a cup of water as a pet. It grew larger and larger, living on trout that the old man caught. Having this pet gave the girl good luck, but finally it became a large water monster, so they buried it in a hole someplace. Later, she met a man and married him, despite the old man's warnings. She had a child who was covered with boils (Kroeber and Gifford 1980:326–329).

C. Hunting and Fishing

C–1. Formula for catching eels, spoken by William Lewis (Hupa) in 1901 (Goddard 1904:252–264). See chapter 7.

C–2. Deer-hunting song, collected from James Anderson (Hupa) by Goddard in 1901. Recording at the Lowie Museum of Anthropology (24–1723). Not transcribed.

C–3. Deer-hunting song, collected from James Anderson (Hupa) by Goddard in 1901. Recording at the Lowie Museum of Anthropology (24–1724). Not transcribed.

C–4. Deer formula, spoken by Senaxon (Hupa) in 1901 (Goddard 1904:319–323). See chapter 8.

C–5. Formula for salmon, spoken by Lame Billy of Weitchpec (Yurok) between 1901 and 1907 (Kroeber 1976:25–27). See chapter 8.

C–6. Formula for deer hunting, spoken by Tskerkr of Gold Bluff (Yurok) between 1901 and 1907. A young man at Oka (a high ridge above the Klamath River near the mouth of Blue Creek) always hunted, but he found no deer because there was no grass there. He went to a place upriver and found a bush whose leaves the deer were feeding on. He planted the bush near Oka and took deer there from then on. The bush was wild honeysuckle or possibly buck brush. Its leaves are used when the formula is spoken, but how they are used is not specified (Kroeber 1976:198–200).

C–7. Formula for salmon, spoken by Stone of Weitchpec (Yurok) between 1901 and 1907 (Kroeber 1976:221–223). See chapter 8.

C–8. Formula and song for taking salmon, spoken by Billy Werk of Weitchpec (Yurok) between 1901 and 1907. This medicine is from the small salmon (Tserhkr). He followed other fish into the sweathouse, even though the owner had told him there was no room for him to lie down there (Kroeber 1976:250–251). No recording of the song could be located. See chapter 8.

C–9. Formula and song for deer hunting, spoken by Domingo of Weitchpec (Yurok) between 1901 and 1907 (Kroeber 1976: 308–311). Recording of song is available at the Lowie Museum of Anthropology (24–823). See chapter 8.

C–10. Formula with song for deer hunting, spoken by Opn of Sregon (Yurok) between 1901 and 1907. An old man lived at Oka with his ten sons and two daughters, and they were terrorized by a monster which always took their deer. The old man offered his daughters to anyone who could kill the monster. Screech Owl managed to do it and later had three sons by the daughters. While sweating himself, he spat in his hand and rubbed the spittle between his hands, singing his deer-hunting song. Using this medicine, he and his two sons killed all the deer they wanted (Kroeber 1976:373–374).

C–11. Formula for salmon, spoken by Barney of Sregon (Yurok) between 1901 and 1907 (Kroeber 1976:378–379). See chapter 8.

C–12. Deer formula, spoken by Tom Hill (Chilula) in 1905. Panther was the older brother of Wildcat. Panther always hunted, and Wildcat always just set snares. They took many deer. One day, Panther's wife told Wildcat that she was tired of dressing hides, so Wildcat left. Panther followed after him and found him inside a house with a woman. Then the two of them went up in the mountains and snared two deer (Goddard 1914*b*:304–305).

C–13. Deer formula, spoken by Tom Hill (Chilula) in 1905. This formula involves a young man who grew up near Orleans, in Karok territory. He and a mountain grew up together. He always hunted deer and never slept, but once he did sleep and had a dream about women. When he awoke, the mountain was gone. He looked for deer but found none. He decided to make medicine. After using a certain herb, the mountain appeared again and deer came his way (Goddard 1914*b*:305–306).

C–14. Deer formula, spoken by Tom Hill (Chilula) in 1905. This text also concerns a young man who always hunted deer and never slept. He fell asleep once and had a dream about women. This spoiled his luck in getting deer. He transformed himself into a certain plant that grew outside the sweathouse, and thus he attracted the deer to him (Goddard 1914*b*:307).

C–15. Deer formula, spoken by Tom Hill (Chilula) in 1905. Raven always went hunting for deer but had no luck. He took a trip by canoe and found an herb that attracted deer in the bow of the canoe. He pulled the boat up behind his house and took deer as they came to browse there (Goddard 1914*b*: 307–308).

C–16. Deer formula, spoken by Tom Hill (Chilula) in 1905. Black Wolf went to visit his ten brothers. He took a special herb and pounded it up while they sat around the fire. Then he rubbed it on them before they went out hunting. Using this medicine they killed many deer. The substance is not identified (Goddard 1914*b*:308–309).

C–17. Formula for deer or money, spoken by Tom Hill (Chilula) in 1905. A young man used to visit two women all the time, but he still got plenty of deer and money because he washed himself with a certain herb. The substance is not identified (Goddard 1914*b*:311).

C–18. Deer medicine song, collected from Hawley of Meta (Yurok) in 1907. Recording at the Lowie Museum of Anthropology (24–889). See chapter 8, example 29.

C–19. Formula with song for killing deer, collected from Stone of Weitchpec (Yurok) in 1907. This was used while holding an arrowhead over a fire. Recording at the Lowie Museum of Anthropology (24–1151). The song has not been transcribed.

C–20. Deer medicine song, collected from Hawley of Meta (Yurok) in 1907. Notes among Kroeber Papers (n.d.: Carton 6; Notebook 67, p. 37). Recording at the Lowie Museum of Anthropology (24–888). See chapter 8.

C–21. Medicine song for hunting bear, collected from Pete Henry (Karok) in 1926. No translation available. Recording at the American Folklife Center, Library of Congress (HHR 13c). Not transcribed.

C–22. Medicine song for hunting bear, collected from Pete Henry (Karok) in 1926. Notes and translation in Roberts (1926*b*). Recording at the American Folklife Center, Library of Congress (HHR 13f). See chapter 8.

C–23. Medicine song for hunting deer, collected from Pete Henry (Karok) in 1926. Notes and translation in Roberts (1926*b*). Recording at the American Folklife Center, Library of Congress (HHR 13g). See chapter 8.

C–24. Medicine song for hunting deer, collected from Pete Henry (Karok) in 1926. Notes and translation in Roberts (1926*b*). Recording at the American Folklife Center, Library of Congress (HHR 14d). See chapter 8.

C–25. Medicine song for hunting deer, collected from Peter Henry (Karok) in 1926. No translation available. Recording at the American Folklife Center, Library of Congress (HHR 16h). Not transcribed.

C–26. Hunting song, collected from Blind Bill (Yurok) in 1927. Recording at the Lowie Museum of Anthropology (24–2723). Not transcribed.

C–27. Formula for taking eels, spoken by Georgia Orcutt (Karok) between 1940 and 1942 (Kroeber and Gifford 1980:293–294). See chapter 8.

C–28. Formula for killing bear, spoken by Mary Ike (Karok) between 1940 and 1942 (Kroeber and Gifford 1980:299–300). See chapter 8.

C–29. Formula with song for luck in hunting, collected from Georgia Orcutt (Karok) between 1940 and 1942. There was a big family, and all the boys were good hunters who slept in the sweathouse. A visitor came from upriver, and they told him to stay in the family house, so he could not follow them to their best hunting place. He followed them anyway, so they caused a fog which made it impossible for him to see the deer. In spite of this, he shot his arrow and killed ten white deer with a single shot. While hunting, one sings the visitor's song. The story is told separately in camp or in the sweathouse (Kroeber and Gifford 1980:300–301).

C–30. Formula with song for luck in hunting, collected from Mary Ike (Karok) between 1940 and 1942. This formula addresses a female spirit who had good luck at hunting even though hunting was taboo for women and she was menstruating as well. She went high up in the mountains and opened her basket so that the opening pointed upriver. Then she turned it in the downriver direction and began to hear noises inside of it. Four deer had fallen inside. The meat could only be eaten by people who were clean, or else it would cause sickness (Kroeber and Gifford 1980:301–302).

C–31. Formula and song to obtain fox pelts for Deerskin Dance costume, collected from Mary Ike (Karok) between 1940 and 1942. A spirit-person instructs humans to obtain a piece of unburned wood from the fire at the First Salmon Ceremony at Amaikiaram. This is placed near the traps, under a rock. The formula also mentions Fox, who sings his song and tries to run past the snare but gets caught (Kroeber and Gifford 1980:309–310).

C–32. Formula with song for deer hunting, collected from Georgia Orcutt (Karok) between 1940 and 1942. An old man lived high in the mountains with his daughter, and he kept all of the deer hidden someplace, in a period before hunting was known. He said that whoever could kill a deer might marry his daughter, because he knew this was impossible. Many tried, but all gave up. They never even saw a deer. Finally, a poor man prayed in the sweathouse and sang his song, whereupon he was able to kill two white deer and claim the daughter. He did not stay with the daughter, but he did offer luck in hunting and luck with women to anybody who used his song (Kroeber and Gifford 1980:319–320).

C–33. Formula for deer hunting, collected from Chester Pepper (Karok) between 1949 and 1950 (Bright 1957:259). See chapter 8.

C–34. Deer-hunting song, collected from Florence Schaughnessy (Yurok) by Robins in 1951. Translation and commentary in Robins and McLeod (1956:594–595). See chapter 8, example 30.

C–35. Hupa deer-hunting song, sung by Jimmy Jackson and recorded by Mary Woodward in 1953. Recording is available at the University of California (Berkeley) Linguistics Laboratory (MA 022). See chapter 8, example 31.

D. Wealth

D–1. Formula for wealth, spoken by Henry Hostler (Hupa) in 1901 (Goddard 1904:336–339). See chapter 8.

D–2. Song for money medicine, sung by Julius Marshall (Hupa) and recorded by P. E. Goddard in 1901. Recording at the Lowie Museum of Anthropology (24–1699). Not transcribed.

D–3. Song for woman to obtain money (Wetsqaaq Song), sung by Weitchpec Susie (Yurok) and recorded by A. L. Kroeber in 1902. Recording at the Lowie Museum of Anthropology (24–545). Notes among Kroeber Papers (n.d.: Carton 6; Notebook 42, p. 48). See chapter 8, example 37.

D–4. Song for woman to obtain money (Meroctan Song), sung by Weitchpec Susie (Yurok) and recorded by A. L. Kroeber in 1902. Recording at the Lowie Museum of Anthropology (24–546). Notes among Kroeber Papers (n.d.: Carton 6; Notebook 42, p. 48). See chapter 8, example 38.

D–5. Song for money (Maoxpir Song), sung by Weitchpec Susie (Yurok) and recorded by A. L. Kroeber in 1902. Recording

at the Lowie Museum of Anthropology (24–547). Notes
among Kroeber Papers (n.d.: Carton 6; Notebook 42, p. 48).
Not transcribed. See chapter 8.

D–6. Sweathouse formula for money, spoken by Billy Werk's wife
(Yurok) and recorded by A. L. Kroeber in 1906. This medicine calls upon Pelintsiik, who instructs the user to gather
sweathouse wood and bathe in order to become rich. Recording and descriptive notes at the Lowie Museum of Anthropology (24–863). Not transcribed.

D–7. Song for money medicine, sung by Tom Hill (Chilula) and
recorded by P. E. Goddard in 1904. Recording at the Lowie
Museum of Anthropology (24–1805). Not transcribed.

D–8. Song for money medicine, sung by Tom Hill (Chilula) and
recorded by P. E. Goddard in 1904. Recording at the Lowie
Museum of Anthropology (24–1807). See chapter 8, example
36.

D–9. Song for money medicine, sung by Tom Hill (Chilula) and
recorded by P. E. Goddard in 1904. Recording at the Lowie
Museum of Anthropology (24–1808). Not transcribed.

D–10. Formula for money or women, spoken by Stone of Weitchpec (Yurok) between 1901 and 1907. There was a stick game
between five brothers from Kewet mountain and another
team from Kenek. Each team put their wives up as stakes,
and the Kewet team won. The youngest brother of the winning team took two of the wives and headed down to Sumig
(Patrick's Point). He offered tobacco and wished that two
beached whales would appear. After this happened, the
people of Sumig went after them, and the young man took
their houses. There was a fight, but the brothers still took
over the town. According to Yurok mythology, porpoises are
the descendants of Kewet Young Man (Kroeber 1976:233–
235). See chapter 9, note 1.

D–11. Formula from Wohpekemeu for money or women, spoken
by Barney of Sregon (Yurok) between 1901 and 1907 (Kroeber 1976:378–379). See chapter 1 and chapter 9, note 1.

D–12. Formula for money or luck, spoken by Doctor of Pekwan
(Yurok) between 1901 and 1907. This formula addresses a
young man who lived behind Pekwan and always gathered

sweathouse wood. He went to a stone chair and cut himself, then began to eat his own blood. After that he gave up food and water, and blood was all he ate. Because of this he obtained whatever he wanted, and when he stopped doing it he died (Kroeber 1976:380–381).

D–13. Formula and song for money or women, collected from Doctor of Pekwan (Yurok) 1901 and 1907. The formula involves a young man from Dry Lagoon who gambled with Kapuloyo, the son of Wohpekemeu. The medicine includes a song, but when it is used the singer must refrain from eating in the presence of other people (Kroeber 1976:385). Recording of song could not be located. See chapter 9, note 1.

D–14. Formula and song for money or women, collected from Doctor of Pekwan (Yurok) between 1901 and 1907. This formula involves Man Dentalium and Woman Dentalium. They headed toward the ends of the world; he traveled upstream and she traveled downriver. The medicine includes a song for gambling, but one must eat apart from others after using it (Kroeber 1976:385). Recording at the Lowie Museum of Anthropology (24–1020). Not transcribed.

D–15. Formula and song for money, collected from Jim of Pekwan (Yurok) between 1901 and 1907. A boy caught a giant dentalium shell while fishing. He kept it in a box, and it gave him good luck. Later he released it. The song used to keep it from leaving the box in which it was kept (Kroeber 1976:387). Recording at the Lowie Museum of Anthropology (24–1021). Not transcribed. See chapter 8.

D–16. Sweathouse wood gathering song, sung by Umiits of Kepel (Yurok) and recorded by A. L. Kroeber in 1906. Recording at the Lowie Museum of Anthropology (24–877). See chapter 8, example 35.

D–17. Money medicine song, sung by Domingo (Yurok) of Weitchpec between 1906 and 1909 (Lowie Museum of Anthropology 24–993). Not transcribed.

D–18. Song for women or money, sung by Johnny Cooper (Yurok) and recorded by A. L. Kroeber in 1907. Recording at the Lowie Museum of Anthropology (24–1146). Not transcribed. See chapter 8 and chapter 9, note 1.

D–19. Formula for money medicine, spoken by Tom Hill (Chilula) in 1905 (Goddard 1914*b*:309–310). See chapter 8.

D–20. Formula and song for money medicine, collected from Tom Hill (Chilula) in 1905. This text involves a person who was a bastard but nonetheless obtained money from all directions because of a song that he used (Goddard 1914*b*:310). Recording of song could not be located. See chapter 8.

D–21. Formula and song to obtain money or women, collected from John Shoemaker (Hupa) by Edward Sapir in 1927. A young man passed by some girls who were digging potatoes downstream from where he lived. They found him handsome, but he did not stay. He went traveling up on Bald Hills and then returned to his own home. He wanted to become a medicine that human beings could use, so he changed himself into an herb that can be found near the streams and lakes where men go to pray for money (Golla, in press: MS pp. 208–210). Recording of song could not be located.

D–22. Formula for obtaining money, spoken by John Shoemaker (Hupa) and written by Edward Sapir in 1927. This text involves two brothers who lived near Chimariko territory (Golla, in press: MS pp. 211–215). See chapter 8. Recording of song could not be located.

D–23. Formula and song for good luck, collected from Sam Brown (Hupa) by Edward Sapir in 1927. This formula involves the Dawn Maiden, who lives in the east where the sun rises. She looks into all the houses early in the morning and gives good luck to anyone who is awake and singing her song. The medicine helps one to obtain things without paying for them (Golla, in press: MS pp. 216–217). Recording of song could not be located.

D–24. Money medicine song, sung by Ewing Davis (Hupa) and recorded by Frank Quinn in 1956. Recording at the Lowie Museum of Anthropology (24–112). Not transcribed.

E. Love Medicine

E–1. Love formula for woman to use, spoken by Emma Lewis (Hupa) in 1901. A very modest woman lived near the mouth of the Klamath River. A man came and visited her but left. Then Mink came and told her that he would never return, for he had two wives across the ocean. She found an herb and made medicine to make him think of her, no matter how many others he was with. Her lost lover was Moon, and after a while he came back (Goddard 1904:305–308).

E–2. Love formula for man to use, spoken by Tom Hill (Chilula) in 1905. This formula concerns Yumantuwinyai, who heard of a girl who would not look at men. He searched for a medicine to use. He found an herb, and rolled its leaves in his hand. Then, he took its root and rolled it five times in his hand. After this, she said that she would go with him. Then, she reached in the water and brought up some dentalia shell money for them to take (Goddard 1914b:297–298). See chapter 8.

E–3. Love formula for man to use, spoken by Tom Hill (Chilula) in 1905. This formula concerns a young man who played a stick game with another. He won everything from him. On returning home, he tried to visit two girls, but they would not open the door. He said that he would leave, and when he did they followed him. Dentalium shell money was scattered all over (Goddard 1914b:298–299). See chapter 9.

E–4. Love medicine for man to use, spoken by Tom Hill (Chilula) in 1905. This medicine involves Yumantuwinyai's illegitimate son. The boy went traveling all over with an herb he had found. He came to a sweathouse where an old man was smoking himself. He asked to enter the old man's family house, where he saw women sitting. But the old man took him back out to the sweathouse and told him not to think about the women, because they were his. The boy answered that women came to him everywhere; then he left and found two women in a place near the eastern water (Goddard 1914b:299–302).

E–5. Love medicine for man to use, spoken by Tom Hill (Chilula) in 1905. This formula concerns a young man who traveled to Mount Shasta carrying an herb that he had found growing by a spring. He found two women there and they followed him home. This also happened when he traveled to other places (Goddard 1914b:302–304).

E–6. Love song for man to use, sung by Weitchpec Henry (Yurok) and recorded by A. L. Kroeber in 1906. Recording at the Lowie Museum of Anthropology (24–824). See chapter 9, example 40.

E–7. Love song for woman to use, sung by Weitchpec Nancy (Yurok) and recorded by A. L. Kroeber in 1906. Recording at the Lowie Museum of Anthropology (24–826). See chapter 9, example 44.

E–8. Love song for woman to use, sung by Minnie (Yurok) and recorded by Weitchpec Frank (for A. L. Kroeber) in 1909. Recording at the Lowie Museum of Anthropology (24–842). See chapter 9, example 43.

E–9. Woman's love song to regain affection, sung by Weitchpec Nancy (Yurok) and recorded by A. L. Kroeber between 1906 and 1909. Recording at the Lowie Museum of Anthropology (24–909). Not transcribed. See chapter 9.

E–10. Love song for man to use, sung by Johnny Cooper and recorded by A. L. Kroeber in 1907. Recording at the Lowie Museum of Anthropology (24–1133). Not transcribed.

E–11. Love song for woman to use, sung by Sara Frank (Yurok) and recorded by A. L. Kroeber in 1907. Recording at the Lowie Museum of Anthropology (24–1137). See chapter 9, example 47.

E–12. Love song for man to use, sung by Tom Hill (Chilula) and recorded by P. E. Goddard in 1905. Recording at the Lowie Museum of Anthropology (24–1810). See chapter 9, example 39.

E–13. Love song for man to use, sung by Tom Hill (Chilula) and recorded by P. E. Goddard in 1905. Recording at the Lowie Museum of Anthropology (24–1813). See chapter 9, example 41.

E–14. Love song for woman to use, sung by Mary Grimes (Tolowa) and recorded by P. E. Goddard in 1901. Recording at the Lowie Museum of Anthropology (24–1861). See chapter 9, example 48.

E–15. Love song for woman to use, sung by Molly Brainerd (Wiyot) and recorded by A. L. Kroeber in 1923. Recording and descriptive notes at the Lowie Museum of Anthropology (24–2536). Not transcribed.

E–16. Love song for woman to use, sung by Molly Brainerd (Wiyot) and collected by A. L. Kroeber in 1923. Recording and descriptive notes at the Lowie Museum of Anthropology (24–2537). See chapter 9, example 45.

E–17. Love song for woman to use, sung by Molly Brainerd (Wiyot) and collected by A. L. Kroeber in 1923. Recording and descriptive notes at the Lowie Museum of Anthropology (24–2538). See chapter 9, example 46.

E–18. Love song for man to use, sung by Blind Bill (Yurok) and recorded by D. N. Lehmer in 1927. Recording at the Lowie Museum of Anthropology (24–2722). Not transcribed. See chapter 9.

E–19. Formula and song to make husband return, collected from Birdie James (Wiyot) in 1922. A couple were married but were no longer good to each other. The man had another lover, so the woman made medicine. She took a stalk of cottonwood and sat by the water, weaving her basket and singing. After ten days, the husband returned. He wanted to come back, but she made him pay money first (Reichard 1925:207).

E–20. Love song for man to use, sung by Bernard Jerry (Karok) in 1926. This song is about two birds who lived on Sugar Loaf Mountain. They were husband and wife, but she went away to live with Eagle. The husband used this song to get her back. The song has no words (Roberts 1926*b*). Recording at the American Folklife Center, Library of Congress (HHR 28a). Not transcribed.

E–21. Love song for man to use, sung by Bernard Jerry (Karok) in 1926. This song is about Coyote. He claimed that he could pick up a stick and sing this song to get a girl (Roberts 1926*b*). Recording at the American Folklife Center, Library of Congress (HHR 28b). Not transcribed.

E–22. Eagle's love song, sung by Mrs. Grant (Karok) in 1926. No translation available. Recording at the American Folklife Center, Library of Congress (HHR 31g). Not transcribed.

E–23. Dog's love song, sung by Mrs. Grant (Karok) in 1926. No translation available. Recording at the American Folklife Center, Library of Congress (HHR 31h). Not transcribed.

E–24. Little Chickenhawk's love song, sung by Mrs. Grant (Karok) in 1926. No translation available. Recording at the American Folklife Center, Library of Congress (HHR 31i). Not transcribed.

E–25. Formula and song for man to get women, collected from John Shoemaker (Hupa) by Edward Sapir in 1927. A dog was so ugly that people would ridicule him when they passed by where he lived, but all the women wanted him after he used this medicine (Golla, in press: MS pp. 199–200). Recording of song could not be located. See chapter 9.

E–26. Formula with song for woman to get a man, collected from Emma Frank (Hupa) by Edward Sapir in 1927. This medicine was given by Seal Maiden, who lived down in Yurok territory near Orick. At sunset she sang her medicine song, and the next day there appeared a young man dressed in a marvelous robe covered with woodpecker scalps. He said that he had come to get her and instructed her to get ready to leave. Then, she went to sleep and awoke in the eastern heaven where he lived (Golla, in press: MS pp. 201–203). Recording of song could not be located.

E–27. Formula with song for man to obtain a woman, collected from Emma Frank (Hupa) by Edward Sapir in 1927. A young man saw some smoke rising out of the ground, and on further inspection he saw that he had discovered a miraculous form of self-igniting fire. He used it to light his pipe and had a smoke. Then he became lonesome and thought about having a woman. He sang his song and two women came to him. The medicine is used with tobacco. While smoking one says, "This smoke will drift into every canyon" (Golla, in press: MS pp. 204–207). Recording of song could not be located.

E–28. Love formula with song for woman to use, collected from Georgia Orcutt (Karok) between 1940 and 1942. A young woman was blown far away when she killed some wind children by accident. A man heard her crying and wanted to marry her. Her crying is the song (Kroeber and Gifford 1980:270–271). See chapter 9. Recording of song could not be located.

E–29. Love medicine for man to recover wife, spoken by Georgia Orcutt (Karok) between 1940 and 1942. Bald Eagle recovers his wife from a thief with the help of Mouse. Formula is recited over water, and the man is supposed to wash himself in the water but not drink it (Kroeber and Gifford 1980:271–272).

E–30. Love medicine with song for man to use, collected from Georgia Orcutt (Karok) between 1940 and 1942 (Kroeber and Gifford 1980:272–274). No recording could be located. See chapter 9.

E–31. Love medicine with song for man to use, collected from Mary Ike (Karok) between 1940 and 1942. Dog was fooling around near some girls, and they went in the house to avoid him. Later they came out when they heard his song. The song has words that relate this story (Kroeber and Gifford 1980: 274–275). No recording could be located. See chapter 9.

E–32. Love formula with song for a man to use, collected from Mary Ike (Karok) between 1940 and 1942. An old dog was unable to pursue women, but they came to him because of a song that he used (Kroeber and Gifford 1980:275). No recording could be located. See chapter 9.

E–33. Love medicine with song for a man to use, collected from Mary Ike (Karok) between 1940 and 1942 (Kroeber and Gifford 1980:275–276). No recording could be located. See chapter 9.

E–34. Love formula with song to help woman keep husband, collected from Georgia Orcutt (Karok) between 1940 and 1942. Sun Young Man was always gone, so his wife Frog said that she wanted to travel with him. While they were traveling through the sky, he threw her into a fire, which consumed her. He had another woman across the ocean. Later he felt so guilty that he gave up the other woman. Frog assembled her bones together and came back to life. Her song will make a husband return to wife whom he has left (Kroeber and Gifford 1980:277). No recording could be located. See chapter 9.

E–35. Love formula with song for man to use, collected from Mary Ike (Karok) between 1940 and 1942. A man was feeling sorry for himself because some girls were laughing at him. He began crying and then the youngest girl came and asked to live with him. He let her stay but continued crying until his tears made a creek (Kroeber and Gifford 1980:278–279). Recording of song could not be located. See chapter 9.

E–36. Love medicine with song for woman to keep husband, collected from Georgia Orcutt (Karok) between 1940 and 1942. The Klamath River formerly had another course, where it flowed over bedrock and had neither sand nor gravel. After it changed its course, cottonwood trees began to grow along the sandbars that developed. Two girls were walking and were followed by boys who heard them singing. A professional formulist speaks the formula and sings the song over cottonwood foliage, which is then given to a client who pays for the medicine (Kroeber and Gifford 1980:280). Recording of song could not be located.

E–37. Formula to cause return of husband who had left, collected from Georgia Orcutt (Karok) between 1940 and 1942. A woman's husband had been gone for some time. She saw him paddling a canoe on the ocean. She made medicine with an herb medicine and threw a stone pestle out across the water at him. This caused him to beach his boat. He asked to return but she would not take him back. The medicine used was a plant called pennyroyal. The woman became transformed into a rock (Kroeber and Gifford 1980:316–317).

E–38. Formula with song for return of a sweetheart, collected from Nettie Reuben (Karok) in 1949 or 1950. Evening Star had a quarrel with his sweetheart and left her. She got lonesome and made a song to get him back. After she sang it, he became lonesome and returned to her. It was only later that he became a star in the sky (Bright 1957:250–251). Recording of song could not be located.

E–39. Formula and song to get a husband, collected from Nettie Reuben (Karok) in 1949 or 1950. All the girls had gathered back of Orleans to gather roots. Some of them came from far away. A local girl wanted to join them, but she was poor and they ridiculed her. After a while they heard her singing, for she had found a husband in the ground. By using her song, girls can find a husband even if they are poor or homely (Bright 1957:251–253). No recording could be located.

E–40. Formula for love medicine, spoken by Chester Pepper (Karok) in 1949 or 1950. Two girls would not come out of their house, which caused much concern. A young man from Klamath Lakes came and made medicine with sand. He put his medicine down at the entrance of the house and his hands on either side of the door. They invited him to come inside, but he left for upriver. They followed him and he married them both (Bright 1957:253–255).

E–41. Formula for the return of a wife, spoken by Chester Pepper (Karok) in 1949 or 1950. Two women wandered around everywhere. They would live with one man for a while, then move on and stay with another. They lived with a man who spent all his time in the sweathouse. When they ran away, a spirit told him how to get them back by using medicine. By rubbing his foot back and forth in the dirt a certain way, he traveled across the ocean and recovered them (Bright 1957:255–257).

E–42. Love song for woman to use, sung by Ella Norris (Yurok) and recorded by Charlotte Heth in 1975. See musical transcription in Keeling (1982a:392–402). Recording on commercial album produced by Heth (1978).

E–43. Love song for woman to use, sung by Aileen Figueroa (Yurok) in 1975. Recording on commercial album produced by Heth (1978). See chapter 9, example 42.

E–44. Love song, sung by Frank Douglas (Yurok) and recorded by Charlotte Heth in 1975. See musical transcription in Keeling (1982a:431–437). Recording on commercial album produced by Heth (1978). See chapter 9.

F. Medicine for Use by Women

F–1. Formula to shorten period of exclusion after menstruation, spoken by Emma Lewis (Hupa) in 1901. The formula describes the deer who come to bathe and drink in a pond. They drool into it and the pond is filled with their spittle. Dentalia come there also, and the pool becomes filled with their saliva. The menstruating woman bathes in this pool. Thus she prevents any bad luck from coming to those who have contact with her. To let her husband and others know that she has protected them, she takes a charred acorn shell and marks a cross upon her right arm (Goddard 1904:310–313). See chapter 9.

F–2. Formula and song for making baskets, collected from Emma Dusky (Hupa) in 1901 (Goddard 1904:324–327). See chapter 9.

F–3. Formula for menstruation, spoken by Weitchpec Susie (Yurok) in 1902 (Kroeber n.d.: Carton 6; Notebook 42, pp. 42–48). See chapter 9.

F–4. Acorn gathering charm song, sung by Phoebe Maddox (Karok) and recorded by Helen Roberts in 1926. Notes and translation in Roberts (1926b). Recording is available at the American Folklife Center, Library of Congress (HHR 9d). See chapter 9, example 50.

F–5. Formula to shorten the menstrual period, spoken by Emma Frank (Hupa) and written by Edward Sapir in 1927. Panther was always hunting, and his sister was menstruating all the time. He told her to bathe in a certain pond of water behind their house. Deer always came to eat the milkweed that grew around the pond. They came in such numbers that they knocked the boards off of Panther's house while going there at night. Panther got tired of that and went away across the ocean (Golla, in press: MS pp. 176–178). See chapter 9.

F–6. Formula for a woman to become lucky and rich, spoken by Georgia Orcutt (Karok) between 1940 and 1942. A woman went fishing with a pole made from hazel wood. She broke the pole into pieces and made a basket from the strips. Using this as a scooper, she fished for shell money above

Katimin and collected quite a bit. While speaking this formula, a person makes a basket plate of hazel strips. Then the plate must be hidden away to avoid possible contamination from an unclean person (Kroeber and Gifford 1980:295–296). See chapter 9.

F–7. Formula for a woman to become lucky and rich, spoken by Georgia Orcutt (Karok) between 1940 and 1942. A woman was making medicine to become wealthy, but an unclean person visited her and spoiled her luck on purpose. She warns humans that women seeking wealth must avoid men and intercourse or else their luck will also be ruined (Kroeber and Gifford 1980:296–297).

F–8. Song for weaver to make sure someone buys her basket, sung by Aileen Figueroa (Yurok) and recorded by Charlotte Heth in 1975. Recording on album produced by Heth (1978). See chapter 9, example 49.

G. Conflict or Revenge

G–1. Formula and song for war, collected from Henry Hostler (Hupa) in 1901 (Goddard 1904:332–335). See chapter 9, example 51.

G–2. War medicine song from Xoltsaitau (translated "lion"), sung by James Anderson (Hupa) and recorded by P. E. Goddard in 1901. Recording at the Lowie Museum of Anthropology (24–1832). Not transcribed.

G–3. Formula and song used over bullets to bring success in killing enemies, collected from Stone (Yurok) by A. L. Kroeber in 1907. Recording and notes at the Lowie Museum of Anthropology (24–1150). See chapter 9, example 53.

G–4. Song to enable murderer to escape when pursued by relatives of the dead, sung by Johnny Cooper (Yurok) and recorded by A. L. Kroeber in 1907. Also sung to ward off sickness from house. Recording and notes at the Lowie Museum of Anthropology (24–1141). See chapter 9, example 57.

G–5. Song for when settlement is made for slain person, sung by Sarah Frank (Yurok) and recorded by A. L. Kroeber in 1907.

Recording at the Lowie Museum of Anthropology (24–1143). See chapter 9, example 59.

G–6. Song of Chickenhawk for fighting, sung by Johnny Cooper (Yurok) and recorded by A. L. Kroeber in 1907. Recording and notes at the Lowie Museum of Anthropology (24–1145). See chapter 9, example 52.

G–7. Song to ward off approach of those seeking revenge for slain relative, sung by Johnny Cooper (Yurok) and recorded by A. L. Kroeber in 1907. Recording at the Lowie Museum of Anthropology (24–1148). See chapter 9, example 58.

G–8. Song for person wishing to meet and succeed in killing enemy, sung by Johnny Cooper (Yurok) and recorded by A. L. Kroeber in 1907. Recording and notes at the Lowie Museum of Anthropology (24–1149). See chapter 9, example 54.

G–9. Fighting song, sung by Ira Stevens (Karok) and recorded by D. N. Lehmer in 1926. Recording and notes at the Lowie Museum of Anthropology (24–2711). Not transcribed. See chapter 9.

G–10. Fighting song, sung by Ira Stevens (Karok) and recorded by D. N. Lehmer in 1926. The museum catalogue has this annotation: "Here comes my enemy. He has on a white shirt and is ready to battle." Recording and notes at the Lowie Museum of Anthropology (24–2712). Not transcribed. See chapter 9.

G–11. Fighting song, sung by Ira Stevens (Karok) and recorded by D. N. Lehmer in 1926. The museum catalogue has this annotation: "Song to put an enemy off his guard." Recording and notes at the Lowie Museum of Anthropology (24–2713). See chapter 9, example 55.

G–12. Fighting song, sung by Ira Stevens (Karok) and recorded by D. N. Lehmer in 1926. The museum catalogue has this annotation: "Do not look my way. Do not look down the river, my enemy." Recording at the Lowie Museum of Anthropology (24–2717). Not transcribed. See chapter 9.

G–13. War song, sung by Blind Bill (Yurok) and recorded by D. N. Lehmer in 1927. This song does not seem to have any words, but the museum catalogue has this annotation: "He kill a man! I won't go to Eureka. You can't arrest me." Recording and notes at the Lowie Museum of Anthropology (24–2720).

G–14. Medicine song for anger, sung by Phoebe Maddox (Karok) and recorded by Helen Roberts in 1926. The text is related to the story of two rocks on the Klamath River near Katimin (Roberts 1926*b*). Recording at the American Folklife Center, Library of Congress (HHR 9e). See chapter 9, example 56.

G–15. Medicine song from Chickenhawk to kill game or enemies, sung by Phoebe Maddox (Karok) and recorded by Helen Roberts in 1926. Notes on song and its use are found in Roberts (1926*b*). Recording at the American Folklife Center, Library of Congress (HHR 46e), but the cylinder was broken. See chapter 9.

G–16. Medicine song from Coyote for fighting, sung by Phoebe Maddox (Karok) and recorded by Helen Roberts in 1926. Many men were angry at Coyote and they had him surrounded inside a house. He sang this song, then threw ashes from the fire into their eyes and managed to escape through their ranks. The words of the song are translated as follows: "I don't care if there are ten rows of you, I will go through" (Roberts 1926*b*). Recording at the American Folklife Center, Library of Congress (HHR 49a). Not transcribed.

G–17. Formula and song "for forgiveness" collected from Mary Marshall (Hupa) by Edward Sapir in 1927. The given title is evidently euphemistic, as this seems to be a medicine for escaping revenge. The formula calls upon Chickenhawk. He kills people but is not killed himself because he prays and burns roots all night. He says, "My enemies will melt away from me." Then he uses the song to make this happen (Golla, in press: MS pp. 193–194). No recording could be located. See chapter 9.

G–18. Formula and song for war, collected from Sam Brown (Hupa) by Edward Sapir in 1927. Black Hawk lived with his sisters up on Redwood Ridge. In the morning, he would go out and kill people, then would come home and sing by himself. One day, he told his sisters that he was going to be killed in a fight to take place the next morning. He revealed this song to them so that humans could become invincible by using it (Golla, in press: MS pp. 195–198). No recording could be located.

G–19. Hate medicine to cause bad luck, from Georgia Orcutt (Karok) between 1940 and 1942 (Kroeber 1976:280–281). See chapter 9.

G–20. Formula to protect person who has committed murder or theft, spoken by Mary Ike (Karok) between 1940 and 1942. This formula concerns a long-nosed creature that was probably either the mouse or shrew. Angry men were looking for him everywhere, but he evaded them by traveling under the ground. As long as a person calls upon him, that person can always travel without being seen (Kroeber and Gifford 1980:297). See chapter 9.

H. Safety in Travel

H–1. Formula and song for going in dangerous places with a canoe, collected from Emma Lewis (Hupa) in 1901. This medicine was given by Snipe. His canoe was very narrow, and it was so shallow that it did not come above his ankle. To make it safe, he made medicine before launching the canoe. He beat on the stern with his paddle and sang this song. He also used the song as he traveled over the water (Goddard 1904:314–316). No recording could be located. See chapter 9.

H–2. Formula for protection from rattlesnakes, spoken by McCann (Hupa) in 1901 (Goddard 1904:317–318). See chapter 9.

H–3. Formula and song to prevent drowning, collected from Captain Spott of Rekwoi (Yurok) between 1901 and 1907. At first the world was only land, and there was no water. Wohpeke-meu was concerned that the world would become overpopulated, so he made water in order that some people would drown. Today, many people drown, but those who know this medicine are saved, even though the water is rough (Kroeber 1976:421–422). No recording could be located.

H–4. Medicine song used in boat when water is rough, sung by Captain Spott of Rekwoi (Yurok) and recorded by A. L. Kroeber between 1906 and 1909. Notes among Kroeber Papers (n.d.: Carton 6; Notebook 67, p. 46). Recording at the Lowie Museum of Anthropology (24–892). See chapter 9, example 60.

H–5. Formula and song used in boat when the water is rough, collected from Captain Spott of Rekwoi (Yurok) between 1901 and 1907 (Kroeber 1976:423). A recording of the song is available at the Lowie Museum of Anthropology (24–894). See chapter 9, example 61.

H–6. Formula and song to protect one from drowning, collected from Captain Spott of Rekwoi (Yurok) between 1901 and 1907 (Kroeber 1976:430). No recording could be located. See chapter 9.

H–7. Medicine song used in boat when water is rough, sung by Captain Spott of Rekwoi (Yurok) and recorded by Kroeber between 1906 and 1909 (Kroeber n.d.: Carton 6; Notebook 17, p. 47). Recording at the Lowie Museum of Anthropology (24–893). See chapter 9, example 62.

H–8. Formula and song for rough water from Seagull, sung by Captain Spott of Rekwoi (Yurok) and recorded by A. L. Kroeber between 1906 and 1909 (Kroeber n.d.: Carton 6; Notebook 67, p. 48). Recording at the Lowie Museum of Anthropology (24–895). See chapter 9, example 63.

H–9. Medicine songs for rough water from each of eleven brothers, sung by Captain Spott of Rekwoi (Yurok) and recorded by A. L. Kroeber between 1906 and 1909. Recordings and notes at the Lowie Museum of Anthropology (24–895 through 24–908). See chapter 9, including example 64, a transcription of 24–901.

H–10. Eagle's medicine for protection from enemies, spoken by Tom Hill (Chilula) in 1905 (Goddard 1914*b*:344–346). See chapter 9.

H–11. Formula to keep rattlesnakes away, spoken by Mary Ike (Karok) between 1940 and 1942. The words call upon Hawk, an enemy of the snake (Kroeber and Gifford 1980:269). See chapter 9.

H–12. Formula for person in capsized boat, spoken by Mary Ike (Karok) between 1940 and 1942. This formula asks a certain spirit to help by throwing the person back up on the river bar (Kroeber and Gifford 1980:269). See chapter 9.

H–13. Formula for crossing the river in a boat, spoken by Mary Ike (Karok) between 1940 and 1942. This involves a flood that covered the world. Mink and Ground Squirrel decided that a male and female of every animal should be brought aboard a boat before the deluge began. The flood covered everything but the tip of Mount Shasta (Kroeber and Gifford 1980:298–299). See chapter 9.

I. Sports and Games

I–1. Formula from Mink for gambling, spoken by Tom Hill (Chilula) in 1905 (Goddard 1914*b*:342–344). See chapter 9.

I–2. Formula and song for success in gambling, collected from Georgia Orcutt (Karok) between 1940 and 1942 (Kroeber and Gifford 1980:294). See chapter 9. No recording of the song could be located.

I–3. Formula for success at stick game, spoken by Georgia Orcutt (Karok) between 1940 and 1942 (Kroeber and Gifford 1980: 307–309). See chapter 9.

I–4. Yurok medicine formula for luck at the stick game, spoken by Mamie Offield (Karok) between 1940 and 1942 (Kroeber and Gifford 1980:325–326). See chapter 9.

I–5. Formula for stick game, spoken by Mamie Offield (Karok) between 1949 and 1950 (Bright 1957:258–259). See chapter 9.

I–6. Formula for wrestling, spoken by Mamie Offield (Karok) between 1949 and 1950 (Bright 1957:260–261). See chapter 9.

J. Purification from Contact with a Corpse

J–1. Formula for purification from contact with a corpse, collected from an unidentified Hupa woman of Yurok ancestry between 1901 and 1907 (Kroeber 1925:71–72). See chapter 9.

J–2. Medicine for purification after corpse contact, spoken by Mack of Weitchpec (Yurok) between 1901 and 1907 (Kroeber 1976:289–291). See chapter 9.

J–3. Formula for purification from corpse contact, spoken by Mary Marshall (Hupa) in 1901 (Goddard 1904:351–359). See chapter 9.

J–4. Medicine for purification from corpse contact, spoken by Tom Hill (Chilula) in 1905. This medicine is for a person who has helped prepare a corpse for burial. The herb used for purifying men is the yerba buena leaf, and water from an abalone shell is used for women. The water is rubbed on the woman's back. The dead person speaks these words as he passes from the world of the living: "Now away from me you want to go. My body do not think about it" (Goddard 1914*b*:347–349).

J–5. Medicine for purification after handling a corpse, spoken by John Shoemaker (Hupa) in 1927 (Golla, in press: MS pp. 183–192). See chapter 9.

J–6. Formula from Spider for purification of a person attending a funeral, spoken by Mary Ike (Karok) between 1940 and 1942 (Kroeber and Gifford 1980:310–311). See chapter 9.

J–7. Medicine for purification of person attending a funeral, spoken by Mary Ike (Karok) between 1940 and 1942 (Kroeber 1976:311–314). See chapter 9.

K. Miscellaneous Types of Medicine

K–1. Song sung if fox cries at one, sung by Johnny Cooper (Yurok) and recorded by A. L. Kroeber in 1907 (Lowie Museum of Anthropology recording 24–1140). Not transcribed.

K–2. Song to drive rain away, from Phoebe Maddox (Karok) in 1926. Notes and translation in Roberts (1926*b*). Recording at the American Folklife Center, Library of Congress (HHR 49c). See chapter 9, example 65.

K–3. Song to drive away rain and bring sunshine, from Mrs. Brigmore (Karok) in 1926. Notes and translation in Roberts (1926*b*). Recording at the American Folklife Center, Library of Congress (HHR 49d). See chapter 9, example 66.

K–4. Formula with song to make it rain, collected from Mary Ike
       (Karok) by Gifford between 1940 and 1942. Grandmother
       told her grandson to set net for salmon, but the rocks were
       covered with ice. She made a fire and told the boy to go up
       on the ridge and sing a certain song. This caused the ice
       to thaw. The ice said, "Old lady, don't be so mean." She
       melted all the ice because one of her grandsons had slipped
       on it and drowned. This is used in frosty weather (Kroeber
       and Gifford 1980:298). No recording of the song could be
       located.

K–5. Formula to make tobacco plant grow quickly, collected from
       Georgia Orcutt (Karok) by Gifford between 1940 and 1942
       (Kroeber and Gifford 1980:302–306). See chapter 9.

K–6. Formula to give a person self-assurance, collected from
       Georgia Orcutt (Karok) by Gifford between 1940 and 1942
       (Kroeber and Gifford 1980:315–316). See chapter 9.

K–7. Song for young man to improve his looks, sung by Ernest
       Marshall (Hupa) and recorded by Frank Quinn in 1956. Re-
       cording at the Lowie Museum of Anthropology (24–120).
       See chapter 9, example 68.

K–8. Song to stop the rain, sung by Ella Norris (Yurok/Tolowa)
       and recorded by Charlotte Heth in 1975. Recording on
       album produced by Heth (1978). See chapter 9, example 67.

Appendix 3
Cantometrics Codings for Various Musical Styles

A. Style of ensemble singing used by males in the Deerskin Dance, the Jump Dance, the Brush Dance, the Kick Dance, and in gambling songs.

1. Social organization   (12) interlock

   It should be noted, however, that the bass part in the Jump Dance is rhythmically independent of the solo part and might be coded (6) discoordinated as defined by Lomax (1976:178).

2. Rhythmic relation of
   vocal group to orchestra   (1) no orchestra or
                                  (4) accompanying

   Principal coding is (1) no orchestra, but with these exceptions: sounds of foot tapping and shell necklaces of singer/dancers that mark each beat in the Brush Dance, a pair of whistles played in unison to mark basic meter in the Deerskin Dance, and a single frame drum that marks each beat in gambling songs.

3. Social organization of
   the orchestra   (1) no orchestra or
                                  (2) one solo instrument or
                                  (4) simple group

   See note for previous line.

4. Musical organization of
   the vocal part   (4) polyphony
5. Tonal blend   (2) very individualized
6. Rhythmic coordination   (3) minimal
7. Musical organization of
   the orchestra   (1) no orchestra or
                                      (3) unison

See note for line 2.

9.[1] Rhythmic coordination
   of orchestra to group   (1) no orchestra or
                                      (4) moderate coordination

See note for line 2.

10. Repetition of text   (5) extreme
11. Overall rhythm-vocal   (4) simple

There is, however, a distinct tendency to add or drop beats, and a strict metric feeling seems to be purposely avoided.

12. Rhythmic relation
    within the vocal group   (4) accompanying
13. Overall rhythm-
    orchestra   (1) no orchestra or
                                     (4) one-beat rhythm or
                                     (5) simple meter

See note for line 2.

14. Rhythmic relation
    within the orchestra   (1) no orchestra or
                                     (3) rhythmic unison

See note for line 2.

15. Melodic shape   (4) descending
16. Melodic form   (1) through-composed or
                                     (4) simple strophe with
                                         much variation.

Early recordings (circa 1900–1910) in various genres are generally coded (10) simple litany with much variation or (8) complex litany with moderate variation.

17. Phrase length	(3)	medium or
	(4)	short
18. Number of phrases	(2)	5 or 7 phrases
	(3)	4 or 8 phrases, asymmetrical
	(5)	3 or 6 phrases, asymmetrical
	(7)	2 phrases, asymmetrical
19. Position of final tone	(1)	lowest note or
	(2)	lowest half
20. Melodic range	(3)	beyond the octave
21. Interval size	(3)	medium
22. Polyphonic type	(6)	counterpoint
23. Embellishment	(4)	slight
24. Tempo	(4)	moderate or
	(5)	fast
25. Volume	(2)	loud or
	(3)	mid
26. Rubato-vocal	(3)	some rubato
27. Rubato-orchestra	(1)	no orchestra or
	(3)	some rubato
28. Glissando	(2)	prominent
29. Melisma	(1)	much
30. Tremolo	(1)	much
31. Glottal	(1)	much
32. Vocal pitch	(2)	high
	(3)	mid
	(4)	low
33. Vocal width	(3)	wide but nasal and
	(1)	narrow
34. Nasality	(2)	much
35. Rasp	(3)	intermittent
36. Accent	(2)	forceful
37. Enunciation	(5)	slurred

B. Style of female singing in the Brush Dance.

    1. Social organization   (12) interlock

    2. Rhythmic relation of
        vocal group to orchestra   (1) no orchestra or
                                 (4) accompanying

      Principal coding is (1) no orchestra, but sounds of foot tapping and rustling of shell necklaces of singer/dancers are heard more or less distinctly in various recordings of Brush Dance songs.

    3. Social organization of
        the orchestra   (1) no orchestra or
                                 (4) simple group

      See note for previous line.

    4. Musical organization of
        the vocal part   (4) polyphony

    5. Tonal blend   (2) very individualized

    6. Rhythmic coordination   (3) minimal

    7. Musical organization of
        the orchestra   (1) no orchestra or
                                 (3) unison

      See note for line 2.

    9. Rhythmic coordination
        of orchestra to group   (1) no orchestra or
                                 (4) moderate

      See note for line 2.

    10. Repetition of text   (4) quite repetitious

    11. Overall rhythm-vocal   (4) simple

    12. Rhythmic relation
        within the vocal group   (4) accompanying

    13. Overall rhythm-
        orchestra   (1) no orchestra or
                                 (4) one-beat rhythm

      See note for line 2.

    14. Rhythmic relation
        within the orchestra   (1) no orchestra or

		(3)	rhythmic unison
	See note for line 2.		
15.	Melodic shape	(3)	undulating or
		(4)	descending
16.	Melodic form	(11)	simple litany with moderate variation or
		(4)	simple strophe with moderate variation
17.	Phrase length	(4)	short
18.	Number of phrases	(5)	3 or 6 phrases, asymmetrical, or
		(8)	1 or 2 phrases, symmetrical
19.	Position of final tone	(2)	lowest half
20.	Melodic range	(2)	within the octave
21.	Interval size	(3)	medium
22.	Polyphonic type	(6)	counterpoint
23.	Embellishment	(4)	slight
24.	Tempo	(5)	fast
25.	Volume	(4)	soft
26.	Rubato-vocal	(4)	strict tempo
27.	Rubato-orchestra	(1)	no orchestra or
		(4)	some rubato
28.	Glissando	(2)	prominent
29.	Melisma	(1)	much
30.	Tremolo	(3)	little or no
31.	Glottal	(3)	little or no
32.	Vocal pitch	(3)	mid
33.	Vocal width	(2)	mid
34.	Nasality	(5)	little
35.	Rasp	(5)	little
36.	Accent	(4)	relaxed
37.	Enunciation	(3)	moderate

C. Style of Flower Dance songs as performed by males or females.

    1. Social organization   (4) social unison, dominant leader

    2. Rhythmic relation of vocal group to orchestra   (4) accompanying

Instruments are a pair of stick rattles which mark each beat in unison.

    3. Social organization of the orchestra   (4) simple group

    4. Musical organization of the vocal part   (3) heterophony

    5. Tonal blend   (2) very individualized

    6. Rhythmic coordination   (4) moderate

    7. Musical organization of the orchestra   (3) unison

    9. [2] Rhythmic coordination of orchestra to group   (4) moderate

    10. Repetition of text   (4) quite repetitious

    11. Overall rhythm-vocal   (4) simple meter

    12. Rhythmic relation within the vocal group   (4) heterophony

    13. Overall rhythm-orchestra   (4) one-beat rhythm

    14. Rhythmic relation within the orchestra   (3) rhythmic unison

    15. Melodic shape   (3) undulating

    16. Melodic form   (11) simple litany with moderate variation

    17. Phrase length   (5) very short

    18. Number of phrases   (8) 1 or 2 phrases, symmetrical

    19. Position of final tone   (3) upper half

Typical ending pattern is coded, rather than the finalis of the body of the song.

20. Melodic range   (1) within the fifth or
                           (2) within the octave
21. Interval size   (3) medium or diatonic
22. Polyphonic type   (1) none
23. Embellishment   (4) slight
24. Tempo   (4) moderate
25. Volume   (4) soft
26. Rubato-vocal   (4) strict tempo
27. Rubato-orchestra   (4) strict tempo
28. Glissando   (3) some
29. Melisma   (3) some
30. Tremolo   (3) little or no
31. Glottal   (1) much or
                           (2) some
32. Vocal pitch   (3) mid
33. Vocal width   (3) wide
34. Nasality   (2) much
35. Rasp   (3) intermittent
36. Accent   (4) relaxed
37. Enunciation   (4) slurred

D. Style of personal medicine songs quite closely related to the
predominant style of male singing (but monophonic).[3]

1. Social organization   (2) solo
2. Rhythmic relation of
   vocal group to orchestra   (1) no orchestra
3. Social organization of
   the orchestra   (1) no orchestra
4. Musical organization of
   the vocal part   (1) monophony
5. Tonal blend   (1) solo
6. Rhythmic coordination   (1) solo
7. Musical organization of
   the orchestra   (1) no orchestra

9. [4] Rhythmic coordination
of orchestra to group   (1) solo

10. Repetition of text   (5) extremely repetitious

11. Overall rhythm-vocal   (4) simple meter or
     (1) free rhythm

12. Rhythmic relation
within the vocal group   (1) solo singer

13. Overall rhythm-
orchestra   (1) no orchestra

14. Rhythmic relation
within the orchestra   (1) no orchestra

15. Melodic shape   (4) descending

16. Melodic form   (6) simple strophe with little
variation

17. Phrase length   (4) short

18. Number of phrases   (2) 5 or 7 phrases or
     (3) 4 or 8 phrases,
asymmetrical
     (5) 3 or 6 phrases,
asymmetrical

19. Position of final tone   (1) lowest note

20. Melodic range   (3) beyond the octave

21. Interval size   (3) medium

22. Polyphonic type   (1) none

23. Embellishment   (4) slight

24. Tempo   (1) extremely slow

25. Volume   (4) soft

26. Rubato-vocal   (1) extreme

27. Rubato-orchestra   (1) no orchestra

28. Glissando   (2) prominent

29. Melisma   (2) some

30. Tremolo   (3) little or none

31. Glottal   (1) much or
     (2) some

32. Vocal pitch   (2) high and
                                       (4) low

Extremely wide melodic range is characteristic.

33. Vocal width   (2) mid
34. Nasality   (2) much
35. Rasp   (4) slight
36. Accent   (3) moderate
37. Enunciation   (3) moderate

E. Style of personal medicine songs in which "sobbing" is evident.

1. Social organization   (2) solo
2. Rhythmic relation of
   vocal group to orchestra   (1) no orchestra
3. Social organization of
   the orchestra   (1) no orchestra
4. Musical organization of
   the vocal part   (1) monophony
5. Tonal blend   (1) solo
6. Rhythmic coordination   (1) solo
7. Musical organization of
   the orchestra   (1) no orchestra
9. [5] Rhythmic coordination
   of orchestra to group   (1) solo
10. Repetition of text   (5) extremely repetitious
11. Overall rhythm-vocal   (1) free rhythm or
                                     (2) irregular rhythm

A sense of meter is often perceptible but always rather weak.

12. Rhythmic relation
    within the vocal group   (1) solo singer
13. Overall rhythm-
    orchestra   (1) no orchestra
14. Rhythmic relation
    within the orchestra   (1) no orchestra

15. Melodic shape   (4) descending
16. Melodic form   (11) simple litany with
                                   moderate variation or
                               (5) simple strophe with
                                   moderate variation or
                               (1) through-composed

Two examples, a money medicine song and a love song, were coded as (1) through-composed, and both were sung by Tom Hill (Chilula). Both songs seemed to be improvised rather than having a fixed melodic form.[6]

17. Phrase length   (4) short or
                               (5) very short

18. Number of phrases   (2) 5 or 7 phrases or
                               (3) 4 or 8 phrases,
                                   asymmetrical
                               (5) 3 or 6 phrases,
                                   assymmetrical or
                               (7) 2 phrases, asymmetrical

19. Position of final tone   (1) lowest note
20. Melodic range   (2) within the octave
21. Interval size   (3) medium
22. Polyphonic type   (1) none
23. Embellishment   (5) little or none
24. Tempo   (2) quite slow or
                               (3) slow

25. Volume   (3) mid or
                               (4) soft

26. Rubato-vocal   (1) extreme
27. Rubato-orchestra   (1) no orchestra
28. Glissando   (1) maximal
29. Melisma   (1) much
30. Tremolo   (1) much
31. Glottal   (1) much
32. Vocal pitch   (3) mid

33.	Vocal width	(1) narrow
34.	Nasality	(1) extreme
35.	Rasp	(4) slight
36.	Accent	(3) moderate
37.	Enunciation	(5) very slurred

F. Style of personal songs that represent speech or singing of spirit-persons or animals.

1.	Social organization	(2) solo
2.	Rhythmic relation of vocal group to orchestra	(1) no orchestra
3.	Social organization of the orchestra	(1) no orchestra
4.	Musical organization of the vocal part	(1) monophony
5.	Tonal blend	(1) solo
6.	Rhythmic coordination	(1) solo
7.	Musical organization of the orchestra	(1) no orchestra
9.[7]	Rhythmic coordination of orchestra to group	(1) solo
10.	Repetition of text	(4) quite repetitious or (5) extremely repetitious

Some songs are entirely sung in vocables while others are entirely comprised of words. In either case, a relatively short text is sung repeatedly.

11.	Overall rhythm-vocal	(4) simple meter
12.	Rhythmic relation within the vocal group	(1) solo singer
13.	Overall rhythm-orchestra	(1) no orchestra
14.	Rhythmic relation within the orchestra	(1) no orchestra
15.	Melodic shape	(3) undulating

16.	Melodic form	(12)	simple litany
17.	Phrase length	(5)	very short
18.	Number of phrases	(8)	1 or 2 phrases, symmetrical
19.	Position of final tone	(1)	lowest note
20.	Melodic range	(1)	within the fifth
21.	Interval size	(4)	wide (mainly thirds)
22.	Polyphonic type	(1)	none
23.	Embellishment	(5)	little or none
24.	Tempo	(4)	moderate
25.	Volume	(4)	soft
26.	Rubato-vocal	(4)	strict tempo
27.	Rubato-orchestra	(1)	no orchestra
28.	Glissando	(3)	some
29.	Melisma	(2)	some or
		(3)	little or none
30.	Tremolo	(3)	little or none
31.	Glottal	(1)	much for Yurok songs
		(2)	some or
		(3)	little or none for Karok songs
32.	Vocal pitch	(3)	mid for Karok songs
		(4)	low for Yurok songs
33.	Vocal width	(2)	mid for Karok songs
		(2)	mid or
		(3)	wide for Yurok songs
34.	Nasality	(2)	much or
35.	Rasp	(2)	great for Yurok songs
		(3)	intermittent for Karok songs
36.	Accent	(3)	moderate or
		(4)	relaxed
37.	Enunciation	(4)	slurred

Notes

Preface

1. While estimates of California's native population circa 1770 vary from a low figure of 84,000 (Kroeber 1953:143) to a high one of 300,000 (Cook 1978:91), few would argue with Kroeber's assertion that this was the most populated territory of comparable size and probably accounted for more than eight percent of the total population north of Mexico (Kroeber 1953:143).

2. A summarized history of the Ethnological Survey of California and other research connected with the collection of sound recordings in California is provided in the introduction to Keeling (1991). Other important sources include Heizer (1978) and Golla (1984).

1: Introduction

1. This account is based on a translation in Kroeber (1976:359–362).

2. This was an actual town located downriver from Pekwan Creek on the Klamath River. Although it was destroyed and rebuilt on account of a flood which occurred in 1862, Indians interviewed circa 1902–1909 still recognized the house pits in which Blue Crane had lived during the pre-human period, and these are indicated on map 12 in Waterman (1920).

3. Victor Golla has informed me that a more literal translation for the element meaning "Hoopa Valley" is "Where the Trails Return" (personal communication, 1987).

4. The nature of the relation of Yurok (and Wiyot) to the Algonkian group or to a form of Proto-Algonkian was once the subject of much controversy; however, linguists now generally agree that a distinct affinity is

evident. The issue is summarized and sources listed at least twice in the *Handbook of North American Indians,* volume 8: *California* (1978:87, 137).

5. By this time, the reader may have noticed a distinct bias toward describing Yurok culture from a male perspective, and this tendency permeates much of the ethnological literature. Early researchers in this region relied mainly on data gathered from Indian men while collecting much less information from women, and this has almost certainly tended to warp our view of Yurok culture. While adhering to the standard ethnographic profile in making these introductory remarks, I have tried to achieve a more balanced picture of beliefs concerning gender and spirituality in the chapters that follow.

6. Kroeber himself was the single most prolific collector, but several others associated with the Department and Museum of Anthropology at the University of California (Berkeley) during these years also contributed greatly. The entire corpus includes 2,712 items that were originally collected on Edison-type cylinder recorders. These and more recent recordings collected on disk, wire, and tape are among the holdings at the Lowie Museum of Anthropology. The collection is described in Keeling (1991).

7. Kroeber does not mention his relationship with Herzog in print, but manuscripts in the Bancroft Library include musical transcriptions bearing Herzog's signature, and Herzog mentions having received assistance from Kroeber and Edward Gifford in his important essay on Mohave and Diegueño music (1928:184).

8. Cantometrics is based upon the hypothesis that every tradition of vocal music tends to symbolize certain behavior patterns that are of great importance for cultural continuity. The methodology measures each style according to thirty-six parameters, and from these ratings Lomax not only develops conclusions concerning musical meaning but also attempts to discern historical connections through which the multitude of world song styles can be shown to derive from ten ancient prototypes or culture areas. Some have criticized the cantometrics methodology as described in Lomax (1968, 1976), and others have questioned Lomax's interpretations of specific musical traditions, but virtually every reviewer has described cantometrics as a major achievement in cross-cultural methodology and one that seems likely to influence the course of ethnomusicology for generations to come.

9. The term "heightened speech" was first used by George List in an essay entitled "The Boundaries of Speech and Song" (1963). In this paper, List attempts to indicate some of the distinctions between song and speech and tries to classify various forms that combine elements of both.

2: Secularization in the Period since 1850

1. The use of the word *wo'gey* to mean "white person" is documented as early as 1851 (Meyer 1855, in Heizer and Mills 1952:126). The idea that the *wo'gey* returned as whites also seems to have been current among Indians very soon after contact, as two versions of the explanation are given in Powers (1877 [1976]:63, 69–70).

2. Despite this critical attitude, I often saw Mr. Rube at dances in Hoopa Valley and was told that he regularly provided regalia for dances at various locations. Before his death during the 1980s, he was very influential among younger Yuroks living downriver from Weitchpec. The overall message of his teachings was far from negative and sought mainly to proclaim Yurok spiritualism as something real and dynamic, rather than just a matter of heritage or tradition.

3. Locals have told me that modern pits came into existence around the turn of the century because they could accommodate a bigger dance than the Indian-style house. This is supported by Kroeber, who indicates that Indians of the period (1890–1900) used both traditional and American-type houses (1925:19) and held the Brush Dance in a modified Indian-style house (1925:61).

4. The information on the Brush Dance is based on an interview conducted at Alice Pratt's home on August 24, 1979. A more complete discussion is found in Keeling (1982a:153–195).

5. "You have four sticks. It has got to be tan oak and madrone, when you're baking that pitch, and then you got to put tobacco on each corner. I always put Bull Durham under here [where the sticks cross each other]."

6. She emphasized that all of her prayers were spoken in the Hupa language, and indeed she offered to conduct her part of the interview in Hupa when we first sat down.

7. Except where noted, this discussion of early contacts between the Yurok Indians and white explorers is based mainly upon information provided by Arnold Pilling in the *Handbook of North American Indians*, volume 8: *California* (Pilling 1978:138–141).

8. Readers seeking further information concerning the genocide against Indians in northwestern California should refer to the excellent studies by Hupa authors Jack Norton (1978) and Byron Nelson (1978).

9. As noted previously, central authority was minimal among all these tribes. Yurok law, summarized in Kroeber (1925:20–22), was based upon a "blood money" principle through which there was compensation for damages based upon claims made by individuals or families. Even in war there was little impulse to act collectively, as was shown during a "war"

which occurred between the Yuroks and Hupas circa 1830–1840. Whether one consults the Hupa version of this incident (Golla, in press) or the Yurok one (Kroeber 1925:50–52) it becomes clear that the conflict was actually waged between families, or at most villages, rather than between tribes.

10. Despite its racist tone, Powers' *Tribes of California* (1877 [1976]) is our single most important source on Indian culture in transition and the following passages will refer to it often. Powers' comment concerning the two types of money comes in a discussion of marriage customs and seems significant enough to be quoted at length.

Divorce is very easily accomplished at the will of the husband, the only indispensable formality being that he must receive back from his father-in-law the money which he paid for his spouse. . . . [But the young men] seldom have shell-money nowadays, and the old Indians prefer that in exchange for their daughters. Besides that, if one paid American money for his wife his father-in-law would squander it [the old generation dislike the white man's, the *wo'gey* money, but hoard up shell-money like true misers], and thus, in the case of divorce he could not recover his gold and silver. (Powers 1877 [1976]:56)

In this connection, Joy Sundberg (Yurok) said that her grandfather and others often received five dollar pieces for ferrying whites across the river, but having no use for the money, they just skipped the coins across the surface of the river for fun (Bommelyn et al. 1976). A similar account of Karok Indians skipping coins across the river like stones is found in Bright (1957:279).

11. The Shaker movement began near Puget Sound in 1881 but did not reach Indians of northwestern California until the 1920s. Although the movement has declined somewhat since reaching a peak around 1940, it continues to be strong among the Tolowa, and there is a Shaker Church among the Yuroks at the town of Johnson's. Major sources on Shakerism include Barnett (1957), Gould and Furukawa (1964), and Valory (1966).

3: The Sacred Landscape

1. These paragraphs are based on information provided in Waterman (1920:189–192).

2. Far from being viewed as a creator-figure, "World-Maker" is not mentioned in other mythological accounts and little is known about him beyond that which is noted here (Waterman 1920:190).

3. The most complete discussion of sorcery is in Valory (1970:102–151).

4. This brief account is based on Gifford's unpublished notes concerning a Hupa version of the ritual (1940*b*).

5. Kroeber also mentions that on finishing the meal, a person was supposed to wash his hands in a basket or wooden basin, then rub them with fragrant pepperwood leaves that had been pulverized by chewing (1925:68).

4: The Sweathouse and the High Country

1. In discussing political organization among Indians of the California region, Kroeber wrote,

The extreme of political anarchy is found in the northwest, where there is scarcely a tendency to group towns into higher political units, and where even a town is not conceived as an essential unit. In practice, a northwestern settlement was likely to act as a body, but it did so either because its inhabitants were kinsmen or because it contained a man of sufficient wealth to have established personal relations of obligation between himself and individual fellow townsmen not related to him in blood. The Yurok, Karok, and Hupa, and probably several of the adjacent groups, simply did not recognize any organization which transcended individuals and kin groups. (Kroeber 1925:830)

2. Spott notes that Yurok employs one word for both "grandfather" and "great-grandfather" (Spott and Kroeber 1942:167).

3. These are called *tsekteya* or *tsekwel* in Yurok (Kroeber 1976:381), and they are known in English as "stone seats" or "stone chairs." They are semicircular walls built of unmortared stones, piled about three or four feet high. These were made as places to cry and shout for help, especially for female Indian doctors seeking to obtain their power-enabling vision. There are photographs of a similar structure in Kroeber and Gifford (1949:143).

4. This name is also given to an amulet for taking salmon (Spott and Kroeber 1942:169).

5. In modern times, Indians often clap this way while playing the gambling game and singing. Though it adds another dimension to the music, they say it is only for luck.

6. Sources on Yurok shamanism include Erikson (1943:261–265), Kroeber (1925:63–68), Powers (1877 [1976]:25–26), Spott and Kroeber (1942:153–166, 219–223), and Valory (1970).

7. The role of confession in Yurok doctoring is described in Erikson (1943:261–262) and in Spott and Kroeber (1942:157–158).

8. The Yurok word *uma'a* refers both to the Indian devil and to the arrows or "pains" that are shot into the victim. As noted in chapter 3, the *uma'a* itself is a nonhuman creature, but its magical "arrows" (*uma'a*) are sometimes obtained by human beings who can then use them to kill or sicken their enemies.

9. In another example cited by Erikson, the Indian doctor saw a man having sex with a woman, even though he had recently been praying for good luck (1943:262).

10. Despite its offensive tone, I quote at length from Powers's account, since it sheds more light on the process used in determining the source of the patient's illness. The methods described here differ slightly from those described in the text above, but variability in such things is to be expected.

There are two classes of shamans—the root doctors and the barking doctors—the latter reminding one of the medieval spagyrics. It is the province of the barking doctor to diagnose the case, which she [most doctors are women] does by squatting down like a dog on his haunches before the patient, and barking at him like that noble and faithful animal for hours altogether. . . .

It will be perceived that the barking doctor is the more important functionary of the two. In addition to her diagnostic functions, she takes care of the "poisoned" cases, which among these superstitious people are very numerous. They believe they frequently fall victim to witches, who cause a snake, frog, lizard, or other noxious reptile to fasten itself to the body and grow through the skin into the viscera. In this case the barking doctor first discovers, *secundem artum,* in what portion of the body the reptile lurks, then commences sucking the place, and sucks until the skin is broken and blood flows. Then, she herself takes an emetic and vomits up a frog or something, which she pretends to have drawn from the patient, but which, of course, she had previously swallowed.

In a case of simple "poisoning," the barking doctor gives the sufferer an emetic, and causes him to vomit into a small basket. The basket is then covered and held before the patient while he names in succession the various persons he suspects of having poisoned him. At each name mentioned the doctor uncovers the basket and looks in. So long as wrong names are mentioned the vomited matter remains; but when the right one is hit upon, presto! it is gone, and when the doctor looks in the basket it is empty. (Powers 1877 [1976]:26)

11. This analysis is based on that of Kroeber (1925:63). While Kroeber found the function of stage three "obscure" at this stage in his research, Spott and Kroeber specifically state that the "pains" come in pairs and that the second must be obtained through a vision quest in the high country (1942:156).

12. These include Erikson (1943:262–267), Spott and Kroeber (1942: 158–164), and Valory (1970:32–72). Erikson's account is based on interviews conducted with Mrs. Founder during a brief field trip in the early 1940s, while Spott's narrative is based on long familiarity with Mrs. Flounder, who was evidently a relative of his. Valory's version is the most detailed; it was based on a biography that was recorded from Robert Spott by Sylvia Beyer, a student of Kroeber's, in 1934 (Valory 1970:32). Valory's bibliography indicates that the Beyer manuscript can be found in the University of California Archives (Bancroft Library), but I was unable to locate the document there.

5: Rituals to Repair the World

1. The transcriptions provided here are simplified somewhat for the purposes of clarity. Pitches are not always so precise or so clearly focused as these notations indicate, nor is the meter so consistent. Sections or whole songs repeated with slight variations are usually represented as if they were identical. Intonation has been "corrected" in some examples, and rhythmic irregularities are also disregarded, except when they are viewed by the author as stylistic.

The special symbols used follow standard practice in ethnomusicology: accidentals are listed in order of occurrence, rather than by Western key signatures; X's are used as noteheads when the pitch is indefinite or not clearly focused; partial bar lines indicate that the meter is flexible rather than strict; small arrows are used when pitch is slightly sharper or flatter than that of the note indicated; and deviations in duration are similarly shown by the use of plus (+) or minus (−) signs.

2. Each component listed below is described in Kroeber and Gifford (1949). This is the single most important source on the religious system, which is also summarized in Kroeber (1925:53–61). Other more specific references are cited below.

3. Also described in Drucker (1936).

4. Also described in Roberts (1932).

5. The Hupa rituals are all centered at or near Takimilding. Besides the discussion in Kroeber and Gifford (1949:56–66), Hupa rituals are described in Gifford (1940b), Goddard (1903–1904), and Golla (In Press).

6. The Weitchpec rituals are described in Kroeber and Gifford (1949:66).

7. Also described in Thompson (1916) and Waterman and Kroeber (1938).

8. Also described in Thompson (1916).

9. See also Spott and Kroeber (1942:172–178).

10. The lengthy narrative from which this was taken was narrated by Mary Socktish (Hupa) in 1940 and translated with the assistance of Sam Brown (Hupa). The idea that people should become filled even though they do not eat much is also expressed in a Hupa Jump Dance formula collected by Goddard (1904:233).

11. Kroeber and Gifford (1949) provide the most complete discussion of the Deerskin Dance as practiced among the Yurok and Karok, while Goldschmidt and Driver (1940) give a very detailed description of the ceremony as practiced among the Hupa. The unpublished notes of Helen Roberts (1926a) also contain descriptions of the Karok Deerskin Dance.

12. This tendency has been discussed in chapter 3, and Kroeber comments upon it repeatedly in footnotes throughout *Yurok Myths* (1976).

The *wo'gey* are said to be crying because they are about to leave the world (1976:310), and they ask that people feel sorry when they remember them (1976:65). Kroeber expands on this tendency in a footnote as follows:

The Yurok are always feeling sorry for people, or wanting them to feel sorry for themselves. More than once, when recording a song or story, I have been asked to remember the teller when he was gone; and once was literally entreated with tears to weep at least a little when I should hear of his death. This last was from a rich man noted for his sharp bargaining. There is no doubt that myths and songs contain to the Yurok an intense association of personality and its perishing. They evince a similar emotion in weeping at the climax of certain dances; and while this is said to be for their dead relatives who used to witness the same scene, it may be suspected that they mingle with their grief some anticipated sorrow for their own end. (Kroeber 1976:65)

13. In earlier times, each major village sent a dance group dressed in regalia which represented the wealth of its inhabitants. Nowadays there are always still at least two "teams" performing in this and other public rituals.

14. This is modified slightly from the diagram in Kroeber and Gifford (1949:69).

15. The sound is referred to as a "grunt" in Goldschmidt and Driver (1940:112).

16. These obsidian blades are described and illustrated in Kroeber (1925:26–27).

17. In example 1 the two whistle parts are indicated as playing at unison and a major second in relation to the main singer's tonal center. This is a typical sonority based on what I heard at various dances rather than a transcription of any specific recording. As noted previously, recording is prohibited at these events and I know of no recording in which the complete Deerskin Dance ensemble can be heard.

18. This solo part was taken from a song sung by Ewing Davis (Hupa) and recorded by Margaret Woodward in 1953.

19. The terminology used here is based upon Lomax's *Folk Song Style and Culture* (1968). Lomax follows *Harvard Dictionary of Music* in establishing the musical phrase as parallel to the spoken sentence (1968:55). He defines a simple strophe as a series of three to eight phrases that are repeated at least twice with no insertions of new materials and no omissions or changes of order (1968:58–59).

20. The formal device of including repeated or new material at a higher pitch level was noted as a distinctive aspect of Yuman Indian music and labeled "the rise" by Herzog (1928:193). Later, in a summary of North American Indian styles, Nettl asserted that this was a general characteristic of Indian music of the California region (1954:18–19). This conclusion

was almost certainly premature, as Nettl failed to address the cultural diversity of the region, and numerous California Indian musical traditions were not documented in the sources he reviewed. It must be admitted that different forms of "the rise" do seem widespread in California, even in musical styles that are otherwise quite different from one another, but the connection between these occurrences is not at all clear and probably owes to coincidence in some cases.

21. One example is a Brush Dance (light) song sung by Aileen Figueroa (Yurok) and recorded by Charlotte Heth in 1976. This song has a melody which is built on a whole tone scale and which outlines a tritone. Sound registrations produced by the melograph Mona (Uppsala University) and a detailed transcription of the song are found in Keeling (1982a: 558–569).

22. A transcription of the Boat Dance song and a photograph of the dancers proceeding downriver in boats are found in Goldschmidt and Driver (1940:111, 135).

23. During the past few decades, the Jump Dance has been performed mainly in Hoopa Valley. Since this is the only place in which I have ever witnessed the ceremony, and since the Hupa Jump Dance is documented rather well, the following discussion focuses on this version of the ritual. The Hupa Jump Dance is described in Barrett (1963) and in Woodruff (1892:53–56); Kroeber and Gifford describe various forms of the dance as performed among the Yurok, Karok, and Hupa (1949:40–44, 61–63, 71–75); and finally the unpublished papers of Helen Roberts contain brief notes on the Karok Jump Dance as described by Phoebe Maddox and Pete Henry (1926a).

24. The manner in which the Hupa formulist and his assistant gather materials and build the fence is described in Barrett (1963:74–78).

25. The baskets vary in size but average just over a foot in length. The elk-horn purses are about half this size but shaped almost exactly the same.

26. Sense of meter is very weak here, largely because of the slow tempo and rhythmic inconsistency. This notation is based upon the singing of Jimmy Jackson (Hupa) in a recording made by Margaret Woodward in 1953. A slightly different rendering of the figure is given in Kroeber and Gifford (1949:74); this is based upon a Jump Dance song sung by Domingo (Yurok) and Billy Werk (Yurok) in 1906 (Lowie Museum of Anthropology recording #24–991). Except for others which might have been made by locals, these are the only recordings in existence.

27. The dancers sing "wo" as the hands are raised, and "hei" as they hop.

6: Rituals to Help Human Beings

1. Major sources on the Brush Dance include Keeling (1982*a*, 1982*b*, 1985), Lindgren (1935), and Woodruff (1892).

2. Frank Douglas (Yurok) gave the term *meyli* (June 14, 1979), and *melo-* is given in Robins (1958:277). The Karok word *hapish* is documented in Kroeber (1925:107), and the Hupa expression *hont naht weht* was mentioned by several persons I knew.

3. Indians describe the heavy songs as slow and the light ones as quick, but they are comparatively moderate (mm 80–100) and fast (mm 110–125) by a comparative standard, as performed today. Archival examples from the early 1900s often seem to be slower.

4. Recorded by the author in 1979 at the home of Dr. and Mrs. Ricklefs in Hoopa Valley.

5. Indian singers use the word "rhythm" in various ways. It is sometimes used to mean something like "vocable," and the question, "Does that song have words?" might be answered, "No, it's only rhythm." For the most part, however, the word refers to that which frames or accompanies the solo part. The patterns shown in example 8 are all called "rhythm," and similar ones used by the soloist (at the beginning of a song or at the end of phrase-groups) are also identified by the same term.

6. This cadential device is also noted in the Jump Dance song transcribed in example 6.

7. As noted in the discussion of Deerskin Dance songs, the B section may be a version of what has been called "the Rise" in Herzog (1928:193) and Nettl (1954:302).

8. Throughout this study, X's have been used to indicate tones that are unfocused in pitch. In this example, these mainly indicate glottal stops or glottal trills that occur in the "rhythm."

9. In the heavy song sung by Elmer Jarnaghan (example 10) there is perhaps another instance of this: there, in section X, Mr. Jarnaghan begins a section with new melodic material and then apparently decides to end it by chanting "rhythm."

10. The recording is available at the Lowie Museum of Anthropology (#24–2730). It is sung entirely in vocables, and at a slightly slower tempo than Mrs. Figueroa's version, but it is obviously the same song. Another version of the song was sung by Frank Douglas (Yurok) and recorded by the author in 1979.

11. The song is available on a commercial recording produced by Heth (1978).

12. In cantometrics terminology the female style would be coded as a litany with slight variation (Lomax 1968:58).

13. In actual context, the end of a girl's song would be signified by one of the male dancers rather than the soloist herself.

14. A Yurok doctor-making dance is described in chapter 4. There are a number of sources in which the Yurok ritual is mentioned or discussed, but the most complete account describes a Hupa Kick Dance. The information presented here was derived largely from this narrative, which was spoken by Sam Brown (Hupa), translated by Edward Sapir in 1927, and subsequently edited by Victor Golla (in press). Readers seeking more detailed information should consult this source, for I have omitted much in the summary given here and made other modifications based on my own research. Brief information on the Karok Kick Dance is found in Roberts (1926a).

15. Sam Brown states that the women dance by jumping in place, and from this it seems likely that they dance by bobbing up and down on the balls of their feet, as in the Brush Dance. In a description of the Yurok Kick Dance, Kroeber notes that this is the only occasion on which women of the community-at-large could enter the sweathouse (1925:64).

16. This refers to the special song that manifests her power-enabling vision and that would also be used in doctoring.

17. Sapir translates the Hupa word for this singing as "they keep reaching for it" and notes that they sing "in a howling fashion at the top of their voices" (Golla, in press).

18. In this connection, readers might recall the account in a previous chapter concerning Mrs. Fanny Flounder (Yurok) and her quest for doctoring power in the high country. She had a vision in which a chicken hawk appeared and offered to become her spiritual guardian (Spott and Kroeber 1942:160). During my own fieldwork, I collected only one Kick Dance song that had words; this was sung by Herman Sherman, Sr. (Hupa), and the text was about someone seeing an eagle in the sky (recorded May 9, 1979).

19. This particular example might be heard in cut time (2/2), but a standard 4/4 meter is more common.

20. Robert Spott (Yurok) speaks a similar formula at the end of a Kick Dance song recorded by R. H. Robins in 1965.

21. The Karok version of the ritual is described in Kroeber (1925:106), Roberts (1926a), and Bright (1978:186), but each of these accounts is quite brief.

22. The account given here is based upon information provided in Goddard (1903–1904:53–54) and in Golla (in press). The latter is the more detailed source and includes two narratives spoken by Sam Brown (Hupa) and translated by Edward Sapir in 1927. Interested readers should consult these sources directly, for I have omitted much and made other modifications in the summary that follows.

23. The dress is made of maple bark that was pounded and ripped up into fringes. The Hupa word for the dress has been translated "grass skirt" (Golla, in press).

24. This part of the ritual is described only in Golla (in press).

25. The Hupa word for the traditional semisubterranean family house.

26. These "hooks" are the same headdresses as those worn by the flint carriers in the Deerskin Dance.

27. This discussion focuses mainly on recordings that were collected from Hupa singers. The corpus is rather small, including eight songs recorded by Margaret Woodward in 1953 and three songs that I recorded in 1979. The same basic style is heard in girls' puberty dance (Ihuk Dance) songs collected from Karok singers by Helen Roberts in 1926.

28. One might expect that the heavy songs would be wordless and more religious in character, but Sam Brown (Hupa) said that there were two heavy songs that the men sung first each evening and that the second one had words that were translated, "Shit floats around." According to him, it was considered important that the girl not laugh at this, nor at anything else that was said or sung; otherwise she would become wrinkled early in life (Golla, in press).

29. The tempo quickens somewhat during section II.

30. The other men's Flower Dance songs (by Ewing Davis) on the Woodward tape are also similar to those transcribed here.

7: Making Medicine

1. This is based on the definition in *Webster's New Twentieth Century Dictionary of the English Language*, unabridged 2d ed. (New York: The Publishers Guild, 1965). There, "Very truly yours" is cited as an example of a formula often used today.

2. In some instances, fasting is also required after making medicine. Georgia Orcutt (Karok) stated that no water is drunk for five days after using a formula (Kroeber and Gifford 1980:263). It was also noted in this study that a Karok herb doctor must neither drink water nor eat salmon or deer meat for five days after making medicine; eel meat may be eaten, but only fresh eel and not dried (1980:265).

3. Wohpekemeu's medicine for childbirth will be described in chapter 8.

4. Yurok attitudes concerning the use of names have been described by Kroeber, who informs us that use of a person's name is considered grossly insulting and that use of a dead person's name is especially taboo (1925:47–48).

5. This text was originally spoken by Billy Werk (Yurok) of Weitch-

pec in 1907. Two different versions are given in Kroeber (1976:246–249), and both were translated with the assistance of an interpreter, probably Weitchpec Frank. The cylinder recording has been transferred onto tape, and is among the holdings at the Lowie Museum of Anthropology (tape #24–981).

6. The formulist in this case would be a woman, and she would be doctoring the man in his family house for pay. Family members and possibly others from the village would be in attendance as she worked. A formulist of this type was known in English as an "herb doctor," which is something quite different from a "medicine woman" (as in the Brush Dance) or an "Indian doctor" (as described in chapter 4 above).

7. Several formulas were employed to purify one who had actually handled a corpse or to terminate a period of mourning for a close relative who had died. The interpretation given here is based on three Yurok texts which were originally spoken by Dave Durban of Weitchpec (Kroeber 1976:305–307), Captain Spott of Rekwoi (Kroeber 1976:426–427), and Johnny Shortman of Welkwau (Kroeber 1976:443–444).

8. Thus it became taboo to carry a corpse past these places in a canoe. A corpse had to be taken ashore at these three places and was carried on the land behind the rocks; then it could be loaded back into the boat again.

9. This text was spoken by Ann of Espeu (Yurok) between 1901 and 1907. The village of Espeu was located near the town of Gold Bluff and most of the events of the narrative take place in this coastal location. A free translation and commentary are found in Kroeber (1976:456–460).

10. In a footnote, Kroeber informs the reader that Kapuloyo is Wohpekemeu's son and that he lives across the ocean at the downstream end of the world, where he spends much of his time dancing or gambling (1976:456). The gambling game mentioned here is the so-called many-stick game played by tribes of this region. In this game a "dealer" holds about fifty slender rods, one of which is marked with blood and ash to serve as the "ace." The dealer divides the bundle taking some of the rods in either hand, and then he invites his opponent to guess which hand holds the ace. The solo part of a gambling song is sung by the dealer while the others on his team sing an ostinato bass pattern and one pounds a drum with a steady five-beat rhythm. The style is exciting and hard to sing, for solo and bass parts are supposed to mesh cleanly in a quickly sung 5/8 meter.

11. Readers will surely note that this formula has many levels of meaning that are not considered here. It is particularly interesting that the formula seems to become a vehicle for the mother's own fantasizing, and thus it apparently serves to comfort her as much as the crying baby.

12. This text was spoken by William Lewis (Hupa) in 1901. It is not a

personal formula but rather one that pertains to the World Renewal complex described in chapter 5. The priest performs the formula for the good of the community and without pay. Interlinear and free translations of the text are found in Goddard (1904:252–264).

13. This Hupa word refers to a spirit or person who interferes with the run of fish, generally by supernatural means, thus causing famine for those upriver.

14. The literal English translation given for what he willed to happen is "Mountain water will go across" (Goddard 1904:253). It is significant to note that eels are indeed not usually found on the Klamath above Weitchpec even though there are some choice places for taking salmon, steelhead, and sturgeon.

15. This text was dictated by Emma Frank (Hupa) to Edward Sapir in 1927. A translation and detailed commentary are found in Golla (in press [MS pp. 171–173]).

16. Footnotes provided indicate that "cough" means flu, "blood sickness" indicates typhoid, and that the term literally meaning "green thing" probably refers to pleurisy or pneumonia (Golla, in press [MS p. 173]).

8: Medicine Songs and Formulas, Part 1

1. This probably refers to the Yurok village of Kenek, near modern Martin's Ferry, a place whose reputation is discussed in Waterman (1920:252).

2. Archival recordings at the Lowie Museum of Anthropology (24–800 and 24–801) reveal that similar sounds were also heard in music for the Fish Dam Dance at Kepel.

3. As a means of depicting relative durations more clearly, I have notated the long-held tones using tied quarter notes. The breath-marks are used to indicate phrasing rather than spots where the singer actually inhaled.

4. Goddard recorded two deer-hunting songs from James Anderson (Hupa) in 1901, and these are in the collection at the Lowie Museum of Anthropology (24–1723 and 24–1724). However, the original cylinder recordings had deteriorated greatly before these could be transferred onto tape, and they are virtually inaudible. George Herzog did collect some recordings among the Hupa during the 1920s; these are mainly of ritual singing rather than individual medicine songs, though the corpus includes shamanistic songs sung by Hettie Stevens (Hupa). These Herzog recordings are at the Archives of Traditional Music at Indiana University (Pre 54-120-F-Herzog).

5. Sung by Tintin (Karok). Recording at the American Folklife Center (HHR 16b).

6. Sung by Pete Henry (Karok). Recording at the American Folklife Center (HHR 14h).

9: Medicine Songs and Formulas, Part 2

1. These include formulas spoken by Stone of Weitchpec (appendix 2, D–10), Barney of Sregon (appendix 2, D–11), and Doctor of Pekwan (appendix 2, D–13). There was also a song "for money or women" collected from Johnny Cooper (appendix 2, D–18).

2. The key signature is incorrect, for the song contains no c-sharp (555 hz) as indicated in the signature. More important, the time signature (6/8) does not agree with the note values in the song. Unfortunately, no recording could be located.

3. Over the course of the recording, the pitch level rises about one-half step (100 cents), but this is not indicated in the transcription.

4. Common names for this flowering bush include mock orange and syringa.

5. The Pleiades are six stars in the constellation Taurus, and it is interesting to note that they are also regarded as sisters in Greek mythology. They were said to be the daughters of Atlas; originally there had been seven, but one sister became lost.

6. According to Yurok cosmology, the sky and the water are closely related, and ocean waves were thought to be caused by the edges of the sky as they fell and struck the sea in a slow but constant rhythm.

7. In one version, eighteen spirit-persons (Kroeber 1976:305).

8. The plant is identified as *hegwomes* (Kroeber 1976:307), but no translation for the name could be found in Robins (1958).

9. Actually the Karok name refers to a particular species of spider, but the species is not identified.

10: Music and Culture History

1. A modern style of music connected with the syncretistic Indian Shaker religion is not considered in the present study.

2. In early (circa 1900–1910) recordings the melodic form is more loosely structured and in cantometrics terminology would be coded (10) simple litany with much variation or (8) complex litany with moderate variation (see appendix 3). The formal device of including repeated or new material at a higher pitch level was noted as a distinctive aspect of

Yuman Indian music and labeled "the rise" by Herzog (1928:193). Later, in his attempt to summarize North American Indian musical styles, Bruno Nettl asserted that this was a general characteristic of California Indian singing (1954:18–19). This conclusion was almost certainly premature, for Nettl failed to address the cultural diversity of the region, and many California Indian musical styles were not considered. Still, various forms of what may be called "the rise" are indeed found widely throughout this area, even in cultures that are otherwise quite different from one another. The significance of these correspondences is difficult to assess at this writing and would require a more detailed analysis of recordings from other California Indian peoples.

3. An aural presentation entitled "Multipart Singing Among the Tribes of California" was given by the author at the annual meeting of the Society for Ethnomusicology in Los Angeles (1984). This included early and recent recordings of multipart singing from the Yurok, Hupa, Pomo, and Diegueño. Among the Pomo and Diegueño polyphony was shown to be rather sporadic but undeniably present. The presentation also included recordings illustrating the social unison texture typical of the Yokuts, Mono, and other central tribes of the San Joaquin Valley and Sierra foothills. That the Diegueño style (of southern California) might be historically related to polyphonic practices of the northern California tribes seems rather unlikely, given the intervening styles and considering that the northern and southern provinces are so different in other aspects of culture, but the possibility of a relationship cannot be categorically denied.

4. The cantometrics methodology includes a relatively systematic categorization of various types of polyphony (Lomax 1976:209–210).

5. The style itself and its apparent implications relating to gender in Yurok and Hupa culture are discussed in two other essays by the author (Keeling 1985, 1989).

6. The corpus includes eight recordings collected by Mary Woodward in 1953 and three collected by Richard Keeling in 1979.

7. Thirteen recordings sung by Phoebe Maddox (Karok) and collected by Helen Roberts in 1926 were considered (American Folklife Center, Library of Congress: HHR 7a–f and 8a–g).

8. A group of thirty-one girls' puberty dance songs as sung by Van Duzen Pete and his wife (both Nongatl) were collected by Goddard in 1907. The recordings are available at the Lowie Museum of Anthropology (24–1732 through 24–1752).

9. A distinct "sobbing" delivery is apparent in Roberts's recordings of the Karok singer Phoebe Maddox, and some of her songs approximate the predominant style in other respects (for example, wider range).

10. See, for example, the deer-hunting song sung by Jimmy Jackson

(example 31) or the "song for a young man to improve his looks" sung by Ernest Marshall (example 68).

11. See, for example, a love song by Mary Grimes (example 48). A "song to stop the rain" sung by Ella Norris (example 67) should also be cited. Though herself of Yurok descent, Ella Norris lived at Crescent City (near the border of Tolowa territory) and knew several Tolowa songs.

12. The love song performed by the Yurok singer Sara Frank (example 47) seems to be an exception to this general rule.

13. Yurok examples include the following, identified by function: song to purify a house after sickness (example 25), songs for deer medicine (examples 27, 28, and 30), song for love medicine (example 40), and song for medicine for rough water (example 65). The two non-Yurok examples were love songs sung by Tom Hill (Chilula) in 1905 (examples 39 and 41).

14. The Yurok examples include the following, identified by function: songs for love medicine (examples 42, 43, and 44), and a song for basket weaving (example 49). The non-Yurok example was a doctoring song sung by Mary Grimes (Tolowa) in 1903 (example 24).

15. The recording was collected by Kroeber in 1907 and is available at the Lowie Museum of Anthropology (24–1146).

16. The recording was collected by Kroeber in 1907 and is available at the Lowie Museum of Anthropology (24–1021).

17. The recording was collected by Goddard in 1901 and is available at the Lowie Museum of Anthropology (24–1699).

18. Examples 29 and 53 are exceptions. These have a narrow melodic range and can also be classified along with the "animal songs" to be discussed next.

19. The "animal songs" are very prominent in the large corpus of Karok songs collected by Helen Roberts in 1926, and the following animals are represented: bear (13 songs), coyote (9 songs), deer (9 songs), snake (6 songs), dog (3 songs), mountain lion (3 songs), quail (3 songs), blue jay (3 songs), chicken hawk (3 songs), wood rat (2 songs), duck (2 songs), frog (2 songs), blue crane (2 songs), lizard (2 songs), mink (2 songs), wildcat, eel, thrush, hummingbird, mouse, catfish, snail, raccoon, beaver, turtle, meadowlark, angleworm, chipmunk, turtledove, bumblebee, robin, eagle, owl, butterfly, squirrel, jacksnipe, fox, skunk, wren, and yellowhammer.

Among the Karok "animal songs" transcribed in this study are songs by Pete Henry (examples 26, 32, 33, and 34), Phoebe Maddox (examples 50, 56, and 65), Ira Stevens (example 55), and Mrs. Brigmore (example 66).

20. Besides the songs of Frank Douglas (Yurok), which were discussed in chapter 3 but not transcribed, this study includes musical transcriptions

of Yurok "animal songs" as sung by Sara Frank (examples 47 and 59), Johnny Cooper (examples 52, 54, 57, and 58), and Captain Spott of Rekwoi (examples 60–63).

21. The Hupa examples in this category were sung by Jimmy Jackson (example 31), Henry Hostler (example 51), and Ernest Marshall (example 68).

22. Tolowa songs in this category were sung by Mary Grimes (example 47) and Ella Norris (example 67).

23. Wiyot examples discussed here were sung by Molly Brainerd (examples 45 and 46).

24. This is true of the "animal songs" by Frank Douglas (Yurok) that are described in chapter 3. The lack of pitch focus in these songs is illustrated by use of sound registrations produced by a melograph in Keeling (1982a:438–442).

25. The chronology is by Kroeber's admission the weakest element in this reconstruction and is only discussed toward the end of the paper; for the most part these estimates or guesses are based upon analysis of shell mounds in the San Francisco Bay area (1923:139–142).

26. Characterizations for this and the following (Aboriginal) period are based largely on information in Spencer, Jennings, et al. (1965, 1977) and in Clark (1962:212–239).

27. It seems important to emphasize here that contacts across the Amerasian Arctic have been continuous and to warn against the interpretation that these only occurred during the Paleo-Indian period as defined above. The most striking evidence of this is the existence of Eskimo-Aleut populations on both sides of the Bering Strait (Erickson 1970:133).

The earliest migrations occurred at a period when the physical characteristics defining the Mongoloid race were less clear than they are today, so that the populations descended from early immigrants tend to have less Mongoloid features than those who came later. By contrast, the Eskimos are distinctly Mongoloid in appearance and have very close cultural affinities with various indigenous peoples of northeastern Asia.

28. Much of the information summarized here is drawn from Clark (1962:229–235).

29. Sources include Bogoraz (1902), Chard (1960), Drucker (1965), Hallowell (1926), Hultkrantz (1979), Ray (1932), and Spencer, Jennings, et al. (1965).

30. The resemblance between a lullaby (B3) on Alan P. Merriam's commercial recording *Songs and Dances of the Flathead Indians* (Merriam 1953) and a basket song as sung by Aileen Figueroa (example 50) is particularly striking.

31. It is interesting to note, however, that a symbology equating crying and singing has also been noted in Gros Ventre music in a recent study by Hatton (1988).

32. This is a point that is touched upon briefly in Herzog (1935*b*:131) but not discussed in Lomax (1968) or Erickson (1970).

11: Crying and Singing

1. In 1985 I gave a lecture on this subject (with recorded examples) that was attended by some Indian people from this area. At the conclusion of my talk, Vivian Hailstone (Yurok/Karok) made the objection that Yuroks and Hupas have "light songs" as well as sacred ones, and that I had neglected to consider them in my presentation. Her criticism was certainly correct, though I also took the remark as indicating tacit acceptance of my thesis (that the sacred songs typically sounded like "sobbing").

2. The original version reads, "À la fin de chaque phrase, on aspire l'air bruyamment, tout à fait comme si l'on sanglotait" (Angulo and d'Harcourt 1931:200).

3. The idea that profuse crying could be cultivated as a cultural habit was perhaps first noted by Charles Darwin in 1872.

Weeping seems to be the primary and natural expression, as we see in children, of suffering of any kind. But the foregoing facts and common experience show us that a frequently repeated effort to restrain weeping, in association with certain states of the mind, does much to check the habit. On the other hand, it appears that the power of weeping can be increased through habit; thus, the Rev. R. Taylor, who long resided in New Zealand, asserts that the women can voluntarily shed tears in abundance; they meet for this purpose to mourn the dead, and they take great pride in crying "in the most affecting manner." (Darwin 1965 [1872]:153, 155)

4. Crying as a textual motive or as a vocal characteristic has been found in a song to make a baby stop crying (appendix 2, A–13), a deer-hunting song (appendix 2, C–18), a bear-hunting formula (appendix 2, C–28), several songs and formulas for love medicine (appendix 2, E–6, E–9, E–12, E–18, E28, E–30, E–33, E–35, and E–43), a song spoken over bullets (appendix 2, G–3), a song for traveling by boat (appendix 2, H–9), and a formula for luck at gambling (appendix 2, I–1). As noted previously in chapter 9, the relationship between wealth medicine and love medicine was rather close, and several men's formulas were used "for money or women" without distinction. The affinity between gambling and wealth is perhaps even greater.

Appendix 3: Cantometrics Codings
for Various Musical Styles

1. Line 8 (tonal blend of orchestra) was removed from the cantometrics coding sheet before the publication of Lomax (1976).

2. Line 8 (tonal blend of orchestra) was removed from the cantometrics coding sheet before the publication of Lomax (1976).

3. The coding is based upon recordings of female singers. That males use this style for personal medicine songs is expected, since they would also perform in this style in ritual contexts. Female singers do not perform in modern public rituals, except for the Brush Dance, but here in private songs their style parallels that of male public singing very closely.

4. Line 8 (tonal blend of orchestra) was removed from the cantometrics coding sheet before the publication of Lomax (1976).

5. Line 8 (tonal blend of orchestra) was removed from the cantometrics coding sheet before the publication of Lomax (1976).

6. The recordings are available at the Lowie Museum of Anthropology (24–1807 and 24–1810).

7. Line 8 (tonal blend of orchestra) was removed from the cantometrics coding sheet before the publication of Lomax (1976).

References Cited

Abraham, Otto, and Erich M. von Hornbostel
  1906   Phonographierte indianermelodien aus Britisch-Columbia. In *Boas Anniversary Volume*. Berthold Laufer, ed. New York: G. E. Stechert. Pages 447–474.

Anderson, E.
  1956   The Hoopa Valley Indian Reservation in Northwestern California: A Study on Its Origins. Master's thesis, University of California, Berkeley.

Angulo, Jaime de, and Marguerite Béclard d'Harcourt
  1931   La musique des indiens de la Californie du Nord. *Journal de la Société des Américanistes de Paris*, n.s., 23(1):189–228. (Translated in Garland 1988.)

Barnett, Homer G.
  1957   *Indian Shakers: A Messianic Cult of the Pacific Northwest*. Carbondale: Southern Illinois University Press.

Barrett, Samuel A.
  1963   The Jump Dance at Hupa, 1962. *Kroeber Anthropological Society Papers* 28:73–85. Berkeley.

Bogoraz, V. G.
  1902   The Folklore of Northwestern Asia As Compared to Northwestern North America. *American Anthropologist* 4:577–683.

Bommelyn, Loren, Aileen Figueroa, Joy Sundberg, and Charlotte Heth
  1976   *Music in the World of the Yurok and Tolowa Indians*. Videotape of interview with transcription. Los Angeles: American Indian Studies Center at the University of California, Los Angeles.
  1977   *Traditional Music of Native Northwest California: Brush*

Dance, Feather Dance, and Gambling Songs. Videotape of interview with transcription. Los Angeles: American Indian Studies Center at the University of California, Los Angeles.

Bright, William

1957   The Karok Language. *University of California Publications in Linguistics* 13. Berkeley.

1978   Karok. In *Handbook of North American Indians,* volume 8: *California*. Robert F. Heizer, ed. Washington, D.C.: Smithsonian Institution. Pages 180–189.

Buckley, Thomas

1982   Menstruation and the Power of Yurok Women: Methods in Cultural Reconstruction. *American Ethnologist* 9:47–60.

Chard, Chester

1960   Northwest Coast–Northeast Asiatic Similarities: A New Hypothesis. In *Men and Cultures: Selected Papers of the Fifth International Congress of Anthropological and Ethnological Studies*. Anthony F. C. Wallace, ed. Philadelphia: University of Pennsylvania. Pages 235–240.

Clark, Grahame

1962   *World Prehistory: An Outline*. London: Cambridge University Press.

Cook, Sherburne F.

1978   Historical Demography. In *University of California Publications in American Archeology and Ethnology*. Robert F. Heizer, vol. ed. Washington, D.C.: Smithsonian Institution. Pages 91–98.

Coy, Owen Cochran

1929   *The Humboldt Bay Region, 1850–1875: A Study in the American Colonization of California*. Los Angeles: California State Historical Association.

Darwin, Charles

1965   *The Expression of the Emotions in Man and Animals*. Chicago: University of Chicago Press. (Reprint of 1872 ed.)

Driver, Harold E.

1941   Culture Element Distributions, xvi: Girls' Puberty Rites in Western North America. *University of California Anthropological Records* 6(2):21–90. Berkeley.

Drucker, Philip

1936   A Karuk World-Renewal Ceremony at Panaminik. *University of California Publications in American Archeology and Ethnology* 35(3):23–28. Berkeley: University of California Press.

1965   *Cultures of the North Pacific Coast*. San Francisco: Chandler Publishing.

Elsasser, Albert B.

1978   Development of Regional Prehistoric Cultures. In *Handbook of the Indians of North America*, volume 8: *California*. Robert F. Heizer, vol. ed. Washington, D.C.: Smithsonian Institution. Pages 37–57.

Erickson, Edwin Erich

1970   The Song Trace: Song Styles and the Ethnohistory of Aboriginal America. Ph.D. dissertation, Columbia University, New York.

Erikson, Erik H.

1943   Observations on the Yurok: Childhood and World Image. *University of California Publications in American Archeology and Ethnology* 35(10):257–302. Berkeley.

1950   *Childhood and Society*. New York: W. W. Norton and Co.

Fry, Winifred S.

1904   Humboldt Indians. In *A Collection of Ethnographical Articles on the California Indians*. Robert F. Heizer, ed. Ramona, Calif.: Ballena Press. Pages 5–14.

Garland, Peter, ed.

1988   *Jaime de Angulo: The Music of the Indians of Northern California*. Santa Fe, N. Mex.: Soundings Press.

Geertz, Clifford

1973   *The Interpretation of Cultures*. New York: Basic Books.

1983   *Local Knowledge: Further Essays in Interpretive Anthropology*. New York: Basic Books.

Gifford, Edward W.

1940*a*   Karok Field Notes, Part II. Unpublished MS. University of California Archives CU 23.1, Box 31 (Valory Guide #179). Berkeley.

1940*b*   Ethnographic Notes on Hupa Ceremonial and Rituals. Unpublished MS. University of California Archives CU 23.1, Box 31 (Valory Guide #171). Berkeley.

Goddard, Pliny E.

1903–1904 Life and Culture of the Hupa. *University of California Publications in American Archeology and Ethnology* 1(1):1–88. Berkeley.

1904   Hupa Texts. *University of California Publications in American Archeology and Ethnology* 1(2):89–368. Berkeley.

1914*a*   Notes on the Chilula Indians of Northwestern California. *University of California Publications in American Archeology and Ethnology* 10(6):265–288. Berkeley.

1914*b*   Chilula Texts. *University of California Publications in American Archeology and Ethnology* 10(7):289–379. Berkeley.

Goldschmidt, Walter R.
1951   Ethics and the Structure of Society: An Ethnological Contribution to the Sociology of Knowledge. *American Anthropologist* 53(4):506–524.

Goldschmidt, Walter R., and Harold E. Driver
1940   The Hupa White Deerskin Dance. *University of California Publications in American Archeology and Ethnology* 35(8): 103–142. Berkeley.

Golla, Victor K., ed.
1984   *The Sapir-Kroeber Correspondence*. Survey of California and Other Indian Languages, Special Report 6. University of California, Berkeley.
In Press   *The Collected Works of Edward Sapir*, volume 14: *Northwestern California*. Berlin: Mouton de Gruyter.

Gould, Richard A.
1966   The Wealth Quest among the Tolowa Indians of Northwestern California. *Proceedings of the American Philosophical Society* 110(1):67–89.

Gould, Richard A., and Theodore P. Furukawa
1964   Aspects of Ceremonial Life among the Indian Shakers of Smith River, California. *Kroeber Anthropological Society Papers* 31:51–67. Berkeley.

Hall, Jody C., and Bruno Nettl
1955   The Musical Style of the Modoc. *Southwestern Journal of Anthropology* 11:58–66.

Hallowell, A. Irving
1926   Bear Ceremonialism in the Northern Hemisphere. *American Anthropologist* 28(1):1–175.

Handbook of the North American Indians, Volume 8: *California*
1978   Robert F. Heizer, ed. Washington, D.C.: Smithsonian Institution.

Harrington, John P.
1932   *Karuk Indian Myths*. Bureau of American Ethnology Bulletin 107. Washington, D.C.

Hatton, Orin T.
1988   We Caused Them to Cry: Power and Performance in Gros Ventre War Expedition Songs. Unpublished MS.

Heizer, Robert F.
1978   History of Research. In *Handbook of North American Indians*, volume 8: *California*. Robert F. Heizer, vol. ed. Washington, D.C.: Smithsonian Institution. Pages 6–15.

Heizer, Robert F., and John E. Mills
1952   *The Four Ages of Tsurai: A Documentary History of the In-dian Village on Trinidad Bay*. Berkeley and Los Angeles: University of California Press.

Herzog, George
1928   The Yuman Musical Style. *Journal of American Folklore* 41:183–231.
1935a   The Plains Ghost Dance and Great Basin Music. *American Anthropologist* 37:403–419.
1935b   Special Song Types in North American Indian Music. *Zeitschrift für Vergleichende Musikwissenschaft* 3:23–33.

Heth, Charlotte W.
1978   *Songs of Love, Luck, Animals, and Magic: Music of the Yurok and Tolowa Indians of Northwestern California*. Disk with liner notes. New World Records NW 297.

Hoijer, Harry
1956   The Chronology of the Athapaskan Languages. *International Journal of American Linguistics* 22(4):219–232.

Hultkrantz, Åke
1979   *The Religions of the American Indians*. Monica Setterwall, trans. Berkeley, Los Angeles, London: University of California Press. (Originally published in Swedish, 1967.)

Keeling, Richard H.
1982a   Songs of the Brush Dance and Their Basis in Oral-Expressive Magic: Music and Culture of the Yurok, Hupa, and Karok Indians of Northwestern California. Ph.D. dissertation, University of California, Los Angeles.
1982b   The "Sobbing" Quality in a Hupa Brush Dance Song. *American Indian Culture and Research Journal* 6(1):25–41. Los Angeles: American Indian Studies Center at the University of California, Los Angeles.
1985   Contrast of Song Performance Style as a Function of Sex Role Polarity in the Hupa Brush Dance. *Ethnomusicology* 29(2):185–212.
1989   Musical Evidence of Female Spiritual Life Among the Yurok. In *Women in North American Indian Music: Six Essays*. Richard Keeling, ed. Special Monograph 6. Bloomington, Ind.: Society for Ethnomusicology. Pages 67–78.
1991   *A Guide to Early Field Recordings (1900–1949) at the Robert H. Lowie Museum of Anthropology*. Berkeley, Los Angeles, Oxford: University of California Press.

Klimek, Stanislaus
1935   Culture Element Distributions, I: The Structure of Califor-

nia Indian Culture. *University of California Publications in American Archeology and Ethnology* 37(1):1–70. Berkeley.

Kroeber, Alfred L.

n.d.   Kroeber Correspondence and Papers: Additions. Unpublished MS on linguistics, ethnology, and ethnomusicology of various Indian cultures of California and adjacent regions. University of California Manuscripts Division, Bancroft Library (Catalogue No. 71/83 C, Cartons 1–11). Berkeley.

1904   Types of Indian Culture in California. *University of California Publications in American Archeology and Ethnology* 2(3):81–103.

1923   The History of Native Culture in California. *University of California Publications in American Archeology and Ethnology* 20:125–142. Berkeley.

1925   *Handbook of the Indians of California*. Bureau of American Ethnology Bulletin 78. Washington, D.C. (Reprinted by Dover Publications, New York, 1976.)

1936   Culture Element Distributions III: Area and Climax. *University of California Publications in American Archeology and Ethnology* 37(3):101–116. Berkeley.

1953   *Cultural and Natural Areas of Native North America*. Berkeley and Los Angeles: University of California Press.

1976   *Yurok Myths*. Berkeley, Los Angeles, London: University of California Press.

Kroeber, Alfred L., and Edward W. Gifford

1949   World Renewal: A Cult System of Native Northwest California. *University of California Anthropological Records* 21(1):1–210. Berkeley.

1980   *Karok Myths*. Berkeley, Los Angeles, London: University of California Press.

Lindgren, Louisa

1935   Brush Dance at Hoopa Reservation. *Indians At Work* 3(5): 43–45 (October 15).

List, George

1963   The Boundaries of Speech and Song. *Ethnomusicology* 7:1–16.

Lomax, Alan

1968   *Folk Song Style and Culture*. Washington, D.C.: American Association for the Advancement of Science.

1976   *Cantometrics: A Method in Musical Anthropology*. Berkeley: University of California Extension Media Center.

Matthiessen, Peter
 1979   Stop the GO Road. *Audubon Magazine* 81(1):49–64 (January).
Merriam, Alan P.
 1953   *Songs and Dances of the Flathead Indians*. Disk with liner notes. Folkways Ethnic Library Album No. FE 4445.
Nelson, Byron
 1978   *Our Home Forever: A Hupa Tribal History*. Hoopa Valley, Calif.: The Hupa Tribe.
Nettl, Bruno
 1954   *North American Musical Styles*. Philadelphia: American Folklore Society.
 1961   Polyphony in North American Indian Music. *Musical Quarterly* 47:354–362.
 1965   The Songs of Ishi: Musical Style of the Yahi Indians. *Musical Quarterly* 51(3):460–477.
Norton, Jack
 1978   *Genocide in Northwest California: When Our Worlds Cried*. San Francisco: California Indian Historical Society.
Pilling, Arnold R.
 1978   Yurok. In *Handbook of North American Indians*, volume 8: *California*. Robert F. Heizer, vol. ed. Washington, D.C.: Smithsonian Institution. Pages 137–154.
Powers, Stephen
 1877   *Tribes of California*. Contributions to North American Ethnology 3. Washington: U.S. Geographical and Geological Survey of the Rocky Mountain Region. (Reprint published by University of California Press, Berkeley, Los Angeles, London, 1976.)
Ray, V. F.
 1932   *The Sanpoil and Nespelem, Salishan Peoples of Northeastern Washington*. Publications in Anthropology 5. Seattle: University of Washington.
Reichard, G. A.
 1925   Wiyot Grammar and Texts. *University of California Publications in American Archeology and Ethnology* 22(1). Berkeley.
Roberts, Helen Hefron
 1926a   Karuk Fieldnotes, Collected at Somes Bar and Orleans Bar, California. Unpublished MS. Archive of Folk Culture, Library of Congress (Manuscript no. KK–14).

1926*b*   Karuk Songs Texts and Translations, Collected at Somes
            Bar and Orleans Bar, California. Unpublished MS. Archive
            of Folk Culture, Library of Congress (Manuscript no. KK–
            15).
1932   The First Salmon Ceremony of the Karuk Indians. *Amer-
            ican Anthropologist* 34(3):426–440.
Robins, R. H.
1958   *The Yurok Language: Grammar, Texts, Lexicon*. University
            of California Publications in Linguistics 15. Berkeley.
Robins, R. H., and Norma McLeod
1956   Five Yurok Songs: A Musical and Textual Analysis. *Bulletin
            of the School of Oriental and African Studies of the Univer-
            sity of London* 18:592–609.
Spencer, Robert F., Jesse D. Jennings, et al.
1965   *The Native Americans: Prehistory and Ethnology of the
            North American Indians*. New York: Harper and Row.
1977   *The Native Americans: Ethnology and Backgrounds of the
            North American Indians*, 2d ed. New York: Harper and
            Row.
Spicer, Edward H.
1969   *A Short History of the Indians of the United States*. New
            York: Van Nostrand Company.
Spott, Robert, and Alfred L. Kroeber
1942   Yurok Narratives. *University of California Publications
            in American Archeology and Ethnology* 35(9):143–256.
            Berkeley.
Thompson, Lucy
1916   *To the American Indian*. Eureka, Calif.: Cummins Print
            Shop.
Valory, Dale K.
1966   The Focus of Indian Shaker Healing. *Kroeber Anthropo-
            logical Society Papers* 35:67–111. Berkeley.
1970   Yurok Doctors and Devils: A Study in Identity, Anxiety,
            and Deviance. Ph.D. dissertation, University of California,
            Berkeley.
1971   *Guide to Ethnological Documents (1–203) of the Depart-
            ment and Museum of Anthropology, University of Califor-
            nia, Berkeley, Now in the University Archives (CU 23.1)*.
            Berkeley: University of California Archeological Facility.
Vennum, Thomas, Jr.
1979   Songs of Love, Luck, Animals, and Magic: Music of the

Yurok and Tolowa Indians. *Ethnomusicology* 23(2):349–352. (Review of Heth 1978.)

Wallace, William J.

1978a   Hupa, Chilula, and Whilkut. In *Handbook of North American Indians,* volume 8: *California.* Robert F. Heizer, vol. ed. Washington, D.C.: Smithsonian Institution. Pages 164–179.

1978b   Music and Musical Instruments. In *Handbook of North American Indians,* volume 8: *California.* Robert F. Heizer, vol. ed. Washington, D.C.: Smithsonian Institution. Pages 642–648.

Waterman, Thomas T.

1920   Yurok Geography. *University of California Publications in American Archeology and Ethnology* 16(5):177–314. Berkeley.

Waterman, Thomas T., and Alfred L. Kroeber

1938   The Kepel Fish Dam. *University of California Publications in American Archeology and Ethnology* 35(6):49–80. Berkeley.

Woodruff, Charles E.

1892   Dances of the Hupa Indians. *American Anthropologist* 5(1):53–61.

General Index

Index of Native Sources

Barney of Sregon (Yurok), 164
Blind Bill (Yurok), 272–273
Bommelyn, Loren (Tolowa), 11, 242
Brainerd, Molly (Wiyot), 178–180
Brigmore, Mrs. (Karok), 205–206
Brown, Sam (Hupa), 19, 21, 115, 262,
 273–274

Cooper, Johnny (Yurok), 166, 188, 189,
 191–193

Davis, Ewing (Hupa), 87–88, 106, 107,
 115, 117, 121
Davis, Fred (Hupa/Chilula), 102
Davis, Shan (Karok), 150, 253–254
Doctor of Pekwan (Yurok), 260–261
Domingo of Weitchpec (Yurok), 106, 108,
 109, 156–157, 251
Douglas, Frank (Yurok), 51, 81, 97–99,
 116, 119, 134, 190
Dusky, Emma (Hupa), 184, 251

Figueroa, Aileen (Yurok), 53, 111–113,
 175, 177, 184–186
Flounder, Fanny (Yurok), 71–73
Frank, Emma (Hupa), 266
Frank, Sara (Yurok), 178, 180, 194

George, Dewey (Yurok), 92
George of Rekwoi (Yurok), 188
Grimes, Mary (Tolowa), 152–153, 181,
 182

Hawley of Meta (Yurok), 89–90, 157–158
Henry, Pete (Karok), 91, 114, 154–155,
 162, 164–165
Hill, Tom (Chilula), 163, 166–167, 171,

174–175, 177, 193–194, 201, 251–252,
 255–256, 263, 277
Hostler, Henry (Hupa), 169–170, 186–
 187, 188
Hostler, Jake (Hupa), 150

Ike Mary (Karok), 136, 147, 148–149,
 150–151, 165, 173–174, 190, 191, 204,
 250, 253, 254, 258, 278

Jack, Abraham (Hupa), 84–85, 98, 123–
 124
Jack, Lucinda (Hupa), 124–126
Jackson, Jimmy (Hupa), 115, 121, 159–
 160
James, Birdie (Wiyot), 265
James, Jerry (Wiyot), 252
Jarnaghan, Elmer (Hupa), 21, 103–105
Jerry, Bernard (Karok), 265
Jim of Pekwan (Yurok), 166
Jones, Sam (Yurok), 100–101

Lame Billy of Weitchpec (Yurok), 164
Lewis, Emma (Hupa), 149–150, 262–263,
 270

McCann (Hupa), 151, 195
McCann, Queen (Hupa), 25
Mack of Weitchpec (Yurok), 135, 146
Maddox, Phoebe (Karok), 186, 187–188,
 191, 192, 204–205, 273
Marshall, Ernest (Hupa), 207
Marshall, Julius (Hupa), 166
Marshall, Minnie (Hupa), 146–147, 148
Matilton, Captain John (Hupa), 29
Meyers, Richard (Yurok/Karok), 20, 35

324

KING ALFRED'S COLLEGE
LIBRARY

Designer: U.C. Press Staff
Compositor: Prestige Typography
Text: 11/13 Caledonia
Display: Caledonia
Printer: BookCrafters
Binder: BookCrafters